CW00421630

D 14

JUDAIC SOURCES AND WESTERN THOUGHT

Judaic Sources and Western Thought

Jerusalem's Enduring Presence

Edited by
JONATHAN A. JACOBS

OXFORD
UNIVERSITY PRESS

OXFORD
UNIVERSITY PRESS

Great Clarendon Street, Oxford OX2 6DP

Oxford University Press is a department of the University of Oxford.
It furthers the University's objective of excellence in research, scholarship,
and education by publishing worldwide in

Oxford New York

Auckland Cape Town Dar es Salaam Hong Kong Karachi
Kuala Lumpur Madrid Melbourne Mexico City Nairobi
New Delhi Shanghai Taipei Toronto

With offices in

Argentina Austria Brazil Chile Czech Republic France Greece
Guatemala Hungary Italy Japan Poland Portugal Singapore
South Korea Switzerland Thailand Turkey Ukraine Vietnam

Oxford is a registered trade mark of Oxford University Press
in the UK and in certain other countries

Published in the United States
by Oxford University Press Inc., New York

British Library Cataloguing in Publication Data

Data available

Library of Congress Cataloging in Publication Data

Data available

Typeset by SPI Publisher Services, Pondicherry, India
Printed in Great Britain
on acid-free paper by
MPG Books Group, Bodmin and King's Lynn

ISBN 978-0-19-958315-7

Table of Contents

List of Contributors

Daniel H. Frank is Professor of Philosophy and Director of the Jewish Studies Program at Purdue University.

Lenn E. Goodman is Professor of Philosophy and Andrew W. Mellon Professor in the Humanities at Vanderbilt University.

Steven Grosby is Professor of Religion at Clemson University.

Edward C. Halper is Professor of Philosophy at the University of Georgia.

Yoram Hazony is Founder and Provost of the Shalem Center, Jerusalem.

Jonathan A. Jacobs is Director of the Institute for Criminal Justice Ethics, Editor of the Journal *Criminal Justice Ethics*, and Professor of Philosophy at John Jay College of Criminal Justice, City University of New York.

Ze'ev Maghen is Professor of Persian Literature and Islamic History at Bar-Ilan University, and a Senior Fellow at the Shalem Center in Jerusalem.

Alan Mittleman is Professor of Jewish Thought at the Jewish Theological Seminary in New York City and Director of the Tikvah Institute for Jewish Thought.

David Novak holds the J. Richard and Dorothy Shiff Chair of Jewish Studies as Professor of the Study of Religion and Professor of Philosophy at the University of Toronto.

Kenneth Seeskin is Philip M. and Ethel Klutznick Professor of Jeweish Civilization at Northwestern University and winner of the Koret Jewish Book Award.

Acknowledgements

Several of the contributors to this work have motivated and shaped my interest in its main concerns in recent years, and I am very grateful to them for that. Inviting them to contribute was, among other things, a way of asking them to carry on educating me in the rich, complex texture of Judaic thought and its significance at the intersection of philosophy, theology, sociology, and history. The authors herein have already made significant contributions in a variety of areas relevant to the main topics of this book. I owe them thanks for writing new work for it. Appearing together in this volume multiplies and reinforces points of contact between their various interests and approaches.

I speak for all of the authors in expressing the hope that these essays might move readers to reconsider some 'received wisdom' about the issues discussed. The success of this book will depend in large measure upon whether scholars and students will be moved to pursue further studies along the lines it sketches out. A great deal remains to be explored concerning Judaic roots and sources of Western thought and ideals, and also how influences of Judaic origin have been transformed by other perspectives and traditions. In addition, much remains to be done concerning the undiminished relevance of Judaic origins to life and thought in the modern and contemporary world. This book is a step in those directions of exploration. It is not a work of polemics or apologetics. It is intended to prompt and to encourage certain perspectives and emphases, with a view to aiding explanation, interpretation, and theorizing.

The proposal for this volume was initially formulated while I was a Visiting Scholar at the Oxford Centre for Hebrew and Jewish Studies in spring and summer 2008. I am very fortunate to have had that opportunity, and I am very grateful to the Centre and its staff. In addition, I would like to thank the Earhart Foundation and the Littauer Foundation for their support of my research and writing during that time.

Tom Perridge at Oxford University Press is owed thanks for his encouraging receptivity to the project early on, for his constructive suggestions at various points in its development, and for his patience while it was being brought to completion. Elizabeth Robottom and

Emma Barber at the Press were very helpful throughout several stages in the development, completion, and production of this volume. My essay borrows from my article, 'The Epistemology of Moral Tradition: A defense of a Maimonidean Thesis', published in *The Review of Metaphysics*, September 2010, and from my *Law, Reason, and Morality in Medieval Jewish Philosophy*, Oxford University Press, 2010. I am grateful to the editors of the journal and at the Press for permission to use material from those publications.

Introduction to Judaic Sources and Western Thought: Jerusalem's Enduring Presence

The essays in this volume identify and explicate Judaic sources of some of the most important ideas of European and Western culture and, in particular, its moral and political thought. One of the main motivations for the volume is that Judaic sources are not only crucial to the history of Western thought, but they contain resources of great value for engaging with enduring issues of politics and morality. Identifying those resources, acknowledging their distinct heritage, and recognizing their continuing relevance can help reveal conceptual texture that otherwise might go unnoticed or misrepresented. It enlarges the stock of ideas and ideals we can deploy in the business of leading our lives and understanding the world and ourselves.

Though the main interest of the volume is with certain currents of thought and a certain sort of overall intellectual disposition with roots in the fundamental texts of Judaism, the essays are not primarily studies of Jewish history or even Jewish intellectual history. This is not to deny a vital role to the Jewish people in the Judaic intellectual heritage; that would be quite untenable, if not absurd. But a primary concern of this volume is to contribute to fuller understanding of ways of conceptualizing key issues in Western thought that owe a great deal to sources distinct from Greek, Roman, and Hellenistic understandings and distinct also from Christian understandings. That is different from a focus on the history of the Jewish people.

Of course, there are multiple, substantial points of contact between Judaic thought and the other understandings mentioned. Still, there are recognizably Judaic ways of formulating and addressing key issues. These essays limn the contours of some of Judaic thought's approaches. It would be fair to say that Jerusalem's enduring presence can be shown largely through examination of certain conceptions of philosophical anthropology—conceptions of human nature, the human condition, and the kinds of significance, concern, and commitment distinctive of our nature and condition. Jerusalem's enduring presence can be seen in distinctive ways of thinking about values, the human prospect, what can be aspired to and hoped for.

Recognizably Judaic understandings have persisted throughout the history of the West, even through significant social and political change. In many cases they have been transformed by later sources of ideas, such as Christianity, and have interacted with others, such as Islamic philosophy and its appropriation of the Greek philosophical heritage. However, such transformations do not mean that Judaic understandings did not persist, develop, and respond in their own way. There are respects in which Spinoza, for instance, is very much a Judaic thinker—or a thinker preoccupied with Judaic ideas—and not just someone educated in them in his youth, later repudiating them. His is a complex case but it is at the same time a study in the fertile friction between Judaic orientations with ancient roots, on the one hand, and conceptions emblematic of early modern thought, on the other.

While the essays are concerned mainly with Western thought it should be observed that their Judaic roots are largely in the Near East and Middle East. Some of the key figures of medieval Jewish thought lived in Arabic-speaking lands and cultural interpenetration between Jews and Muslims was often more extensive than that between Jews and Christians. It could be argued that the cultural background of many of the key ideas studied here is not Western. Still, the influences studied are being explored for their impact on Western thought. That is one of a number of spheres in which such influence could be studied. It is, by any plausible reckoning, a very important one. There are different ways of distinguishing spheres, including geographical, cultural, religious, social, economic, and others. The volume does not attempt to define 'Western' with some specific formulation of the features by which spheres might be defined. From the discussions themselves it should be evident what sort of influences are the focus of interest and where they have been especially important.

The essays focus on the period from antiquity to early modern times. The modern world clearly has features distinguishing it from antiquity and the medieval world. But there are continuities as well, and exploring Judaic ideas enables us to 'place' modernity more accurately and to discern continuities and contrasts with what came before. Part of what is interesting and important about Judaic ideas is that they are not 'domesticated', so to speak, to one or another historical period. Their depth and significance is attested to by their persistent relevance and how they remain responsive to the world. This is not because of dogmatic immunity to changed reality; the essays herein make that clear. Instead, the enduring relevance of Judaic conceptions and orientations speaks to their original wisdom. They have not been rendered obsolete or shown to be jejune even by changes in the conditions in which human beings live, revolutionary human achievements, and changes in the understanding of nature.

Given the complexity of human culture and human history, and given how contested are the interpretations of them, a study of even one significant current of thought is a highly ambitious project. This collection does not claim to be exhaustive in any respect. Nor is it primarily a work of intellectual history, though each contributor exhibits conscientiousness regarding the history of thought. Its intention is to survey the conceptual landscape in order to bring into relief certain overall perspectives on human nature, the world, and moral and political life. The essays purport to show why it is illuminating to take seriously the notion of Judaic moral and political thought, a Judaic culture, along with Greek, Roman, and Christian culture. Doing so is an important part of negotiating the self-understanding of the West.

For several centuries it has been widely thought—both among intellectuals and among 'common' people—that Judaism has been theologically, morally, and politically superseded. To put it bluntly, it has been widely held that Judaism is 'over'; that the ways in which it has been superseded leave for it no role but stubborn anachronism. That sort of intellectual, moral, and spiritual condescension has a long and unhappy history. But whatever the condition of the Jewish people (in their own eyes or in the view of others) there is no doubting that there is an enduring *Judaic* Jerusalem in a sense that is not confined to issues having to do with the state of Israel or the Jewish people. It includes ways of seeing the most basic and most important things, and it offers rich, penetrating insights apt for informing explanatory and normative conceptions *now*, as well as in earlier times. The significance of Judaic ideas is not confined to resonances and survivals in Christian, Islamic, and secular thought.

At the same time, this is not to suggest that there is an intellectual monolith—'Judaic thought and culture'. Nor is it an attempt to argue that all of the most important ideals of Western culture have Judaic roots, in some sort of triumphalist exercise of 'competitive culture'. The essays show that there are important intellectual resources of a distinctly Judaic character, to think *with*, not just to find out *about*. We are not suggesting that there is a Judaic *system* of thought or that Judaic ideas are amenable to articulation in a *summa*. But the conceptions and ideals discussed are not just a haphazard collection, either. They include and they reflect guiding orientations of thought, and by examining some specific issues those orientations can be made an explanatorily significant focus in their own right.

The notion of 'the Judaic' should be distinguished from the notion of 'the Jewish'. Of course there are important links between what is Jewish and what is Judaic. Yet there is an important historical case we can look to for some guidance concerning the difference between Judaic and Jewish. When seventeenth-century Christians accused other Christians of judaizing, sometimes the gravamen was that the 'offender' held that there is a significant teaching in the Hebrew Bible, the importance of which could be independent of how the Hebrew Bible foreshadowed and anticipated the New Testament. The charge might be made against maintaining that there is wisdom concerning the nature of the rule of law or nationhood or freedom of the will in the Hebrew Bible, such wisdom having philosophical significance in its own right. Or, the charge of judaizing might be made against maintaining that the Hebrew Bible is a source of deep ethical truths without reference to the 'New Law' of the New Testament. The willingness to read the Hebrew Bible as a book that stands on its own (in its own language) often elicited an attribution of guilt by association, the alleged guilt of the Jews implicating Judaic thought as guilty, too.

Some of the Christian Hebraists of the seventeenth century are notable for having argued that Judaic thought merited close study for its relevance to moral and political life. That is not to say that there was an agreed, well-defined characterization of 'the Judaic', or that those thinkers did not also read the Hebrew Bible as the Old Testament. But it was recognized as intellectually fruitful to study and to learn from Judaic conceptions in ways that are not wholly absorbed by their role as preparation for, and as prefiguring Christian ones. Why not use the term 'Hebraic', then, as it is used in speaking of the Christian Hebraists of the early modern period? Many of those figures thought it especially important to learn Hebrew language, which they saw as a key to understanding what I am referring to as 'Judaic' ideas. In many respects, they were correct. Knowledge of Hebrew affords access to meaning in highly valuable ways. But the concern of the present volume is with ideas, which, while they may have had original formulation in Hebrew texts, have gone on to have very wide cultural significance, whether or not that significance has been transmitted through Hebrew language. To be sure, for some non-Jews their importance is intimately associated with their roots in Hebrew texts. That was the case for many of the Christian Hebraists. But their importance is not limited to their formulation in Hebrew texts. There are many people for whom the ideas are significant, and to whom it would not occur that the ideas might be better understood through study of their roots in Hebrew. In fact, many such people might not even have a clear idea of which aspects of the relevant conceptions are traceable to Judaic rather than Christian sources.

Some currents of recent European and American culture have been quite willing to see Judaic and Christian roots as a single, complex source, shaping a shared culture. The formulations 'Judeo-Christian culture' and 'Judeo-Christian heritage' have a good deal of currency in both academic and non-academic contexts. For example, they occur in editorial rhetoric concerning a diversity of topics, from questions about what undergraduate liberal arts curricula should include, to the American national self-conception, to issues of global politics, among other matters. There generally is not much careful consideration of these expressions. Unfortunately, much can be obscured or misrepresented by usage of the conception 'Judeo-Christian' in a summary, uncritical way. It can make for a kind of specious fluency, an appearance of an important, clear meaning when, in fact, users may have little in mind except the idiom itself and perhaps a few vague generalizations.

It is true that contemporary Jews and Christians, and many secular-minded people of Jewish or Christian background can point to certain values and conceptions that might be said to constitute a Judeo-Christian tradition. These would likely include the value of the individual—the individual's priceless moral worth—and our having equal moral standing despite differences in individuals' virtues, vices, and actions. An important kind of moral egalitarianism is traceable to Judaic and Christian roots. There are also ways in which the values of justice, compassion, humility, and freedom have pronounced origins in Judaic and Christian thought. Those origins are not uniquely Judaic and Christian but they have paradigmatic grounds there.

Still, the notion of a Judeo-Christian culture or tradition is actually rather recent, and its employment is often not very sensitive to whether Jews and Christians in earlier times saw themselves as inheriting, participating in, or upholding such a tradition. There have been periods—the seventeenth century is especially notable in this regard—during which Christians had a heightened interest in Judaic roots and early Jewish history. English and Dutch scholars and political thinkers of the period are among the most prominent examples, including Grotius, Selden, Milton, Harrington, and even, to some extent, Hobbes and Locke. But it is doubtful that historically there has been much shared consciousness of a Judeo-Christian tradition or that it was *important* to many people to think in such terms. During the Middle Ages some thinkers regarded the common monotheism of Judaism, Christianity, and Islam as a significant bond (Maimonides is a good example) but there was also awareness of clear and significant differences between the faith-traditions, and the differences often motivated mutual alienation despite the common bond of monotheism. Sometimes there was vilification, violence, and persecution as well. If, in our time, it seems that there is *one* 'Jerusalem' from which arose one complex, Judeo-Christian culture, it is helpful to be reminded that matters have not always been seen that way.

What if, upon consideration, we should find that the Judaic roots and elements are actually different from the Christian roots and elements in interesting and significant ways? Clearly, there are important respects in which Judaic thought is not easily absorbed into the Christian providential *telos*. What if the absorption depends upon much being read back into and onto Judaic ideas, including much that *changes* them in order to make them absorbable? These essays will provide the reader with resources for considering such matters. The more Jerusalem's enduring presence is studied, the more clarity we can attain regarding relations between Judaic thought and other currents that have contributed to Western culture. For instance, the moral psychologies of Judaic thought on the one hand, and Greco-Roman, and Christian thought on the other, differ in important respects. Of course, there are important roles for repentance, forgiveness, compassion, humility, and the concern for justice in both Judaism and Christianity. Yet, their conceptions of the metaphysics of moral agency and of some of an agent's central, guiding concerns are different.

For example, in Christianity the understanding of salvation and of how human beings can return to God involves elements without clear Judaic counterparts. These include the Christian meaning of the Fall, God becoming man, the mystery of the Trinity, and Christ's passion. There is a distinct metaphysics of salvific agency in Christianity. In both faith-traditions there are prayers beseeching God to turn us toward Him. That, and related notions of repentance and moral reorientation are indeed common to Judaic and Christian religion. However, Christianity involves a decidedly non-Judaic notion of our being *remade* through salvific agency. It is notable that, for example, Maimonides insists that, in the messianic era, neither the world nor human nature will be fundamentally changed. There will be peace, Israel will not be oppressed, and humankind will be devoted to study of Torah. The emphasis is on freedom and knowledge (and their mutual reinforcement), not on the world and human beings being made anew.

In some important currents of Judaic thought there is a pronounced role for coming closer to God through enlarged and deepened understanding, attained through fulfilling the commandments and reflection upon them. *Deuteronomy* 4:5–8 is often quoted by Jewish thinkers: 'Behold, I have taught you statutes and ordinances...Observe therefore and do them; for this is your wisdom and your understanding in the sight of the people...And what great nation is there, that hath statutes and ordinances so righteous as all this law...?' For many thinkers the issue of 'the reasons of the commandments' and human understanding of the justifications of the commandments is intimately connected with the notion of approaching God through comprehension of the created order and Torah. Through God's graciousness, the world was created, the Law given, and human beings can lead lives that bring them closer to God through fulfilment of the commandments, including the commandment to seek understanding. Not all currents of Judaic thought are so rationalistic. But that is an excellent example of the spiral of mutual reinforcement of practical activity and theoretical understanding found in some important Judaic conceptions of what it means to fulfil the commandments.

Judaic and Christian ideas of providence and redemption are not just variants of a common faith-commitment and anthropology. There are deep differences with implications extending into multiple aspects of human self-understanding, of appropriate ideals, ethical requirements, conceptions of human limitations, and how all of these are related to each other. Secularists may see these as no more than differences of detail between conceptions that are intellectually disqualified anyway, on account of being so much at odds with naturalistic conceptualization and explanation. But that perspective cuts us off from more than just the real complexity of intellectual history. It is sometimes also a kind of willful blindness to deep insights into the human condition, human aspiration, possibility, and limits. If one reads the Hebrew Bible as a collection of historical and factual propositions, to be tested for truth in the same ways that other empirical propositions are tested, it requires little effort to conclude that it appears to be a collection of dubious assertions, inconsistencies, and untestable claims. But for many centuries readers of the text have approached it with more sophistication than that and there is no reason to abdicate sophistication simply because our scientific understanding is now much greater.

This is not to suggest that there is *one* Judaic conception and *one* Christian conception of any of the matters mentioned here. That is far from the case. Nonetheless, there are matters of overall orientation, of guiding perspective and disposition, which, in many respects, distinguish Judaic thought from Christian and from Greek and Hellenistic thought. For example, Genesis can be read as a compressed yet inexhaustibly rich anthropology, as an account of how features of human nature with profound moral and existential significance entered the world and of what human lives are like, given that we have those features. Both the content and the presentation of its conception of human beings differ in significant ways from what we find in Greek, Roman, and Christian thought.

In Exodus there are insights into the nature and significance of human freedom, its relation to law and reason, and the relations between the individual and a people. The Judaic conception of freedom, law, and nationhood and how they are related has a distinct character, however much it has been interwoven with other conceptions. These jointly constitute key elements of the Western intellectual heritage, the complexity of which is due in part to differences between Judaic ideas and those with other roots. For instance, differences between the Judaic notion of nationhood, and the Christian notion of a church ramify in manifold, significant ways, including conceptions of past and future and our relation to them. Those differences *matter* in several ways, and they have practical (in the sense of *ethically* relevant) implications.

Christians find a great deal of prefiguration of the New Testament in the Hebrew Bible and they read the two books as a unified body of sacred text. Moreover, there are important common themes, especially concerning moral life and human beings' treatment of other human beings. I am not anxious to find or to create as much space and difference as possible between the two Scriptures. Still, the ways in which the Hebrew Bible can be read and appreciated as a 'complete' work, and the lessons that can be drawn from it separately from Christian (and Islamic) readings and interpretations merit consideration in their own right, in terms of depth of meaning, character of influence, and continuing relevance.

Many of the essays in this volume take up philosophical issues or address issues from a philosophical perspective. Hence, it may strike some readers as unexpected that there is no direct discussion of the 'Athens and Jerusalem' or 'Athens versus Jerusalem' issue in the essays. The main concern is with the content of specific conceptions and the durability of their relevance to the human condition and human self-understanding. The essays explore how Judaic contributions enable us to negotiate numerous substantive matters, rather than adjudicating the question of whether there is a non-negotiable antinomy between reason and revelation. The essays indicate several respects in which focusing on the Judaic Jerusalem's enduring presence enlarges the stock of conceptions, insights, and ideals with which fundamental moral and political issues can be addressed. The 'Athens and Jerusalem' issue might seem especially important because exploration of the interpenetration of philosophy and revelation—whether, and in what ways that interpenetration is genuine and illuminating—bears so heavily on questions about roots, sources, and their influence. From the essays the reader will be able to discern where their authors stand on that issue, despite its not being the primary topical focus of any of them.

This Introduction has not offered a specific characterization, no less definition, of 'Judaic'. The reader is invited to consider the essays that follow, to see what contours of 'the Judaic' are traced out or suggested. However, we can say that there is discernible in Judaic thought a combination of alertness to the limitations of human nature along with responsiveness to what transcends it, and an aspiration to understand the implications of both for action, for thought, and for their relations with each other.

With the foregoing as orientation to the volume, the remainder of this Introduction supplies a brief summary of the main themes and arguments of the essays.

The ten essays are organized into five Parts. In the first Part, 'Some Judaic Roots', Alan Mittleman and Kenneth Seeskin address some fundamental issues concerning the nature of value and what we might call 'normative perspective'. They look at how Judaic—and especially biblical—sources are origins for important, distinctive kinds of understanding.

In 'The Goodness of Being' Mittleman discusses the philosophical aspects of the biblical notion of the world's goodness. His account employs concepts from recent meteathical debates, and it articulates elements of a realist interpretation of the biblical conception of good and its most significant implications for moral value and other kinds of value. Mittleman argues that there is a philosophically important and defensible conception of the goodness of being in the Bible. Not only is it amenable to being explained in philosophical terms, it also has considerable merit inasmuch as it illuminates key ideas and concerns for moral thought and valuative thought in general. In addition, he argues that, while the biblical conception of good is not teleological in an Aristotelian sense, the goodness of being can have motivational significance in that human beings can respond to the recognition of the goodness of being by enacting and actualizing good. Good is real and it is also *realizable* through deliberate human action, which can be a response to the encounter with good. Good can be motivationally *attractive*. Pain, suffering, and tragedy are not to be explained away as merely illusory but there is durable, incorruptible goodness in the very being of things. Human beings can know and appreciate that good, and they can respond to it through affirming it and realizing it in their lives.

That is a distinctively and unavoidably human task and it is a crucial part of what it is to imitate God. Given the realist status of goodness, given the way in which being is to be understood in terms of value, we need not fear that value is ultimately merely expressive or projective, that the world is valuatively vacuous, or that the ground and source of value might cease to be or be rendered inefficacious.

In 'Judaism and the Idea of a Better Future' Kenneth Seeskin explores the notion of the future and how that is integrally related to very basic perspectives and commitments concerning the human predicament and the human prospect. He contrasts this view not only with Christian and Kantian conceptions but also with the Greco-Roman views, in which human beings are condemned to repeat the mistakes of the past, failing to learn in ways that could morally reconstruct the human world. There is a connection with Mittleman's themes in that Seeskin argues that an important Judaic idea of the future denies that the human predicament is ultimately tragic. It asserts that genuine, enduring good can be realized by human effort (though, there is nothing inevitable about that kind of progress). Seeskin's essay is a philosophical exploration of a conception of messianism according to which we can realistically hope for a better future without succumbing to superstition, waiting for an apocalyptic transformation or engaging in utopian speculation.

In some of its most influential forms thought of the future is connected with the notion of human depravity (as in Christianity) or the notion of perfection unattainable by human beings (as in Kant's moral thought and in Cohen's). If the human condition is ultimately tragic, that could motivate a kind of catastrophic demoralization. How can we avoid that without erring in the direction of implausible optimism requiring complete human transformation? Seeskin explains how the concept of the Messiah can be demythologized, how we can retain the idea that human life is not tragic without succumbing to fanaticism. He argues that there are strong moral grounds for believing that there can be a future time when things will be set right, understood along the lines of Maimonides' view that the age of the Messiah will be one in which human beings are devoted to truth and to justice even though human nature will not have been changed in radical ways. The project of bettering ourselves and improving the world is never complete, yet, neither is it hopeless, beyond our capacity. That age will be an end to history in the sense that it will reflect the fact that the Law can be fulfilled in ways it is within the power of human beings to achieve.

Both Mittleman and Seeskin's essays exhibit the non-mysterious conception of value in Judaic thought. In addition, they point out respects in which biblically rooted ideas remain powerfully relevant to modern debates concerning the nature of value and the plausibility of guiding conceptions of the human prospect and project at the most fundamental levels. There are several respects in which ancient Judaic ideas have heightened relevance and plausibility in light of modern debates.

In the second Part, 'Judaic Culture and Politics', Steven Grosby's and Yoram Hazony's essays explicate ways in which it is important to recognize a distinct Judaic culture, especially a culture of the polity, the main ideals and categories of which sharply distinguish it from cultures with Greek and Roman provenance. In 'Hebraism: The Third Culture' Grosby argues that Hebraic culture (a notion close to what has been referred to so far as 'Judaic') is indeed a heuristically productive historiographical category. The essay argues for Hebraism as an illuminatingly distinct, complex conception of a people, of law, of politics, and theology. Somewhat more than the other essays, this one outlines the contours of an *explanatory* (in the sense of *methodological*) approach to the normative character and significance of Judaic ideas. Indeed, several crucially important early modern thinkers (and important actors in politics) sought to retrieve it as normatively authoritative. The Christian Hebraism of the Reformation brought this culture into relief, not as intellectual archaeology but as authoritative. It went on to have real importance in the British presence in North America, having a profound impact on the formation of political culture of the New World. Grosby shows that conceptions of the primacy of the legislative body in governance, the ideal of a republican order of free and equal individuals, and the subordination of the ruler to the law are owed to Hebraic culture, however much this may be disguised by the interpenetration of other sources and influences.

Hazony's 'The Political Thought of the Biblical History, Genesis–Kings' explicates some fundamentally important political ideas in ways that complement Grosby's analysis. Hazony argues that there is a central, unified political teaching in the Bible, one that can be distinguished from the multitude of diverse political purposes to which the Bible has been put. He identifies the chief books in the Bible in which an important political narrative is presented (Genesis to Kings), and he argues that its political import is both deliberate and significant. There is not just one political teaching but there is a core teaching in the story of the rise, and then decline, of the Israelite people and their state. The narrative of the deliverance of Israel— once from bondage in Egypt and once from anarchy in the era of Judges—is the main vehicle for the presentation of biblical political teaching. Moses delivers Israel from the imperial state and David delivers Israel from disintegration and civil war. The limited state—in contrast to the empire, illustrated by Egypt, and the political dissolution of the period of the judges—is the best political form human beings can achieve. A state, with limited powers, limited claims upon citizens, ruling by law, and having limited ambitions in regard to its neighbours offers the most promising and stable political possibility. There is political *thought* in the Bible, not just political history, and its relevance is not limited to antiquity. Hazony explicates the considerable political awareness and insight in the texts on which he focuses, finding in them a rich fabric of understanding of individual and social psychology and the complex interaction of principles, ideals, and human tendencies.

Hazony's and Grosby's essays highlight the political sophistication and depth of Judaic thought and also the way in which its insights remain strongly relevant to fundamental issues of politics. These essays focus on some of the most important components of the political anthropology of the Bible and Hebraic thought. In connection with the preceding two essays these contribute content and contour to that anthropology.

The next two essays are by Jonathan Jacobs and David Novak. In this Part, 'Fundamental Elements of Morality and Moral Psychology', the authors explore the contribution of Judaic resources to the conceptual architecture of moral thought. Looking at approaches to 'the reasons of the commandments' in 'Tradition, Rationality and Moral Life: Medieval Judaism's Insight' Jacobs argues that there is an important current of rationalism in medieval Jewish philosophy, combining an aspiration to supply rational justifications for moral requirements, with humility regarding the extent to which rational justifications can be ascertained. Moreover, this current of thought, to which Saadia and Maimonides are especially important, includes materials for an appreciation of the complex role of tradition in rational morality. Jacobs argues that the medievals fashioned a view in which tradition is a mode of transmitting moral commitments, the rationality of which may not be fully evident, though fulfilling the tradition's requirements enables agents to more fully grasp the justifications of those requirements. Tradition can be a way of being anchored to truths that come into view through fulfilling the requirements of tradition. The epistemology of this view overlaps with, but is distinct from practical wisdom and natural law approaches. It is relevant to enduring questions concerning the rational justification of moral requirements and to the way in which moral understanding can be deepened and enlarged. It is important also in respect of the conception of the relations between practice and understanding, and how their spiral of mutual reinforcement is crucial to human excellence.

In 'Natural Law and Jewish Philosophy' Novak explicates the ways in which Jewish sources and the rabbinic tradition supply a conception of the relation between rational justification and the theistic ground of moral requirements that illuminates natural law theorizing. The particularism of Jewish perspective and tradition can be a means of access to universal moral values and principles, rather than distancing Judaism from them. He argues that the Noahide commandments, the interpretation of which has been central to debates about whether Judaism contains a conception of rational, natural law, are best understood as reflecting God's creative wisdom, discoverable when humans recognize the necessary divine grounding of all cogent human claims on each other. He maintains that a view of the Noahide commandments as natural law corresponds best with classical Jewish sources, and that it presents the most coherent approach to appreciating the ongoing normative significance of these laws and the ideas and ideals they concretize. Novak claims that natural law categories of thought are a sound way of articulating the universally valid standards of justice in Jewish moral thought. Natural law provides a conceptual idiom for the rights and duties religious Jews regard as having a divine source and which are many of the same rights and duties secular persons recognize. He argues that there is much to be gained by a rethinking of natural law. It could be significant in at least two ways. One is that it would show that many of the fundamentals of natural law are present in distinctively Judaic thought and sources. Another is that a rethinking by contemporary Jews would bring into relief the significance of universally valid justifications of theologically grounded moral and political commitments.

Jacobs and Novak arrive at different conclusions regarding Judaic moral thought and natural law. Their differences indicate some of the internal dialectic of Judaic thought and highlight some of the most important and contested issues of moral epistemology, especially in its relevance to the universality of moral values.

The next pair of essays constitute the Part, 'Medieval and Modern Politics: Maimonides and Spinoza on Reason and Revelation'. In it Daniel Frank and Edward Halper explicate the continuing relevance of Maimonides and Spinoza to fundamental issues concerning political life and political thought, and their discussions have some thematic connections with the immediately preceding pair of essays. A central concern of Frank's and Halper's essays is the rationality, and the appropriate role of concrete practices in political life. Both Maimonides and Spinoza regarded political life as necessary to human perfection. They had sharply contrasting views of the role and authority of tradition, while sharing some insights concerning the significance of specific, concrete practices and the differences they make to the dispositions of members of a political community.

In 'The Politics of Fear: Idolatry and Superstition in Maimonides and Spinoza' Frank shows how Maimonides' work offers a psychological history of humankind from contemplative repose in Eden, to idolatrous worship, to Abrahamic monotheism, to (again) idolatrous worship, to (finally) Mosaic prophecy. The divine law is meant to bind the community in a kind of worship and way of life that is the antithesis of idolatrous worship. Love of God replaces irrational fear, and communal worship replaces idolatrous practice. In the *Tractatus Theologico-Politicus* Spinoza commences with a description of superstition, that mental state resultant upon the wayward emotions of hope and fear. To overcome or at least mitigate superstition Spinoza offers humankind a different kind of divine law, the inexorable laws of nature (whose study is physics), and a way of life, devoted to justice, charity, and love of one's neighbour. This, he argues, would liberate citizens from the (idolatrous) pomp of religion, as well as the civil unrest consequent upon religious intolerance. Frank explains how what might appear to be a parochial dispute *within* Judaism is in fact part of a much broader debate in political philosophy about human nature, the limits of the civil authority, and the possibility of communal consensus. The ways in which Maimonides' and Spinoza's thought wrestled with the interpretation of religion and its (broadly) political significance affords insight into important, universal concerns.

Halper focuses on religious law and how its fulfilment has significant communal benefits, even if agents do not recognize how those benefits are achieved. He highlights motivational issues and how obedience to the commandments shapes dispositions crucial to a well-ordered community, largely through redirecting desire and imagination. In fact, Torah accomplishes this surreptitiously. While people see themselves as serving God through following religious laws, that activity cultivates traits and dispositions important to communal life and a healthy social world. Both Maimonides and Spinoza held that desire and imagination can distract and disorient the intellect. According to Halper, the religious laws are 'political devices' to mould citizens' characters so that they are motivated to act rightly. (He explains how Maimonides and Spinoza draw their ideas concerning this matter from the Torah's parable of expulsion from the Garden of Eden.) Maimonides recognized the religious laws as divine, while Spinoza was famously much more critical of them. He argued that the Hebrew state was fatally flawed but also claimed that it had the merit of inducing citizens to obey its law from love, rather than fear. In his unfinished *Political Treatise* Spinoza introduced what amount to secular alternatives to Torah's religious laws, with different laws for different states. In short, Halper sees Maimonides and Spinoza as analysing the political significance of Torah's laws, and as acknowledging their significance for creating and shaping motivation. Thus, Torah was an important model for political philosophy, containing insights into fundamental issues concerning political obligation and the justification of political institutions.

As in the immediately preceding pair of essays, here too there is fertile disagreement. Frank and Halper bring out the complexity of Judaic thought concerning reason in politics while recognizing the relevance of biblically based political thought, even for questions concerning the modern liberal polity. Rationalist commonalities are often overshadowed by differences in Maimonides' and Spinoza's conceptions of what sorts of practices and requirements are suitable to attaining political goods. Spinoza's thought is not as complete a departure from Judaic roots and sources as it may appear. In some ways, it is a distinctively modern development of them. These essays help place these two thinkers in the larger, overall story of how the central, enduring problems of political thought and political life are to be formulated and addressed.

The final pair of essays, in the Part, 'Moral Personality: Enduring Influences and Continued Borrowings', concern the significance of the individual. Both essays explore the topic through comparing Judaic sources and interpretations with Islamic counterparts. One reason for that is that both Judaism and Islam are strongly legalistic and yet in each tradition there are vitally important, outstandingly spirited and independent individuals. The essays explore features of moral personality and conceptions of the individual as a locus of intrinsic, inestimable worth. In 'Dancing in Chains: The Coexistence of Legalism and Exuberance in Judaic and Islamic Tradition' Ze'ev Maghen explains how apparent antitheses of law and exemplary individuality are, in fact, *merely* apparent, and how spirited, even revolutionary individuality is valued by both traditions. Maghen looks into ways in which the comprehensive legalism of Judaic and Islamic thought is not an impediment to freedom or a constraining imposition on individuality. This is an approach to the relationship between law and freedom that can do much to correct persistent misinterpretations of the Judaic conception of moral personality.

Goodman's essay looks at how the medieval Aristotelian emphasis on kind-specific natures is reconcilable with the Judaic emphasis on the inestimable worth and importance of the individual. Goodman argues that the concept of the individual, rooted in biblical monotheism, has critical implications for morals, for politics, and indeed for aesthetics. In morals it is the root of a very particular way of articulating the ideas of human dignity, privacy, and worth. In politics, those roots support a construal of desert in terms of rights, both negative and positive. And in art we see a parallel appreciation of creativity in the artist and of the unique, original artwork. His treatment of the issue looks at it through the medieval appropriation of Greek philosophy by Islamic and Jewish thinkers. Avicenna's relocation of the principle of individuation, not in our embodiment but in our consciousness is an important development of the conception of the individual. Among the philosophers who follow it up are Ibn Bajja, Ibn Tufayl, and Maimonides. Even al-Ghazali, powerful critic of the Greco-Arabic tradition in Islamic philosophy, and of Avicenna in particular, makes use of Avicenna's solution. So does Maimonides, taking up the work of his Muslim predecessors, philosophically finding its deepest original roots in the Hebrew Bible.

The way in which Maghen and Goodman show the braiding of Judaic sources and perspectives with Islamic thought illustrates some of the mutual influences between the two traditions, including the naturalness of the cohabitation of scripture and philosophy in them. The essays also show how ancient themes have been elaborated and interpreted by later thinkers who saw themselves as being faithful to origins rather than departing from them. Medieval thought offers many excellent examples of ancient sources being seen as ever-relevant guides containing inexhaustible wisdom rather than primitive myth or sub-rational consolation.

In some ways, something similar can be said about the early modern Christian Hebraists. While they may have sought to escape a charge of judaizing they were unabashed in claiming to find deeply significant relevance in ancient Judaic sources and conceptions. It is striking that they saw its relevance most prominently in regard to urgently practical matters of politics.

The essays in this volume reflect the judgement that much is to be gained by studying Jerusalem's enduring presence in medieval and early modern times, and the judgement that we can continue to find much of value in Jerusalem's enduring presence even now. Its presence is not a result of the tenacity of unreason in the face of more adequate and illuminating accounts of the relevant issues. It is not a matter of *clinging* to something but of continually *finding* wisdom, insight, and guidance despite changes in philosophical idiom, political reality, and scientific understanding. Interest in Judaic origins reflects willingness to consider how ancient roots and sources might sustain living convictions and shape illuminating perspectives, notwithstanding the antiquity of their origins. The passage of time multiplies the influences and contexts with which Judaic conceptions interact and the ways they are developed and revised. Nevertheless, it is possible to appreciate their distinctness and significance, and our comprehension of the past and ourselves can be enlarged and deepened by that appreciation.

Part I

Some Judaic Roots

1

The Durability of Goodness

Alan Mittleman

As for me, nearness to God is good. Psalm 73:28

The first creation account of Genesis, unlike the Mesopotamian creation stories, portrays God as evaluating his own work. At six points in the process of creation, God sees that what he has done is good and, ultimately, very good.[1] The conspicuous repetition of 'good' (*tov*) in the account invites an exploration of the relationship between axiology and ontology, value and being, in Scripture. The impulse to locate radical value in being—to affirm that human life is fundamentally good—is typical, even constitutive of biblical and Judaic thought. In what follows we will explore this strand of the metaphysics of the Hebrew Bible on the assumption that Scripture opens itself to a metaphysical articulation. This metaphysics can be compared to other ancient metaphysical views, such as those of Plato and Aristotle. The Bible does not offer an argument in a formal sense. But an argument can be gleaned from its texts and made on its behalf.[2]

---

[1] One could argue that the Egyptian and Akkadian creation stories imply that the orderly whole which the gods form is good. What is lacking, however, is an explicit recognition, articulated in divine speech, that the creation is good. Explicit invocation of the concept of the good vis-à-vis the creation is found in Plato's *Timaeus*. See, e.g., *Timaeus* 30a, 53b. Here, however, the speaker, Timaeus, surmises that God acts for the best. God himself, as it were, is not speaking about his work.

[2] This essay is very much indebted to the work of Prof. Lenn Goodman, especially to his magisterial *God of Abraham* (New York: Oxford University Press, 1996) viii, in which he explores the 'nexus between God and values'.

It is not at all obvious, from a modern point of view, that such a project is possible. After Spinoza the Bible has been approached, at least among intellectuals, as an expression of a particular time-bound culture notably lacking in philosophical or scientific interest. At best the Bible encodes moral, not metaphysical, teaching. Spinoza and his heirs believed that the interest of medieval writers, such as Maimonides, in extracting the philosophical teaching of the Bible and displaying its complex relationship with the Platonic and Aristotelian traditions was completely groundless. The ancient (Philo) and medieval authors were imposing their own alien philosophical views on the biblical text. There is, of course, some truth in this assertion. On the other hand, they sidestep an abiding problem and render it invisible. The medieval authors pursued a philosophical exegesis of Scripture because they believed, correctly, that truth was unified. The truth which they humbly accepted in the Greek traditions could not, they believed, fundamentally contradict the truth which they thought was revealed in the biblical tradition. They were not cultural relativists or epistemological pluralists, at least not in the modern sense. Spinoza was willing to let the Bible remain meaningful in a reductive, moral sense but he did not permit the Bible to teach truth in a metaphysical sense. This approach only gets us so far. In fact, it stands in tension with the deep reasons that motivate readers, both scholarly and lay, to explore Scripture in the first place. If Scripture is just another collection of ancient literature without abiding claims to truth, why invest inordinate effort in decoding its cultural specificity? To the extent that moderns retain a theological interest in Scripture, rather than an exclusively historical one, they cannot evade the question of truth.[3]

What understandings of the good or, at the risk of reification, of goodness emerge from Scripture? I intend to look at a few key texts

---

[3] Not only debunkers of the philosophical content or potential of Scripture, such as Spinoza and his descendants, but defenders of the theoretical content of Scripture, such as Thorlief Boman disagree with the approach taken here. Boman argues, in his *Hebrew Thought Compared with Greek*, that the biblical creation accounts are not comparable with a philosophical account, such as Plato's *Timaeus*, since the biblical accounts do not aim at a 'scientific' explanation of the world but rather are a confession of the power and goodness of Israel's God as revealed in the exodus. That is, 'creation' is simply an artefact of 'redemption'; the creation stories are really about the founding of history, not about the way world is in and of itself. See Thorlief Boman, *Hebrew Thought Compared with Greek* (New York: W.W. Norton & Co., 1970) 172–5.

that focus on the good at the intersection of ontology and axiology, being and value. By value, I mean primarily moral value but, admittedly, the distinction between moral and other forms of value is not hard and fast. A central locus of biblical teaching on the good is found in the first three chapters of Genesis. Arguably, God's evaluation of the world as good is not an invocation of moral value since, at this stage, the goodness of the world is still irrelevant to moral conduct as no moral agents (other than God) exist.[4] Nonetheless, it would seem odd to think of the goodness of creation in a wholly non-moral, say, purely aesthetic or epistemic sense. Even if goodness here were to mean well-formed or fit to function, as Leon Kass maintains, the being of a well-formed whole is of prime significance for moral value. The goodness of the world is not irrelevant to the goodness of human character or conduct. Good character and conduct, we might say, are instances of a more fundamental goodness—the goodness of being. Just as Plato's postulation of the good in epistemological and metaphysical terms in *Republic* 509b relates integrally to the good as an ethical and political ideal in the rest of his thought (eg *Republic* 540a, *Gorgias* 507a), so too the evaluation of the world as good in Genesis, chapter 1 grounds a moral and lawful way of life.[5] The first section of

[4] cf. Leon R. Kass, *The Beginning of Wisdom* (New York: Free Press, 2003) 39. '"Good" as used throughout Genesis 1 cannot mean *morally* good: when "God saw the light that it was good", He could not have seen that the light was honest or just or law-abiding. The meaning of "good" seems rather to embrace notions like the following: (1) fit to the intention; (2) fit to itself and its work, that is, able to function for itself and in relation to the unfolding whole; and especially (3) complete, perfect, fully formed, clear and distinct, and fully what it is. A being is good insofar as it is fully formed and fully fit to do its proper work.'

[5] A strong challenge to the view that the creation is good *at all* is found in Edward L. Greenstein, 'Presenting Genesis 1, Constructively and Deconstructively,' *Prooftexts* 21, 1996, 1–22. Greenstein argues based on texts that reflect the primordial *Chaoskampf*, as well as Genesis 6:1–4, that God is actually rather malevolent. The repeated use of 'good' in Genesis 1 signifies only 'pleasing to the tastes' of God (*Elohim*, which he ominously translates as 'the Powers' to distance a biblical understanding of divinity from ours, where 'God' inevitably triggers association with its etymological cousin, 'good'). But divine taste 'does not mean that it was all good, or good at all, in the moral sense'. 'God may be pleased with creation, and it may for some reason need to be the way it is—but that does not in and of itself mean that creation is good or makes for goodness.' '[I]t has not been made essentially, inalterably good; it already contains the elements of its own corruption. And these, of course, have been made or left there by God.' Whatever merit this highly provocative reading has as biblical exegesis, it seems to me to fail philosophically. Greenstein claims that 'it makes no sense to interpret the term "good" in Genesis 1 valuatively [*sic*], because "good" can only mean good in contrast to bad, just as darkness can be recognized only in contrast to light', but then

this essay sketches out some of the implications of the goodness of creation.

But what is the relationship between this moral and lawful way of life, rooted as it is in the goodness of creation, and the God who brought the world into being? How are the goodness of creation and the goodness of God related? Is the way of life simply a protracted act of obedience to divine will or does it have a rational basis as a response to the goodness, with which God, in his goodness, endowed creation? The latter explanatory framework, long favoured by the rationalist stream of Jewish thought, grounds law and ethics, the Jewish way of life, in the imitation of God, whose goodness must be actualized by his human partners in the midst of a world compatible with that purpose. That is the stance which I shall develop here.

The Bible frequently prompts us to praise God because 'He is good' (*ki tov*: e.g., Psalm 136:1). On the Bible's own account, this is more than an exclamation of approbation; it is a description. Consider such a statement in the light of Exodus 33:19 where God tells Moses that 'I will make all my goodness [*tuvi*] pass before you.' Moses had requested to experience 'your presence' (*kavodkha*) but, as a human being, he could not do so and remain alive. God thus reveals all of Himself that can be revealed to a human, namely, His goodness. To say then that God is good is to do more than commend; it is to describe. It is, on the biblical account, to track a fact about the divine nature. How does the goodness of God relate to the goodness of the world? Is *tov* used in the same sense in both statements? It would not be radical to say that the acknowledgement of the goodness of the world qua creation is an *acknowledgement* of the divine—the heavens tell of the glory (*kavod*) of God (Psalms 19:2). But, given the ontological status of the good vis-à-vis God in Exodus 33:19, could we say that the experience of the goodness of the world is an *experience* of the divine or that the realization of goodness in the world is a *realization* of the divine? This sounds rather Spinozist. It seems to violate the

---

goes on to claim that good implies pleasing to God's tastes. One cannot have it both ways. 'Pleasing to tastes' is inherently evaluative. Furthermore, are we really to believe that God's 'tastes' are wholly disjointed from God's moral attributes? Greenstein claims that this view, which portrays an essentially arbitrary and violent God, better captures the tragedy of 'our experience of reality'. I would say, by contrast, that it privileges a tragic reading of our experience by ignoring the deeper implications of the biblical metaphysics.

transcendence of God, a key theme for both the Bible, at least in its most rationalized texts, and subsequent Judaism.

What then is the difference between a suitably biblical and Judaic concept of God and the good? Is God equivalent to goodness, as Plato's god seems to be? In biblical terms, the divine will always, by definition, exceed any embodiment of divinity within the world, thus goodness can be said to disclose the divine but not to comprehend or exhaust it. But is this not also true of the good? That is the case on Plato's account where the good is ultimately beyond being (*Republic* 509a) or, to put it in a more epistemological way, the good is sovereign over other concepts.[6] The goodness of God and the goodness of creation are linked in biblical and Jewish thought. The affirmation of goodness and, crucially, its enactment in human conduct, orient the life of the Jew. To illustrate this, we will consider some rabbinic texts which draw from this mutually implicated radical goodness profound consequences for human orientation and conduct. That is the focus of the second part of this essay.

The goodness of creation and the goodness of God make for what I would like to call the durability of goodness—the fundamental, non-defeasible goodness of being. I believe that the intuition of a goodness underlying life, despite the infinite adversities encountered in the midst of life, is one of the most significant contributions made by the Bible and Jewish thought to world civilization. More precisely: the conceptual framework, the work of naming, affirming, and supporting that the Bible provides for the intuition of fundamental goodness is a signal contribution. All that is recognizably human—from the love of knowledge, to the love of justice, to the love of beauty—is launched in recognition of an underlying goodness which both contemplation and action seek to grasp, instantiate, and further. All cultures arguably respond to that goodness in original ways. The response of biblical and Jewish thought is to identify human life with goodness under the description of the holy (*kadosh*). Sacrality or holiness fixes the good as an indefeasible characteristic of human persons, derived from an ultimate source in the goodness or holiness of God. Again, all cultures arguably assign or discover sacred value in some people, places or things, setting these extraordinary items apart from the profane members of their class. But the biblical culture

---

[6] Iris Murdoch, *The Sovereignty of Good* (London: Routledge, 2003) esp. 75–101.

posits the sacredness of *all* human beings; all are made in the image of God (Genesis 1:26–27). The underlying goodness of being is linked to the goodness of God. Humans are to actualize the goodness of their being by following the manifest pattern of divine goodness.

It is striking that Greek thought, which puts a high premium on the metaphysical status and ethical consequences of goodness, constructs goodness vis-à-vis persons in a dramatically different way. Greek thought evaluates the worth of life, of human being as such, differently from biblical and Jewish thought. Aristotle, infamously, thought that some human beings are slaves by nature (*Politics* I:5). Their lives are worth less, have intrinsically less potential for *eudaimonia* (*Nicomachean Ethics* X:6). Plato's caste system, in *Republic*, Book III, rests on cognate beliefs. (The Stoics, of course, offer a more egalitarian view.) Another indication of fundamental difference is the value assigned to suicide among these various traditions. For Plato, suicide was objectionable because it harmed the gods by depriving them of their possession (ie, oneself) (*Phaedo* 62b–c) or because it violated a social norm of manliness (*Laws*, IX, 573 c–e)—not because it violated a fundamental *ḥuqat ḥayyim*, a law or norm of life. Under certain circumstances, which are more expansive for Plato than for the Bible or Judaism, suicide is appropriate. For the Stoics, suicide could be noble or praiseworthy under the right conditions.[7] Noble persons are in their own possession (contra Socrates in the *Phaedo*) and can dispose of themselves as reason deems fit. From a biblical and Jewish point of view, this is an offence against the goodness of life and the God of life. The third section of this essay, through a study of the last chapter of the Book of Jonah, will explore the insistent biblical affirmation of the value of life. Jonah begs God to take his life from him, as his life no longer seems good to him. God refuses and tries to get Jonah, through dialogue, to recognize the enduring goodness of life. That good is more fundamental and enduring than evil is here affirmed.

By the 'durability of goodness' I mean to allude to the important work of Martha Nussbaum, *The Fragility of Goodness*. There Nussbaum takes up a matter of fundamental importance in Greek tragedy and philosophy, the problem of moral luck. Luck (*tuche*) refers to the

---

[7] See, e.g., the letter (#70) on suicide of the Roman Stoic, Seneca. Moses Hadas, trans., *The Stoic Philosophy of Seneca: Essays and Letters* (New York: W.W. Norton & Co., 1958) 202–7.

innumerable conditions, both internal and external, that shape our lives and impinge on our ability to govern ourselves as we would wish, virtuously, to do. Nussbaum's analysis leads her to affirm the tragic character of human life, that is, the wisdom found within traditions of tragedy and philosophy as it draws on tragedy. Tragedy captures the incomparability of value. The world is so arranged that, given the constraints of luck, our choice of one valuable course of action or way of life precludes others. The good is fragile in the sense that the conditions which make it possible also often make it impossible to realize. Isaiah Berlin, committed to a similar view, put the case categorically: 'The notion of the perfect whole, the ultimate solution, in which all good things coexist, seems to me to be not merely unattainable—that is a truism—but conceptually incoherent; I do not know what is meant by a harmony of this kind. Some among the Great Goods cannot live together. That is a conceptual truth. We are doomed to choose, and every choice may entail an irreparable loss.'[8] Here, incomparable and incommensurable goods ('value pluralism') are constantly in conflict with one another. To choose one good is to choose against another good. There is no way of ranking or ordering goods such that the inevitable trade-offs can be harmonized.

The Bible offers a different vision. It does not diminish the tragic dimensions of life—witness the parallel to Agamemnon in the story of Jephthah in Judges 11—but it enwraps tragedy in a higher wisdom where the good is not defeated by circumstance and contingency. It offers a way of looking at and living beyond moral luck: even though one walks through the valley of the shadow of death, one is not alone or abandoned. A table is set for one in the presence of one's enemies (Psalm 23). There is affirmation in the midst of hardship and suffering, the reality of which is neither denied nor minimized. The good endures. Nor does one need to go beyond our earthly existence, either metaphysically or 'experientially' (eg in the Socratic afterlife of *Gorgias* 523a–527e or *Apology* 41b). The good endures in the midst of being insofar as God, who is 'near to all who call Him' (Psalms 145:18) has placed it there. Furthermore, the way of life which biblical and Jewish teaching means to inculcate is premised on an ordered and doable good. Trade-offs there inevitably are but they need not be tragic.

---

[8] Isaiah Berlin, *The Crooked Timber of Humanity* (Princeton: Princeton University Press, 1990) 13.

Tragedy, its wisdom notwithstanding, is not the last word for a person whose convictions are shaped by the biblical view. It is this view that has moved the Jewish people over the centuries to endure when they might have taken another course, the course avowed by Jonah when he said, 'I would rather die than live' (Jonah 4:8). That sturdy conviction of the blessing of life, despite the enormity of adversity, was taken up by Christianity and enshrined in its central symbol: the victory of life over death, of good over evil, in the resurrection of a crucified man. Judaism, of course, does not go down that road. The resurrection of an entire people, again and again, is its natural-miraculous testimony. Despite the difference in idiom, there is a common underlying axiological instinct. Judaism and Christianity have together shaped the moral culture of the West, holding a hopeful biblical affirmation of life in tension with the tragic sensibility of the Greeks. The loss of the intellectual salience of the biblical affirmation, among contemporary moral philosophers such as Nussbaum, Berlin, Williams, Hampshire and others, results in a new appreciation of tragedy. Whatever wisdom or nobility that might confer, however, it seems to me fundamentally misguided. Were the goodness of being to be abandoned or repudiated, the sacred worth of persons would be jeopardized, hanging by a thread of inherited convention or Camus's absurdist rebellion against nihilism.

1. THE GOODNESS OF CREATION

At first glance, it may seem unremarkable that God should express satisfaction with the results of his unfolding plan. After all, Scripture, as the rabbis put it, speaks according to the language of man (B. Nedarim 3a). It is natural for a skilled artisan to take pleasure, to find goodness, in the fruit of his labour. But this analogy is not exactly correct. God is not expressing, at the most literal level, satisfaction in his work. God is not reporting on his own psychological state, as it were, implying an emotivist account of 'good'. Rather, God 'sees' (*v'yar*) that objects, which now have an ontological status of their own, are good.[9] God observes an objective goodness. God's satisfaction, as it were, is

---

[9] The NJPS translation of the phrase *v'yar elohim ki-tov*, 'and God saw that this is good,' seems preferable to me on this count to Speiser's translation, 'and God was

an appropriate response to the goodness of the world that he has created. Divine action, the action of creation, installs an aboriginal goodness in the works of creation. God acknowledges that goodness post facto. Thus, goodness appears as a property of created things and eventually as a property of the entire system of creation. The whole is 'very good' (*tov meod*). Precisely what this means in Scripture itself is not transparent. The rabbis, in a striking formulation based on the phonetic resemblance of 'very' (*meod*) and 'death' (*mot*) say that both life and death, the ultimate constituents of the whole, are good.[10]

The Bible thus asserts a thesis about the fundamental goodness of nature, of the entirety of life, of being—without, of course, using any of these words to mark the objects or states that are good. This claim is radical. It implies that both individual classes of beings and being as a whole are good. It leaves open whether this good may be subverted, diminished, effaced, abused or destroyed or whether this good is durable and enduring.[11] But this much is clear on the account of Genesis 1: the good belongs to being. It is neither beyond being, the property of God alone, nor a destination or achievement of being such that the failure to achieve it would mean the non-existence of the

pleased with what he saw'. Speiser asserts, 'This phrase, which serves as a formal refrain, means literally "saw that it was good," or rather "saw how good it was" . . . but Heb. "good" has a broader range than its English equivalent.' (E.A. Speiser, trans., *The Anchor Bible*: Genesis (Garden City: Doubleday & Co., 1964) 4–5.) That Hebrew *tov* has a broader range than English *good* should not warrant the shift in emphasis from the goodness of things to the satisfaction of their maker.

[10] *Bereshit Rabba* 9:5, where 'very good' is related to death. See also 9:11 where it is related to punishment. Cassuto relates 'very good' to the harmony of the whole. See U. Cassuto, *From Adam to Noah: A Commentary on Genesis I–V* (Hebrew), (Jerusalem: Magnes Press, 1953) 37.

[11] Contemporary biblical scholarship has explored the different theological or philosophical implications of the various creation accounts, including not just Genesis, chapters 1 and 2 but fragments found in Psalms, Job, and the prophets. The wholly good, stable, and unrivalled cosmic order of Genesis 1 may well be a late development in the history of ancient Israel. The longer story is that of an underlying chaos, which still threatens the cosmos, but is kept at bay by divine might, love, and covenantal fidelity, which is in turn reinforced by human covenantal action. Given this entirely likely history of ideas, our inquiry may be framed as a metaphysical analysis of one particular stream—from my point of view, the deepest and most truth-bearing stream—of Israelite and Jewish thought. See Jon Levenson, *Creation and the Persistence of Evil* (Princeton: Princeton University Press, 1994). The idea, central to this essay, that primordial goodness requires participation and action to be instantiated fits well with this evolutionary view of scriptural thought.

good. The good belongs to being. Does it also belong to becoming? How does the good fare in the course of time?

It is significant that unlike after the creation of light, dry land and seas, vegetation, sun, moon and stars, birds and fish, and land animals, God does not pronounce the creation of the first human pair as good. It may be the case, as Leon Kass argues, that the text is calling attention to the unfinished character of the human. As beings endowed with choice, human beings can choose to become good or not. The absence of divine evaluation may function as a significant pointer toward this distinctive feature of the human vis-à-vis the remainder of creation. On the other hand, the final statement—And God saw all that He had made, and found it very good (Genesis 1:31)—may be read simply to include the human pair. Furthermore, the fact that the humans were made in the image of God (1:27) and that God is ultimately revealed to be good (Exodus 33:19) may obviate the need for explicit evaluation. Nonetheless, if we want to stay within the bounds of the present narrative, we should probably locate some significance in the omission.

The possibility that the omission is significant is buttressed by reference to the second creation narrative in Genesis, chapter 2. There, the stages of creation are not judged to be good. Indeed, the relevant use of 'good' in the story—let us leave aside for a moment the tree of the knowledge of good and evil—is that it is *not* good (*lo tov*) for man to be alone (2:18). The original human condition does not reflect an underlying goodness or, less severely, it reflects a still truncated goodness. (Privation is only possible given the existence of that which is, in the relevant instance, lacking.) It is only when woman is created that human life fully reflects goodness. Here goodness is not primarily aboriginal but achieved, albeit mostly without human effort. (The man does have to notice, celebrate, and name the woman in Genesis 2:23.) In this story, to the extent that human beings participate in the goodness of the created world, they do so as beings who are becoming or, at least, as beings who have become fit to be with one another. It is in their completed form as social beings, more precisely as sexual and social beings fit to be paired with one another, that they participate in and express goodness. Although one could think of the achievement of this condition as a primordial fait accompli and therefore as fundamental to creation per se (as in Genesis, chapter 1), the inclusion of a dimension of development—

so crucial in the teaching of Aristotle on the good—seems pertinent here, as well.

The good is thus *both* part of the founding of the world *and* part of the process of the emergence of the world, as the world is given to human beings in their sexual and social nature. It inflects both being and becoming. Human beings, however, do not *know* this. The growth of human knowledge is part of the emergence of goodness. The first human pair experiences goodness in a primordial way but they do not fully discern, acknowledge, or cognize it. (The man's joyful celebration of the woman in 2:23, however, suggests at least a threshold level of recognition.) God saw that what He had done was good but humans cannot see that their Edenic world is good until they transgress God's command and eat of the 'tree of the knowledge of good and evil'. It is one thing to experience the good, another to know it (and yet another to do it). A baby experiences the goodness of its mother's nurturing love, but only the mother can know (and do) good; can know, at least, in a linguistic, fully cognitive way. If the first creation story installs goodness in being as a fait accompli, the second story ties it to a process of becoming which appears, immediately, as fraught. Is the good not, then, fragile?

The story of Genesis, chapter 2 suggests a tragic dimension to goodness, familiar to Greek thought. The goodness that we gain in achieving our full humanity (as beings capable of knowledge) also involves irreparable loss. Goodness is defeasible, not durable. The full stature of humanity is purchased at a horrific cost. Is this what the Bible is telling us? If so, then the affirmation of value would necessarily entail the conflict of values and tragedy would be inevitable. Let us consider an influential medieval interpretation of this text—that of Maimonides—which aims to reject a tragic reading almost completely. In *Guide* I:2, Maimonides takes an anonymous interlocutor to task for suggesting that God had intended humans to be without moral reason. Furthermore, the interlocutor maintained, humans would have been better off without knowledge. For knowledge, with which came expulsion from the Garden and mortality, although the highest human excellence, was also a kind of curse. On the interlocutor's reading, the Bible is expressive of a tragic sensibility. Maimonides differs radically, becoming incensed—his language is rather abusive—by this view. He denies that God intended for human beings to remain in ignorance by claiming that their creation in the *imago dei already* invested them with knowledge. They had from the outset knowledge of the true and false, that is, they had theoretical knowledge, knowledge of the highest kind. But they also had some sort of primordial practical or moral knowledge for had they not had an ability to make moral distinctions, they could not have grasped God's statement—'Of every tree of the garden you are free to eat; but as for the tree of the knowledge of good and bad, you must not eat of it; for as soon as you eat of it, you shall die' (Genesis 2:16–17)—as a commandment. On Maimonides' view, Adam and Eve already had a form of moral knowledge. What they gained was a lesser form of evaluative judgement, *conventional* knowledge. They became able to judge of 'fine and bad' as persons in political society do.[12] They thus became able to enter a political state where conventional evaluative distinctions, for example, the convention against nakedness, became salient.

Maimonides construes 'but God knows that as soon as you eat of it your eyes will be opened and you will be like divine beings (*elohim*) who know good and bad' (Genesis 3:5) to mean 'you will be as rulers'. The Hebrew *elohim*, as Maimonides points out, can mean 'rulers governing the cities', and is so translated by the ancient Aramaic Targum Onkelos (*ravravin*). Thus, the 'fall' was a melancholy passage from a purely contemplative state to the order of action, of politics. Moral reasoning straddles both realms. Ethics is not fully at home in the theoretical realm of true metaphysical knowledge about the ultimate nature of reality but neither is it a mere sub-species of conventional judgements about the noble and the base within political society. Some apprehension of goodness—in Maimonides' non-tragic vision—is prelapsarian.

Maimonides' tack is to argue that the concept of a commandment would be unintelligible to a being without a notion of obedience or authority or rightness—in short, to a being devoid of moral judgement—therefore Adam and Eve must have had moral judgement prior to their eating from the tree. (Let us leave aside the question of the relation of the right to the good.) But is this a good argument? Perhaps not. In Genesis 1:22, God tells the fish and the birds to 'be

---

[12] Ibn Tibbon translates the Arabic as '*ha-meguneh v'ha-naeh*', Kafih, however, translates as '*tov v'ra*' and criticizes Ibn Tibbon in a note. See Moshe ben Maimon, *Moreh Nevuchim*, Yosef David Kafih, trans. (Jerusalem: Mossad Ha-Rav Kook, 1972) 19. Maimonides' commentator, Shem Tov ibn Falquera, also takes the Arabic to mean '*tov v'ra*', as does Lenn Goodman, who translates alliteratively as 'fair and foul'.

fertile and increase'. Are we to suppose that the fish and birds had a threshold knowledge of normativity? This verse employs the grammatical form of a command but we should not assume the capacity for rational response on the part of the creatures so commanded. Perhaps the closest analogy is the sense in which one commands one's dog. Such statements are meaningful to the commander and, within a limited range, to the dog without there being a full complement of moral abilities in place. In this sense, the human persons commanded at Genesis 2:16 to abstain from eating the fruit of the tree of the knowledge of good and evil could be assumed to have a rudimentary grasp of authority and obedience, of right and wrong, but no more. They were not fully capable of practical reasoning until they lapsed into transgression of the divine command and their eyes were opened to the fullness of moral reality before them. But this does not dispel the tragic estimation of the human condition; it ties the good inextricably to the bad. Genesis would then resemble *Protagoras* in the sense that Plato's account of human origins (*Protagoras* 320d–322d) anchors the unique value, or at least the unique characteristics, of the human in an act of transgression. In order for man to flourish, someone had to sin.

Maimonides wants to reject this tragic conclusion. His strategy entails ranking kinds of knowledge (and the goods which they represent). Whatever capacity for evaluative judgement Adam and Eve had prior to their transgression, full moral knowledge follows only after sin but *full moral knowledge is inferior to theoretical knowledge*. It is higher to contemplate and know the basic facts of the universe than to form judgements of 'fine and bad' about them. Evaluative judgement correlates with political existence (see the parallel, once again, in *Protagoras* 322c where Zeus gives men justice and the political art as an afterthought to preserve the species) rather than with the perfection of the contemplative. Tragedy is averted by downgrading the significance of life as it is lived in the polis. The durability of the good is preserved by delimiting the range of the good. Theoretical contemplation is the highest good; moral judgement is a lesser good. (At the end of the *Guide*, Maimonides moderates (and complicates) this view by associating the theoretical contemplation of God with a *life of action* in imitation of God's goodness.[13] The good revealed to

---

[13] cf. *Guide* III:54.

thought can, indeed, *must* also be lived. This is the deeper biblical and Jewish truth but it is hard to see how Maimonides can affirm it without contradicting himself. In *Guide* III:54, he struggles to reconcile the biblical truth with the 'Greek' truth of the superiority of pure intellection. The goodness of life cannot be fully grasped, actualized and instantiated through contemplative retreat from the world into a kind of Jewish *ataraxia*. God calls us into the world to develop its inherent but embryonic goodness as best we can.)

Maimonides is right when he implies that goodness is a property that requires a social order for its full instantiation. Many uses of *good* describe how well an x fulfils its function under a certain conception. One sees this clearly in Aristotle's idea of human goodness, where the goodness of man (qua man) has to do with fulfilling the essential, constitutive function of a human being, which is to reason both theoretically and practically, with the highest value placed on the former. The logical relation between *good* and statements that describe functions or roles supports Maimonides' view that 'fine and bad' are correlated to social or political existence. But that is evidently not the view embedded in Genesis, chapter 1. There the good is not an artefact of human sociality; it is descriptive (and evaluative) of the world per se. The problem remains then, how we can maintain this without being compelled to read Genesis, chapter 2 as a tragic coda, a necessary compromise of the good. Unless we accept Maimonides' stratagem of ranking the moral and political expressions of the good below theoretical or contemplative expressions we seem to be stuck with a tragic clash between those apparently conflicting sets of expressions.

The way out of this is to argue that the good is not static, nor is it zero sum. Although original to creation, it grows in scope and power as an emergent property.[14] The good emerges from creation towards its full amplitude in a partnership, in biblical terms, a covenant, between Creator and creature, God and man. Plato is able, in the *Timaeus*, to see the creation as a copy of the good. His universe is a

---

[14] So Goodman: 'It is the conative character of being that leads me to equate being with value. If being were static, there would be little basis for this claim, and no one, of course, to make it. I do not think of value as a property of things, natural or nonnatural, or supervenient. Rather, I think of being itself as a value. The value of being is its essence in Spinoza's sense, its conative project' in 'Value and the Dynamics of Being' *The Review of Metaphysics*, September 2007, Vol. LXI, No. 1, Issue No. 241, 72–3.

near perfect derivation of perfect forms. Perfection, the true good, however, lies outside of the order of time and change. The *demiourgos* shapes materials that are not good (*Timaeus* 53b) into a universe that is good. But it is good only insofar as it reflects something necessary and changeless; the ideal, geometrical objects that are the forms of the physical elements which compose the universe. The true good is atemporal; the good available within the world is at best a 'moving image of eternity' (*Timaeus* 37d). Time imitates eternity for Plato; eternity alone is perfect. Genesis, in contrast, ties goodness to time. The good marks stages in the unfolding of time, in the work of days. The good emerges in time. So too, the recognition of value, of the primordial but dynamic goodness of creation, develops in time. It develops in the encounter between man and world, in the growing concourse among created beings.

The good drives the time-bound unfolding of the human. The good launches those activities most characteristic of human beings, especially the quest for knowledge symbolized by the tree of the knowledge of *tov v'ra*. For Plato, 'the Good makes things known, is what we might perhaps express by saying that goodness is fundamental in any explanation.'[15] In analogizing the Good to the sun, Plato claims that the idea of the Good must be conceived 'as being the cause of knowledge, and of truth, in so far as known' (*Republic* VI:508e). The sun's light links the eye to the visible things, enabling visibility. So too the Good gives truth to the objects of knowledge and the power of knowing to the knower. The sun, which is greater than light, because it is its source, also nurtures and sustains the world through its light. Thus, the Good does not just make 'things knowable, but actually makes them what they are'.[16] For Plato, the Good is both a logical and an ontological condition for knowing. In its narrative way, the Bible makes a similar point. The desire to know precedes the quest for knowledge. Adam and Eve had, so to speak, an apprehension that knowledge was a fundamental good before they ate from the tree. Eve believed that 'the tree was desirable as a

---

[15] Annas continues: 'Plato holds not only that facts and values are not radically different kinds of thing, known in different ways, but that values are fundamental to explaining facts.' Julia Annas, *An Introduction to Plato's Republic* (Oxford: Clarendon Press, 1981) 246.

[16] ibid.

source of wisdom' (Genesis 3:6).[17] One must already be aware of the goodness of knowledge in order to desire its consummation in wisdom. Or to put it in a less psychological way: the good is the pre-condition for knowledge.

Beyond the story as such, the status of knowledge as a fundamental good can be inferred in a wholly secular, merely epistemological way from the paradoxical status of scepticism. A sceptical challenge to the value of knowledge attests, ironically, to its primacy and its goodness. The claim, 'there is no genuine knowledge' is a knowledge claim. The question, 'Can we know anything?' seeks an answer, which would count as a bit of knowledge. Doubt compels us to infer that knowledge per se has an intrinsic value, an inherent goodness. The value of knowledge—regardless of the ends to which it is put or the complications towards which it leads—indicates its status as a fundamental good.[18] As beings who seek to know, we seek to advance and give form to an underlying good. Without the goodness of knowledge, the quest for knowledge cannot get off the ground. The search for knowledge aims to complete the arc of goodness sensed at the initiation of the search. It aims to extend the rational order, which Plato took as a token of the good, from one realm to another, from seed to mature tree.

The Bible's postulation of the goodness of creation requires the course of time. The goodness of the completed order, of the *tov meod*, is rediscovered infinitely in the exploration of that order. But this is more than anamnesis. The shaping of new, emergent systems of order by human beings in covenantal partnership with the Creator actualizes and extends goodness.[19] From this point of view, the Edenic lapse is not a tragic fall but a difficult passage. It is part of what differentiates a Platonic universe from a Judaic one. Human beings

[17] Significantly, the desirability of wisdom (*nehmad ha-etz l'haskil*) runs parallel in the verse to 'the tree was good for eating (*ki tov ha-etz l'maachal*) and a delight to the eyes'. The goodness of eating and the desirability or goodness of knowledge, although not equivalent, resemble one another.

[18] John Finnis, *Natural Law and Natural Rights* (Oxford: Oxford University Press, 1996) 59–69.

[19] 'From the earliest coalescence of particles, to the fusion of new elements "cooked" in the stars, to complex, self-regulating systems like the Krebs and citric cycles, to the thought processes of human beings, the great theme in cosmic history is not stasis but emergence, projection of ever more complex and ambitious projects, the rise of ever more autonomous *and ever more interdependent beings.*' Goodman, 'Value and the Dynamics of Being' 71–2.

were not designed to be temporal shadows of eternal forms but to be persons—God's active partners in time, naming the creatures, developing their communion with one another, and keeping and guarding the Garden. Man and woman were given to one another in an incipiently personal way; Adam knows loneliness in his isolation and fulfilment in his sociality. Adam and Eve work together and so mark and spend time with one another. Their Edenic world is not entirely unlike our post-Edenic one. To fulfil the tasks for which they were designed they must leave the Garden and work to evoke the goodness of order in the world. The passage is painful—the sting of transgression cannot be removed—but the logic of their journey was set at the beginning when goodness was proclaimed to reside in the world and set on a course of emergence that required the cooperation of incipiently good creatures. As persons, they are to grow in uniqueness, interdependence and complexity, fully exposed to the vicissitudes and contingencies of history yet capable of adaptation, continual affirmation and development of the good. These are not Platonic guardians who, if they cognize the Form of the Good, want to remain above history and must be compelled to reenter the cave to govern the lesser beings who live there. For Adam and Eve, goodness is in their midst, both within the Garden and within the larger creation. The world does not lose its goodness when they are expelled from Eden. Rather, the possibilities for furthering its goodness are multiplied. The good is not beyond being; its pursuit entails suffering, but does not require a tragic compromise.

2. GOD AND GOODNESS

'Taste and see how good the LORD is,' the Psalmist proclaims, 'happy the man who takes refuge in Him.' 'Fear the LORD, you His consecrated ones, for those who fear Him lack nothing. Lions have been reduced to starvation, but those who turn to the LORD shall not lack any good' (Psalm 34:9–11). The goodness of God is so palpable for the Psalmist that it can be perceived, not merely conceived. To live in awe of this God, to turn to him, secures the fundamental goods of life. The proper response to the goodness of God, grasped in the experience of the goodness of being, is to do good. The psalm continues: 'Shun evil and do good, seek amity and pursue it' (Psalm 34:15).

That those who turn to God 'shall not lack any good' is a familiar thought to traditional Jews. The psalm as a whole is recited following the Grace after meals. The critical verse fragment ('shall not lack any good') was also embedded into the final blessing of the Grace. (Grace after meals is recited after every meal, which, in Jewish law, is constituted by the inclusion of bread.) The final blessing is a compact essay on goodness in the rabbinic understanding:

> Blessed are you, Lord our God, King of the universe. O God, you are our Father, our King, our Redeemer, the Holy One of Jacob, the Shepherd of Israel, the good King who does good to all [*ha-melekh ha-tov v'ha-metiv la-kol*]. For on each and every day, he has done good, he does good, and he will do good for us [*hu hetiv, hu metiv, hu yeitiv lanu*] . . . And let him never cause us to lack any kind of goodness.

The alliterative play with the root for goodness (*tov*) delights. What is remarkable about the text, however, is not its poetic charm but the narrative that lies behind it. In the Babylonian Talmud's discussion of the origins of the Grace after meals, the first three blessings that make up the core of the text are ascribed to Moses, Joshua, and David and Solomon. The final blessing, under consideration here, is ascribed to the rabbis at Jabneh, after the carnage of the failed Bar Kochba revolt (132–135 CE). The Talmud states (B. Berakhot 48b):

> The benediction 'Who is good and bestows good' was instituted in Jabneh with reference to those who were slain in Bethar. For R. Mattena said: On the day on which permission was given to bury those slain in Bethar, they ordained in Jabneh that 'Who is good and bestows good' should be said: 'Who is good', because they did not putrefy, and 'Who bestows good', because they were allowed to be buried.

In this shocking explanation, God's goodness is found in the (miraculous) fact that the corpses of the Jewish warriors did not putrefy. (One is reminded of Father Zosima in *The Brothers Karamazov*.) But it is also found in the (miraculous) permission the Romans gave the Jews to bury their dead. The occasion might have been remembered as a painful, humiliating defeat which could well support a tragic, resigned, or pessimistic orientation to human existence. Instead, the rabbis, without scanting the pain and horror of the war, found evidence of God's goodness in its midst. This is not a Pollyannaish attitude. It is one of stark confrontation with suffering and evil out of which, nonetheless, some measure of courage to persevere may be found. Some measure of hope in Israel's future may be affirmed. Daily ritual reenacts this discovery of God's goodness.

God's own being, 'perceived' by the Psalmist and affirmed by the rabbis as good, models how human beings are to experience, realize and advance goodness in the world. As Maimonides taught at the end of the *Guide*, God's goodness is the pattern humans are to emulate in order to educe and consummate the goodness of creation. Were we left in nature without divine action as our pattern, we might succumb to the evidence, always abundant, that weighs against the primacy of the good. We might run in terror from the field of corpses, so to speak, rather than perform a final act of mercy towards them. Jewish ethics and law, understood by the tradition to originate in the good will of the divine, channels human inclinations, dispositions and desires into duties and responsibilities which coordinate with virtues and aspirations to excellence. Jewish ethics is both deontic and aretaic. The most excellent life is one of gratitude to the Creator for having given one being. It is a life of rational response to the goodness of being. Yet it also accepts the mitzvot—the teachings and commandments of God—as the mode by which gratitude is expressed and goodness furthered in the world. The Torah commands 'Do what is right and good in the sight of the LORD' (Deut. 6:18). The mitzvot are held to be the framework in which primordial human instincts toward the right and the good are disciplined and validated through coherence with the divine pattern of goodness.[20]

How does God come to represent goodness rather than sheer power, will, or *mysterium tremendum*? As noted above, when Moses asks to see God's presence, God responds that He will make his goodness, not his presence, pass before Moses (Exodus 33:18–19a). No man can see his presence and live. God will cause his goodness to pass before Moses. What can that mean? The enigmatic answer may be found in the next clauses 'and I will proclaim before you the name LORD, and the grace that I grant and the compassion that I show' (Exodus 33:19b). For the biblical author, no less than for Plato, the name indicates the essential, constitutive qualities of the entity so named.[21] But those

---

[20] See especially the commentary of Nahmanides *ad loc* for a nuanced analysis of how commandment/duty and virtue work together.

[21] For Plato, see, e.g., Cratylus 390e (but compare 439b, where Socrates expresses scepticism that the name gets us toward knowledge of the thing).

essential, constitutive qualities are not substances but *values*. The values conveyed by God's name are enumerated in Exodus 34:5–7:

> The LORD came down in a cloud; He stood with him there, and proclaimed the name LORD. The LORD passed before him and proclaimed: 'The LORD! The LORD! A God compassionate and gracious, slow to anger, abounding in kindness and faithfulness, extending kindness to the thousandth generation, forgiving iniquity, transgression, and sin; yet He does not remit all punishment, but visits the iniquity of parents upon children and children's children, upon the third and fourth generations.'

These qualities, all of which are emulable (although in normative tradition only the positive ones should be emulated by man), conceptualize God's being qua goodness and its normative consequences. God's being is not reified; it is understood as value. Later authors, notably Maimonides and Hermann Cohen, constitute the divine goodness along the lines of norms for action rather than ontic properties. Whether as Maimonides' 'attributes of action' or Cohen's regulative ideals, the divine goodness *is* equivalent to an ideal pattern of action rather than a predicate that names a property of God, as yellow names the property of a thing that bears it. Another way of putting this is to say that goodness is a matter of God's action rather than God's essence—and action is all that we can know.[22] This is a rationalist position, of course, and is somewhat removed from the atmosphere and beliefs of popular piety.

Some textual support for this reading of God's goodness is found in the theophany of Exodus 33:19, cited above. The translation used supra elides slightly the redundancy of the Hebrew. More literally, the translation reads, 'and I will grant the grace that I will grant and show the compassion that I will show.' The pleonasm recalls Exodus 3:14, God's mysterious naming of Himself as 'I Am That I Am' or 'I Will Be What I Will Be'. The latter statement was also taken by Jewish tradition in a normative direction. As the Talmud understood it: 'Just as I am with you in the current oppression, I will be with you in the oppression caused by future kingdoms' (Berachot 9b). God's mysterious expression of being is taken as a statement of value, of the

---

[22] For Cohen's view, see Hermann Cohen, *Ethics of Maimonides*, Almut Sh. Bruckstein, trans. (Madison: University of Wisconsin Press, 2004) 68–72 (paras 66–8). cf. Hermann Cohen, *Religion of Reason Out of the Sources of Judaism*, Simon Kaplan, trans. (Atlanta: Scholars Press, 1995) Chapter VI.

value of covenantal loyalty: As He is reliably with Israel now, He will be reliably with Israel in the future. Whether that ethicizing interpretation is wholly salient within the original biblical context is hard to say. Perhaps in context it means 'My nature will become evident from My actions'.[23] At any rate, the seeming redundancy of Exodus, chapter 33 ('I will grant the grace that I will grant . . .') recalls the earlier one in Exodus, chapter 3. Arguably, the Bible itself prompts us to read ontological statements in an axiological way.

Rabbinic Judaism grounds the aretaic side of Jewish ethics on the imitation of God. God, despite his incomprehensible otherness, is domesticated, as it were, to the requirements of the doable good. A classic Talmudic text argues:

> R. Hama son of R. Hanina further said: What means the text: Ye shall walk after the Lord your God? Is it, then, possible for a human being to walk after the *Shechinah*; for has it not been said: For the Lord thy God is a devouring fire? But [the meaning is] to walk after the attributes of the Holy One, blessed be He. As He clothes the naked, for it is written: And the Lord God made for Adam and for his wife coats of skin, and clothed them, so do thou also clothe the naked. The Holy One, blessed be He, visited the sick, for it is written: And the Lord appeared unto him by the oaks of Mamre, so do thou also visit the sick. The Holy One, blessed be He, comforted mourners, for it is written: And it came to pass after the death of Abraham, that God blessed Isaac his son, so do thou also comfort mourners. The Holy one, blessed be He, buried the dead, for it is written: And He buried him in the valley, so do thou also bury the dead. (B. Sotah 14a)

The good is done in the context of a covenant between humans and God. God commands man to act, as well as how to act, in consequence of his primordial experience of the goodness of being. In the prophet Micah's famous words: 'He has told you, O man, what is good and what the LORD requires of you: Only to do justice, and to love goodness, and to walk modestly with your God', Micah 6:8.[24] The covenantal bond structures the tasks that are set before human

---

[23] *Jewish Study Bible*, Exodus 3:14, *ad loc*. William H.C. Propp points out that the function of such so-called idem per idem rhetorical devices is 'to be vague, whether to convey infinite potentiality or to conceal information, by defining a thing as itself . . . One possible inference is that "I will be who I will be" means "I can be and can do anything", providing an interpretation of the name "Yahweh".' See William H.C. Propp, *The Anchor Bible: Exodus 1–19* (New York: Doubleday, 1999) 225.

[24] For the fundamental role this verse plays in rabbinic Judaism, see Makkot 23b–24a; Sukkah 49b.

beings. The tasks are not arbitrary; they flow from the premise of the goodness of being, refer to a pattern modelled by the goodness of God, and aim to realize the implications of that conjoint goodness fully in the projects of our lives.

The goodness of God, as the pattern for human action, resembles in some ways Plato's Form of the Good but departs from it significantly, as well. Biblical understandings of the good differ from the Platonic one not only in the radical goodness of being, but in the entanglement of the good with persons. God speaks as a person, not as an impersonal representation of the Form of the Good. God himself has a dynamic relationship with the goodness of creation; it is like his own goodness but unlike it as well. 'God is good' and 'Creation is good' need not set up identities and equivalences among 'God', the 'good', and 'creation'. For Plato, the impersonality of the good, its elevation to a Form, to the Form of Forms, separates the good *Lebenswelt* of evaluations, assessments, social roles and functions, as well as any positive connection with selfhood. The Guardians return to the cave because of a justice that

> prescribes disinterestedly what is best for all [519e–520a]. They do not go down because it is better for them; they would be happier and better off doing philosophy. Nor do they sacrifice themselves altruistically for others . . . They go down because they realize that it is best—simply *best*, not best *for* any particular group of people. They know what is really good, not good relative to the interests or situation of anyone. And it demands their return; so they go. Their motivation is thus very abstract. They are not seeking their own happiness. Nor are they seeking that of others. They are simply doing what is impersonally best; they make an impersonal response to an impersonal demand . . . They take a wholly impersonal attitude to their own happiness, along with everybody else's; and this is because their judgements are made in the light of the impersonal Good, the separated Form which is what is simply *good*, not good relative to anything.[25]

The separation of the Good came at too high a cost, as Aristotle clearly saw (*Nicomachean Ethics* I:6). But Aristotle also paid a price by immanentizing the good.[26] Aristotle's good inheres wholly in the

---

[25] Annas, *An Introduction to Plato's Republic*, 266–7.

[26] Hermann Cohen objects strenuously to Aristotle's critique of Plato as a compromise of the 'strict rationality of ethics' and as a concession to hedonism. See Cohen, *Ethics of Maimonides*, 50–2. Aristotle 'turns ethics into a matter of psychological description

functions of things and beings, and in the projects of persons. The good can be retarded by bad fortune. Boys cannot be said to be *eudaimon* until their lives are over and one can assess the course of life as a whole (*Nicomachean Ethics* I:9). As Nussbaum puts it, Aristotle's 'ethical anthropocentrism is a special development of a general argument denying that our belief commitments do, or can, attach themselves to objects that are altogether independent of and more stable than human thought and language.'[27]

Between Plato's elevation of the good and Aristotle's relegation of it to the vagaries of moral luck, the Bible takes a middle position. God as person is not equivalent to an impersonal form of the good. God is wholly good but, unless we follow the stringent rationalism of a Hermann Cohen, remains irreducible to goodness. Goodness has its highest instantiation in personhood. It is personhood that orders goodness rather than, as in Plato, the other way around. The goodness of creation reaches its most articulate expression in the lives of persons. The work that persons do together to build interdependent lives, when patterned after the goodness of God, fulfils the incipient goodness of creation. The Bible proposes an understanding of goodness that suggests an onto-logical dimension, as in Plato, with a practical, moral teleological dimen-sion, as in Aristotle. Unlike Aristotle, whose good can be destroyed by tragedy, the Bible's good remains durable because of its source in an enduring God. Unlike Plato, whose good cannot be destroyed by tragedy because it is beyond being, the biblical good is continuously rediscovered in the midst of life, tragedy notwithstanding. Human experience, as the experience of unique, sacred persons has inherent worth regardless of its deficiencies, miseries, or outcomes. The last chapter of the Book of Jonah exemplifies this with both economy and power.

3. A DIALOGUE ON GOODNESS

Jonah, chapter 4 presents a dialogue between God and the emotional, embittered prophet. The people of Nineveh repented of their evil

---

and historical development, a sort of knowledge, in which assumption and probability prevail rather than certainty and demonstration' on Cohen's view (at 52).

[27] Martha C. Nussbaum, The *Fragility of Goodness: Luck and Ethics in Greek Tragedy and Philosophy* (Cambridge: Cambridge University Press, 2001) 238.

when they heard Jonah's call. 'The people of Nineveh believed God. They proclaimed a fast and great and small alike put on sackcloth' (Jonah 3:5). Jonah is bitterly disappointed by this mass repentance. 'This displeased Jonah greatly, and he was grieved' (Jonah 4:1). It is unclear why he was displeased. Later commentators impute a personal concern to him—people would think that he was a false prophet (Rashi)—or a public concern—he knew what Assyria would eventually do to Israel (Radak). Within the text, however, Jonah might be claiming that God, not he, had failed. God did not act as He should have acted according to, for example, Exodus 34:7: 'yet He does not remit all punishment, but visits the iniquity of parents upon children and children's children, upon the third and fourth generations' (cf. Numbers 14:18). Jonah has been let down by God; he is angry and disappointed.

It would go too far to say that he is suffering from anomie or that the plausibility structure of his cosmos has crumbled. It is not that the world has suddenly become absurd, that its illusions have become unsustainable. Jonah knew in advance that this might happen; that God was capable of acting like this. He explains that he had initially fled from God and spurned his mission because he knew, alluding to Exodus 34:6, 'that You are a compassionate and gracious God, slow to anger, abounding in kindness, renouncing punishment.' The last phrase, 'renouncing punishment' (*niham al ha-ra'ah*) is not, of course, found in the original Exodus (and Numbers) statements—it is Jonah's addition and stands in tension with Exodus 34:7, 'He does *not* remit punishment.'[28] Why Jonah wants God to conform to His wrath rather than His mercy is unclear. At any rate, God is not capricious or absent—there is no drama here approaching the enormity of Job's situation.

Although not yet Joban, Jonah is so angry (*v'yiḥar lo*) that he tells God that He should take his life (*nafshi*) from him—that 'my death would be better than my life' (*tov moti me-ḥayyai*) (Jonah 4:3). God replies: 'Are you that deeply grieved?' (*ha-hatev harah lecha*) (Jonah 4:4). Note that God's reply uses an adverbial form of *tov, hatev*. Although it cannot be translated literally with sense, the subtle play on the notion of goodness seems significant. Colloquially, we could translate God's remark as 'Are you good and mad?' Jonah perverts the

---

[28] The phrase *niham al ha-ra'ah* is found in Joel 2:13; portions of the thirteen attributes recur in Pss. 86:15, 103:8, and 145:8.

goodness of being by claiming that death is more good (*tov me-*) than life. God archly asks whether Jonah is 'well angered,' good and mad, as if to imply that Jonah, having perverted goodness, still experiences at least perverse instances of it. Goodness finds a way.

What follows is didactic. God, through examples, shows Jonah what elemental goodness is like. He reminds Jonah of the simple goodness of human life. Jonah retreats from the city to see what will happen and builds a booth. But then God causes a lush plant to grow over the booth, sheltering him from the sun. The vine saves him *me-ra'ato*, from the evil, of the harsh sunlight. Significantly, the word is the same as that used in Jonah 4:2, there translated as 'punishment'. It is not right in Jonah's eyes for God to renounce 'punishment' (*ha-ra'ah*) on the Assyrians but it is welcome for God to save him from the evil (*me-ra'ato*) of the sun. Jonah takes simple delight ('great joy') in the plant and the shade, experiencing on a basic level goodness qua pleasure. God leads him back from the absolute negation of the goodness of life through primordial experiences. But pleasure, as Plato well knew, is flickering and an insufficient basis for the concept of the good. God kills the plant—a worm He prepares consumes it—and then, for good measure, rouses a strong east wind to exacerbate the harsh sun. Jonah repeats his plaintive cry for God to take his life, for 'my death would be better than my life' (Jonah 4:8). But then God, having failed to convince Jonah of the goodness of life through shelter and shade, tries to reason with him. He approaches Jonah as a person should be approached, not with carrots and sticks, pleasures and pains, but with the giving of reasons. God puts it to Jonah:

> You cared about the plant, which you did not work for and which you did not grow; which appeared overnight and perished overnight. And should I not care about Nineveh, that great city, in which there are more than a hundred and twenty thousand persons who do not yet know their right hand from their left, and many beasts as well? (Jonah 4:10–11)

In this a fortiori argument, God invites Jonah to consider the weakness of his own position. He cares for something that mattered to him, although his own investment in it was negligible, but he will not allow God to care for persons that matter to Him when His commitment to them is substantial. The book ends with the question. There are no threats, no miraculous displays, only the invitation to reason. Presumably Jonah and the reader will draw the only logical answer.

Jonah should renounce his anger, retreat from his bitter despondency and reverse the perverse judgement that death is better than life.

Jonah needs not only to be convinced that God made the right choice in pardoning Nineveh, he needs to be convinced that life is better than death. God's strategy was to re-educate Jonah in the fundamental goodness of being. The strategy was subtle. Jonah was invited to enter a dialogue based on reasons, to interrogate the logic of caring. Caring—a way of exercising love and responsibility for the world—is premised on the goodness of the world. The world is worth caring for. Life claims us and makes claims upon us. It is this which Jonah is induced to consider. A logic unfolds which will undermine his bitter certainty. He is invited by God to choose life (cf. Deuteronomy 30:19).

God's invitation to Jonah stands as an invitation to all. To choose life fully is to choose to emulate a 'living God' and to live according to the 'laws of life'. On the Bible's telling, this entails affirmation of the priority of the good. Evil is not on a par with goodness. Those thoughts, desires, acts, projects, consequences, and events that we recognize as evil are so recognized because they violate a more primordial normativity that we know as the good. We recognize injustice because we have an incipient concept of justice. More to the point, we work to overcome injustice because of our conviction of the priority of the just. Were justice and injustice, good and evil, equal and opposite, we would, like the ass in Zeno's paradox, not know which way to turn. That we do know, when we think rightly, attests to the sovereignty of the good.

In the language of Maimonides, evil is a privation.[29] Evil gets a grip on human choice when ignorance is allowed to arrest knowledge. When knowledge of the good flourishes and leads, when the tasks that God imposes on us to advance the good orient our action, evil is revealed as insubstantial. Isaiah's famous prophecy—'I am the LORD and there is none else; I form light and create darkness, I make weal and create woe [*oseh shalom u'bore ra*]'—appears to give evil (*ra*) parity with the good.[30] Whatever polemical point Isaiah was making, perhaps against Zoroastrian dualism on behalf of the undivided sovereignty of God, the verse should not be read as endorsement of an amoral God beyond good and evil. The Jewish tradition could not

---

[29] *Guide* III:10.   [30] Isaiah 45:7.

accept such a reading. The Rabbis embedded the statement into the daily liturgy and rewrote the problematic 'evil' as 'everything' (*ha-kol*). More subtly, Maimonides, as well as the influential medieval commentator, Rabbi David Kimchi, noted that the text used different verbs for the positive and negative predicates that follow. God 'forms' (*yotzer*) light (*or*) and weal (*shalom*) but 'creates' (*bore*) darkness (*hoshek*) and woe (*ra*). The rare word *bore* is used also in Genesis, chapter 1, where God brings existence out of nothingness. The use of *bore* by Isaiah is thus meant to convey the originary nothingness of darkness and woe; they come from nothing, not from the positive ground of the good. They are privations of the good, not 'formed' powers in their own right. One creates darkness, Maimonides avers, by blowing out a lamp and terminating its stream of light. The lamp and light have priority; the darkness is privative.[31] One can object to the logic of this argument, but it speaks to the insistence of the Jewish tradition that evil is ordered by a more potent, more real normativity.[32] As Moses puts it in his valedictory address to the nation: 'The Rock! His deeds are perfect, Yea, all His ways are just; A faithful God, never false, True and upright is He' (Deuteronomy 32:4).

4. CONCLUSION

Goodness is durable. It is a property of God and created being. On the biblical account, goodness inheres in the mere fact of being. Yet it is also actualized in the tasks and projects of persons. It is sometimes, even often, derailed by those projects. There is evil in the world, but evil is not ultimate nor is good ultimately destroyed. The goodness of being is not a refuge. We cannot flee to it and wish away suffering or horror. It is not a magic charm. It does not protect us against illness, adversity, oppression or cruelty. It gives us rather a standard by which

---

[31] *Guide* III:10. cf. Kimchi (Radak) on Isaiah 45:7 *ad loc.*

[32] A complex exception of sorts to this judgement is found in the medieval mystical tradition of Judaism, kabbalah. There, evil is reified, given a substantial status, as well as an etiology in the divine nature. Evil represents an imbalance in the system of instantiations (*sefirot*) which form the being of the divine. Nonetheless, even within this system evil serves a higher purpose—the restoration of the unity of the divine and the perfection of the human. For an overview, see Moshe Hallamish, *An Introduction to the Kabbalah* (Albany: State University of New York Press, 1999) Chapter 10.

to judge those assaults on the sacredness of persons and a reason to do something about them, to the extent that we are able. The goodness of being is not a delusion or a fantasy; it is that tangle of fact and value that launches thought. It is both origin and goal. A durable goodness grounds and orients our work in the world. It is prior to our work but also dependent upon it. It endures, in a meaningful sense, only insofar as we endure, only insofar as persons seek together to flourish. It does not adjudicate all conflicts of value or dispel every particular tragedy. It is a transcendent norm, a reference point. The biblical view insists that being is based in value; that goodness arises as soon as something overcomes nothing. Goodness is not an infallible guide. For that, the Jewish tradition looks to divine law and the emulable goodness of God. We can lose awareness of it, but it cannot be lost. To trust in God is to affirm the durability of the goodness of being.

2

Judaism and the Idea of the Future

Kenneth Seeskin

I begin with a simple point of clarification. By *future* I do not mean the fact that there is always another moment in time waiting to appear but the hope that what will appear could be different from and better than what we have now. From the outset, the Hebrew Bible is future oriented. It opens with the dramatic claim, 'In the beginning...,' which, on any reasonable interpretation, implies that it is legitimate to ask about the middle and end as well. The linear structure of the narrative is confirmed by the fact that many of the stories in the Torah involve journeys. But unlike the Odyssey, where the title character returns to his home in Ithaca, these stories generally involve people going to places they have never seen before.[1] For example, Abraham is asked to leave the home of his father and go to a land God will show him, and a whole generation of Israelites led by Moses is asked to leave Egypt and go to the Promised Land.

In addition to the theme of futurity, there is also the theme of novelty. For the most part, the events narrated in the Torah are not variations on a familiar theme but turning points which change forever the way we view human behaviour: the fall from Eden, the flood, the call of Abraham, the exodus from Egypt, and the giving of the Law at Sinai. It is in this context that we can appreciate Isaiah 43:18–19: 'Do not remember the former things, or consider the things of old. I am about to do something new.'

---

[1] For the comparison with Homer's *Odyssey*, I am indebted to Michael Walzer, *Exodus and Revolution* (New York: Basic Books, 1985) 10–17, cf. Walzer, 10–17. Erich Auerbach, 'Odysseus' Scar' in *Mimesis* (Princeton: Princeton University Press, 1953) 13.

The biblical view of history has become so much a part of our way of thinking that we need to step back to appreciate how things could be otherwise.

For the ancient Greeks the world is eternal, and the order we perceive is rooted in the essential nature of things. In the Introduction to his *History of the Peloponnesian War*, Thucydides writes:[2]

> The absence of the fabulous may make my work dull. But I shall be satisfied if it be thought useful by those who wish to know the exact character of events now past which, human nature being what it is, will recur in similar or analogous forms. It has not been composed to win temporary applause but as a lasting possession.

Nothing in Thucydides' account of the war rules out the possibility that over the course of history, empires will rise and fall and the political map of the world change. On the contrary, he is saying that such upheavals are inevitable. His point is that however devastating, these upheavals will not alter human nature so that the categories we now use to explain it will apply equally well in other contexts.

This view contrasts sharply with that of the Hebrew prophets, whose overriding conviction is that no matter how bad things are at present, the day is coming when all wrongs will be righted and justice will prevail. Whether we think of this as a future time (the Day of the Lord) or the ascendancy of a particular person (the Days of the Messiah) is insignificant. The point is that if things could—and eventually will—get better, the way they are is not the way they have to be. Though mankind now lives in deplorable conditions, and the histories of individual people may have terrible endings, no cosmic principle guarantees that the strong will always prevail, that the weak will always suffer, or that disaster is inevitable. If anything, history suggests that the God who liberated Israel from Egyptian bondage will once again hear the cries of the oppressed and step in to redeem his people.

The central claim of this essay is that the idea of the future is not just a way of coping with misfortune, but, more importantly, a presupposition of moral behaviour. As Immanuel Kant put it: 'Without this hope for better times the human heart would never have been warmed by a serious desire to do something useful for the

---

[2] Thucydides, *The Peloponnesian War*, 1.22.

common good'.[3] Simply put: there would be no reason to work for the common good unless we believe our efforts have some chance to succeed. This is another way of saying that our behaviour will be better if we are convinced that the human condition is not tragic— that morality does not impose a Sisyphean labour in which failure is the only outcome.

Acceptance of this view changes significantly the way we view human behaviour. It is not enough to say that there are eternal standards of right and wrong or even that if we live rightly, we will be better off. Beyond the question of right and wrong, is the need to confront the future with optimism—not only that one's own circumstances will improve but that oppression of any kind will cease. It is in this sense that Hermann Cohen, following in the footsteps of Kant, could say that the Hebrew prophets are the first idealists of history and that their vision begot the concept of history as 'the being of the *future*.'[4] We can see this in the evolution of the concept of *Messiah*: literally the anointed one of God. Originally it referred to an existing King (e.g., 1 Samuel 2:10, 2 Samuel 5:3, 23:1, Psalms 89:20) or priest. But after the Babylonian exile, it came to refer to a future King or redeemer who would restore political sovereignty and end oppression.

Again the contrast with the ancient Greeks is instructive. In the first place, it is not clear that the Greek *elpis* corresponds to *hope* in the sense in which we now use it. While *elpis* implies expectation, several scholars have pointed out that it is not necessarily expectation of good.[5] Even when it does imply expectation of good, *elpis* is not necessarily a virtue, let alone a presupposition of moral action. In the *Nicomachean Ethics* (III.8), Aristotle argues that hope or confidence is opposed to courage on the grounds that courage involves confronting fear, while those who are hopeful, either because of skill or past experience, do not have fear.[6]

---

[3] Immanuel Kant, *On the Old Saw: That It May Be Right In Theory But It Won't Work In Practice*, E.B. Ashton, trans. (Philadelphia: University of Pennsylvania Press, 1974) 77.

[4] Hermann Cohen, *Religion of Reason Out of the Sources of Judaism*, Simon Kaplan, trans. (1972 rpt. Atlanta: Scholars Press, 1995) 262.

[5] On this point, see Clifford H. Moore, *The Religious Thought of the Greeks*, 2nd edn. (Cambridge: Harvard University Press, 1925) 37, as well as Pietro Pucci, *Hesiod and the Language of Poetry* (Baltimore: Johns Hopkins Press, 1977) 124.

[6] For an informative discussion of hope in Aristotle, see G. Scott Gravlee, 'Aristotle on Hope', *Journal of the History of Philosophy* 38.4 (2000) 461–77.

It follows that while hopefulness may resemble courage, it is not the real thing. Elsewhere, in the *Rhetoric* (II.5), he indicates that those who become completely dejected and give up all hope *also* cease to fear. The problem is that they become resigned to their fate and cease to have normal human emotions. He concludes that without hope and fear, no one would deliberate: a person would just go on being dejected. This insight is true and important; unfortunately Aristotle does little to develop it, and after making his point, lets the matter drop.

So far from letting the matter drop, the prophets are absolutely committed to the view that dejection is not final. To be sure, they did not make their case on the basis of argument alone. Even the most hardened of readers cannot fail to be swayed by the force with which Isaiah (11:9) proclaims that 'The earth shall be full of the knowledge of the Lord, as the waters cover the sea' or Ezekiel (37:5) tells the bones in the desert 'I will cause breath to enter you and you shall live again.' In time these images and the sentiments behind them became an essential part of the Western philosophic tradition—so much so that in the *Critique of Pure Reason*, Kant could say that the central questions of philosophy are three in number: 'What can I know?' 'What should I do?' and 'What can I hope for?' The first two would have made perfect sense to an ancient Greek audience; the latter would have struck them as silly.

1. HOPE AND ITS DANGERS

Compelling as they are, the prophetic utterances cited above mask a serious problem. If hope for a better future has its upside in preventing people from falling into despair, it also has a downside. As Gershom Scholem wrote: 'There is something grand about living in hope, but at the same time there is something profoundly unreal about it.'[7]

Needless to say, the history of Judaism is littered with false hopes, false messiahs, and wild speculation about the circumstances in which the true one will appear. Though hope is needed when things get

---

[7] Gershom Scholem, *The Messianic Idea in Judaism* (New York: Schocken Books, 1971) 35.

difficult, it is precisely when things get difficult that people are most susceptible to folly. Such folly expresses itself in either of two ways.

The first way it expresses itself is the vision of apocalypse. For many of the prophets, justice cannot be done unless all sin is exposed and punished. Thus Amos (8–9) claims the day of the Lord will not be a joyous time but a bitter, awful one when no light will shine and famine will destroy the land. The punishment will be so severe that no one from those in Sheol to those at the top of Mount Carmel will escape. Jeremiah (4) tells us the earth will be waste and void, the heavens will have no light, the mountains will quake, cities will lie in ruins, and 'disaster will follow upon disaster'. Isaiah (6) goes so far as to ask God to stop up the people's ears and shut their eyes so that cities will lie in waste and the land will be totally desolate.

Again from Scholem: 'Jewish messianism is in its origin and by its nature . . . a theory of catastrophe.'[8] While this is obviously over-stated—not all Jewish messianism is apocalyptic—it allows us to see something important: the belief that oppression and injustice are so prevalent nothing short of a full-blown cataclysm will be needed to rid the earth of them. There are numerous precedents for this view. Recall that God too destroyed humanity during the flood, destroyed the cities of Sodom and Gomorrah, and threatens to destroy the Jewish people after the Gold Calf episode. It is hardly surprising then that the Talmud sometimes expresses reservations about the Messiah, for example, 'Let the Messiah come, but let me not live to see it.'[9]

In addition to general fear of a cataclysm, this sentiment may represent uneasiness with the idea of a leader better known for military prowess than for faithful observance of the commandments. Will such a leader insist that the commandments be performed when the dangers have been eliminated or will he suggest that they can now be abrogated? Uncertainty over the answer may have led some rabbis to wonder whether it was worth taking the risk to find out.

The second way it expresses itself is the vision of what will follow the apocalypse: a world totally unlike this one, where peace will reign, death will be overcome, haughtiness and pride eliminated, and idolatry give way to worship of the true God. From Isaiah onward, this vision was extended to include the restoration of a divinely appointed King from the house of David, political sovereignty for Israel, the

---

[8] ibid 7.   [9] *Sanhedrin* 98a.

ingathering of the exiles, the rebuilding of the Temple in Jerusalem, and resurrection of the dead. The problem is that false hopes not only leave people disappointed, in many cases, they make a bad situation worse. Here one thinks of Bar Kochba ('son of the star'), who ruled as King (*nasi*) of Israel for a short period of time, was proclaimed as Messiah by no less an authority than Rabbi Akiba, but was eventually defeated by a scorched earth policy meant to teach the Jews a lesson for all time.

The defeat of Bar Kochba and the devastation that followed raised the same question over again: What is the proper response to catastrophe—despair or hope? If the latter, why has hope gone unanswered thus far? Given the speculative nature of the question, and the dire circumstances in which they found themselves, the rabbis of the Talmud were unable to reach a single answer. On the one hand, there are rabbinic texts that claim the Messiah will come if Israel were to mend its ways: repent for a single day or observe a single Sabbath in accordance with the Law.[10] The rationale for this view is clear: it is not enough to wait for God to intervene; people can hasten the coming of the Messiah by improving the quality of their behaviour. Rather than a Herculean effort, what is required is a sincere desire not to repeat past mistakes.

On the other hand, *Sanhedrin* 97a tells us, in the name of various rabbis, that when the Messiah comes: (1) scholars will be few in number, and as for the rest, their eyes will fail through sorrow and grief. Multitudes of trouble and evil decrees will be promulgated anew, each new evil coming with haste before the other has ended; (2) the house of assembly will be for harlots, Galilee in ruins, Gablan lie desolate, the border inhabitants wander about from city to city, receiving no hospitality, the wisdom of scribes in disfavour, God-fearing men despised, people dog-faced, and truth entirely lacking; (3) young men will insult the old, and old men will stand before the young, daughters will rise up against their mothers, and daughters-in-law against their mothers-in-law; (4) impudence will increase, esteem be perverted, wine expensive despite an ample supply of grapes, the Kingdom converted to heresy. Again the rationale for this view is clear: no matter how bad things may get, one should never abandon hope that the Messiah is on his way.

---

[10] See, e.g., *Sanhedrin* 97b; Taanit 64a. cf. *Yoma* 86b; *Shabbat* 118b.

2. HOPE DEMYSTIFIED

From a philosophic perspective, the question is: How does one retain
the legitimate part of the idea of the future and jettison the mythology? This brings us to Maimonides. On the centrality of belief in the
coming of the Messiah, Maimonides has no doubt:[11]

> King Messiah will arise and restore the kingdom of David to its former
> state and original sovereignty . . . He who does not believe in a restor-
> ation or does not wait the coming of the Messiah denies not only the
> teachings of the prophets but also those of the Law of Moses our
> Teacher.

Faced with the excesses to which speculation had led, Maimonides
opts for what Scholem terms a restorative as opposed to an apocalyptic conception of the Messiah. Citing Ecclesiastes 3:14 ('Whatso-
ever God doeth, it shall be forever'), Maimonides argues that nothing
God has made admits of excess or deficiency. Thus all references to
cosmic upheaval in the works of the prophets should be read as
references to the overthrow of political regimes not to disruptions
of the natural order. In fact, Maimonides follows a rabbinic view
according to which the only difference between life now and life then
is that Israel will make peace with the rest of the nations, regain
political sovereignty, and be able to focus its attention on study and
worship.[12] In regard to everything else the Messiah is supposed to do,
Maimonides writes: 'Do not think that the King Messiah will have to
perform signs and wonders, bring anything new into being, revive the
dead, or do similar things. It is not so.'[13]

Not surprisingly, Maimonides has nothing but contempt for those
who think rivers will flow with wine, the earth will bring forth baked
bread, or that people will become angels. In his opinion, there will still
be rich and poor, strong and weak. Although it will be easier to
provide for the necessities of life, people will still have to sow and
reap. All this is to say that the Messiah will be a political leader, not a
miracle worker. In time, the Messiah himself will die a natural death.

---

[11] *MT* 14, Kings and Wars, 11.1.
[12] Perek Ḥeleq. *MT* 14, Kings and Wars, 11.3, 12.1. For rabbinic sources, see
Berakhot 34b, *Shabbat* 63a, 151b, *Sanhedrin* 91b, 99a.
[13] *MT* 14, Kings and Wars, 11. 3.

Not only does this take the miraculous element out of messianism, it also purges messianism of hedonistic overtones. While restoring sovereignty to Israel will make it easier to earn a living, Maimonides insists that the purpose of doing so will not be to enjoy material comforts but to have time to pursue spiritual and intellectual goals. The Messiah will put an end to persecution of Israel *so that* Israel can fulfil the commandments, devote itself to study and worship, and lead the rest of humanity in the same direction. In the words of *Mishneh Torah* 14, Kings and Wars, 12.4:[14]

> The sages and prophets did not long for the days of the Messiah that Israel might exercise dominion over the world, rule the heathens, or be exalted by the nations, or that it might eat, drink, and rejoice. Their aspiration was that Israel be free to devote itself to the Law and its wisdom . . .

Because the Law and its wisdom are eternal and focus on God's governance of the natural order, there is no reason to suppose that that governance will change. For Maimonides the return of sovereignty to the Jewish people is a blessing precisely because it will allow people to restore the Temple, reestablish the priestly cult, and be in a position to fulfil all the commandments as they were originally intended to be fulfilled.

Maimonides' view is significant because while it envisions a new and different age, it does not assert that age will be ushered in by superhuman or supernatural feats. Making peace with the rest of the nations is within human capacity. So is abandoning one's obsession with material things and devoting oneself to study. In short, the end of history is an event that occurs *within* history, the perfection of the human species rather than its transformation into something different. Thus Maimonides makes a sharp distinction between the days of the Messiah, a future time in this world, and the world to come, a purely intellectual realm in which the mind survives and the body is left behind. According to him, we long for the former in order to prepare for the latter.[15]

---

[14] cf. *MT* 1, Repentance, 9.2: 'Hence all Israelites, their prophets and sages, longed for the advent of Messianic times, that they might have relief from the wicked tyranny that does not permit them properly to occupy themselves with the study of the Torah and the observance of the commandments; that they might have ease, devote themselves to getting wisdom, and thus attain to life in the world to come.'

[15] *MT* 1, Repentance, 9.2.

I take this to mean that during the days of the Messiah, we will still have to confront the fact of human fallibility. People will still need to gather for sacred assemblies, mourn the dead, and call upon God in times of distress. And there will still be occasions for confessing sin and seeking repentance. All this is a way of saying that Maimonides does not conceive of the days of the Messiah as a time when people will shed their earthly nature and become angelic. Judges will have to decide cases, and political leaders will have to enlist popular support. In a word, Maimonides' conception of the Messiah is deflationary. Rather than an earthly paradise, the Messiah will usher in an age where we can put aside the things in life that are of little account and focus our attention on the pursuit of truth. Everything else is a throwback to mythology.

3. HOPE AS A MORAL IDEAL

Putting Jewish philosophy aside for the moment, the philosophic problem we face is how to make belief in the idea of the future more than just wishful thinking. We saw that Kant's claim about hope for better times amounts to more than the observation that if I approach the future with optimism, *my* fortunes are likely to improve; rather his claim is that hope for better times will make us more likely to work for the improvement of the common good. Kant's strategy then is to transform the concept of hope from a personal feeling involving luck or fortune to a concern for all of humanity. In addition to its hedonistic implications, luck or fortune has the disadvantage that it can lead to inactivity. Why work for something that fortune may bring about on its own?

To this we should add that as we normally think of it, hope is directed to something whose prospects are neither assured nor impossible. If it makes no sense to hope that the sun will rise in the East tomorrow, it makes no sense to hope that someone will square the circle. In regard to assurance, Kant argues at some length that while we can hope that the human condition will improve over time, we will never be in a position to know that it will.[16] This means that historical

---

[16] See Immanuel Kant, *Conflict of the Faculties*, Mary J. Gregor, trans. (Lincoln, NB: University of Nebraska Press, 1979) 141–71.

evidence alone is never decisive. Sometimes it appears that the human situation is getting better, sometimes that it is getting worse, sometimes that it is going along in the same old way. No one is in a position to assess all of history and say which is right.

Indeed once we look at history from a global perspective, and introduce a distinction between the conscious intentions of the protagonists and the historical consequences of their actions—what Hegel referred to as 'the cunning of reason' (*List der Vernunft*)—it becomes nearly impossible to say which actions advance the cause of human progress and which do not.[17] Joseph's brothers committed evil by selling him into slavery, but as he himself comes to see (Genesis 45:5), the ultimate effect of this action was to save life.[18] So too, one might argue, the destruction of the Second Temple, the conviction of Albert Dreyfus, or the Japanese bombing of Pearl Harbor led to consequences quite different from what the protagonists intended. Even if we were to take a single moment in history and ask whether things were moving in a positive direction, to answer with certainty, one would have to look into the souls of the actors and assess the purity of their motives, an impossible feat for anyone but God.

Rather than a prediction based on empirical evidence, hope in Kant's sense is better understood as a moral presupposition. Morality demands that we work to promote the highest good. Doing so would make no sense unless we believe the highest good is possible to achieve. In this way, practical reason asks us to adopt an attitude that theoretical reason cannot establish on its own. We are asked to view history *as if* the human condition were improving in order that we may be motivated to contribute to that improvement. Even this formulation may be too weak. Not only must the highest good be possible in principle but our efforts to achieve it must have some likelihood of success. As Kant puts it: Although 'What is to result from this right conduct of ours?' is not, strictly speaking, the concern of morality, neither can it be viewed as a matter of indifference.[19]

---

[17] Hegel, *Reason in History*, Robert Hartman, trans. (Upper Saddle River, N.J.: Prentice-Hall, 1997) 43–4.

[18] Here I am indebted to Aviezer Ravitzky, *Messianism, Zionism, and Jewish Religious Radicalism*, Michael Swirsky and Jonathan Chipman, trans. (Chicago: University of Chicago Press, 1993) 112.

[19] Kant, *Religion within the Limits of Reason Alone*, Theodore M. Greene and Hoyt H. Hudson, trans. (1934, rpt. New York: Harper & Row, 1960) 4.

His point is this. The obligation to do our duty is unconditional. Therefore we are obliged to do it even if we are convinced our actions will not change anything. The fact is however that such a belief would have a devastating affect on human behaviour. As we saw, people need to think that their actions can—or will—make a difference. That is why hope for a better future, though it may not be justified on theoretical grounds, is justified on moral grounds.

It is at this point that Hermann Cohen enters the picture. Cohen credits Maimonides with severing any connection between the days of the Messiah and either visions of an apocalypse or return to a primeval state of innocence.[20] He also emphasizes that for Maimonides, the Messiah will not just rule over Israel but will have a decisive impact on the rest of humanity. Along these lines, it is noteworthy that in uncensored versions of *Mishneh Torah* (14, Kings and Wars, 11), we find the suggestion that for all their errors, Jesus and Mohammed may have paved the way for the Messiah by assisting in the transition from paganism to monotheism.

Still Cohen parts company with Maimonides in three respects. First, where Maimonides pictures the emergence of an extraordinary individual who will usher in a new age, Cohen's view is limited to the age itself. Technically it is not even an age, but, as we will see, the ideal towards which all ages point. Second, where Maimonides makes the restoration of political sovereignty to Israel an essential part of his understanding of the Messiah, Cohen argues that messianism is by nature a universal idea so that any suggestion of particularity undermines its integrity. Third, Maimonides sees the coming of the Messiah as something that will take place at a specific time in the future. Although he warns us not to speculate on when it will happen, he has no doubt that there will come a point when the Messiah will actually walk the earth. For Cohen any conception of the Messiah as an individual with a particular lineage or nationality takes us back to an empirical concept with all the distortions and limitations that implies. Rather than a person who walks the earth, the Messiah refers to the moral perfection of the human race.

Although these differences can be explained by a shift from a medieval to a modern perspective, the difference between Kant and Cohen and Maimonides runs deeper. As a Christian, Kant begins by

---

[20] Cohen, *Religion of Reason*, 248–50, 310–12.

accepting the idea of depravity: all human behaviour is tainted by selfishness, and the problem is so great that no amount of effort will ever be sufficient for us to overcome it. Although Cohen's rhetoric is not as sharp, he begins from roughly the same place. Alternatively, the goal we are seeking is that of holiness, a complete fit between our intentions and the demands of the moral law (*II Critique*, 122). So the task of going from the condition in which we now find ourselves to that towards which we are striving is infinite.

We saw however that according to Maimonides, there is no possibility of shedding our nature as human beings and becoming angelic. Even in the days of the Messiah, we will still have to deal with the fact of human fallibility. For Maimonides, then, the task before us may be formidable, but there is no reason to think it is infinite. On the contrary, when citing the famous parable of the four rabbis who entered *pardes*, he praises Akiba for recognizing that we have to stay within our limits (*Guide* 1.32, 68–9).

Let us return to the evidence from Kant and Cohen. The end of history requires the attainment of virtue. But, Kant continues, this is 'a perfection of which no rational being in the world of sense is at any time capable' (see above). In other words, human action is and will always be tainted by selfishness. If so, how can we be obliged to act for the sake of a universal law? Here Kant retreats. Thus: 'It is man's duty to *strive* for this perfection, but not to *reach* it (in this life), and his compliance with this duty can, accordingly, consist only in continual progress.' And again: 'Only endless progress from lower to higher stages of moral perfection is possible to a rational but finite being' (*II Critique*, 27).

The same is true for Cohen, who argues that the process of moral improvement or self-sanctification is infinite. With respect to the Messiah, this implies that 'his coming is not an actual end, but means merely the infinity of his coming, which in turn means the infinity of development.'[21] Cohen's messianic age then is always in the future. As Steven Schwarzschild argued: 'the Messiah not only has not come but also will never have come . . . [rather] he will always be coming.' To use Cohen's metaphor, we can approach the age of the Messiah as a function approaches its limit—approach but never actually reach.

----

[21] *Religion of Reason*, 314–15.

This view has several advantages. First it exposes the folly of trying to calculate the exact moment the Messiah will arrive. Second it frees us from the task of trying to determine which, if any, pretenders to the claim of Messiah are genuine. Third it avoids an embarrassing question. When the second Temple was destroyed in 70 AD, animal sacrifice ended as a form of worship because there was no longer a place in which to perform it. But many of the standard prayers in Judaism follow the restorative model, asking God to send the Messiah and sanction the rebuilding of the Temple. As committed a rationalist as Maimonides argues that if this should happen, animal sacrifice would have to be reinstituted.[22]

Does anyone really want this? The overwhelming answer is no. But because the Torah commands that animal sacrifice be done in the Temple, it would be hard to find a reason for *not* doing it once the Temple is rebuilt. If, on the other hand, the Messiah never comes, people can continue praying for the Messiah without facing the question of what to do if their prayers are answered.

From a philosophic perspective, an infinitely delayed Messiah rids us of the conceit of thinking that the end of history has already been reached. More than one political movement has prepared itself for the Battle of Armageddon, after which a new order will be installed and history redeemed. Both Lenin and Hitler made such claims on behalf of totalitarian regimes that set out to save civilization and destroy any kind of opposition. Norman Cohn is right to say that given our liberal sensibilities, not only the rhetoric but the actions of these movements are barely comprehensible.[23] But the strangeness of their doctrines derives from the fact that we tend to look at them in a vacuum, not recognizing that apocalyptic urgency has deep roots in European history—roots that take it all the way back to ancient times and people's susceptibility to messianic fervour. By putting the end of history into the infinite future, we have grounds for rejecting anyone who claims we are on the verge of reaching it now.

---

[22] *MT* 14, Kings and Wars, 11. 1. 3.
[23] Norman Cohn, *The Pursuit of the Millennium* (1957 rpt. London: Pimlico, 2004) 288.

4. THE POSSIBILITY OF FULFILMENT

We may conclude that infinite delay has much to recommend it. The problem is, as Franz Rosenzweig put it, that if the Messiah is not coming for all eternity, he is not coming.[24] If we get ever closer to the ideal but never actually reach it, it is hard to avoid the conclusion that the ideal cannot be reached. No matter how much progress we make, there will still be an infinite amount left to complete. As long as the goal of history lies beyond the reach of history, we get what Scholem called a life lived in deferment. In a sense we are back with Sisyphus and endless frustration.

Consider this. I can ask you to walk from the White House to Capital Hill because the distance can be covered in a short period of time. I can ask you to walk from the Brooklyn Bridge to the Golden Gate Bridge even though the distance is much greater. In a science fiction novel, I could ask you to walk to a distant star because even though it might require millions of years to get there, we are still talking about finite time. But what sense would it make to ask you to walk to a place that is infinitely far off *and tell you not to lose hope in trying to get there*? If we get ever closer to the ideal but never actually reach it, it is hard to avoid the conclusion that the ideal cannot be reached by human effort. After all, no matter how much progress we may make, there will still be an infinite amount of progress left to complete. So rather than a reasonable hope of success, this alternative, in Steven Schwarzschild's opinion, gives us a guarantee of relative failure.[25]

Why do Kant and Cohen think human behaviour will always be deficient no matter how much progress we make? Both turn to Scripture for support. Kant cites Romans 3:9–10 ('They are all under sin, there is none righteous (in the spirit of the law)') and 7:15 ('What I would do, that I do not'). Cohen cites Ecclesiastes 7:20 ('Surely there is not a just man on the earth who does good and sins not'). Beyond scriptural reasons are philosophic.

---

[24] For discussion, see Steven S. Schwarzschild, *The Pursuit of the Ideal*, Menachem Kellner, ed. (Albany: SUNY Press, 1990) 211, esp. fn. 16. Note that on this issue Schwarzschild once took a position similar to Rosenzweig. Thus 19: 'for progress to be possible there must be a logical guarantee of the eventual attainability of the goal of progress...' See in addition fn. 15, 356.

[25] *Pursuit*, 19.

Kant is afraid that if we admit the demands of morality can be fulfilled, we will be guilty of lowering the standards of morality to suit our own needs. According to him, the demands of morality are established a priori, which means that their validity has nothing to do with human efforts to fulfil them. This results in commands that are 'stern, unindulgent, truly commanding.'[26] He concludes that the advantage of Christian morality over the schools of the ancient world is that it conceives of the moral law with 'purity and rigor' and culminates in precepts that are 'pure and uncompromising'.[27] Unlike the schools of the ancient world, Christianity assumes we are in a fallen state and, in Kant's words, destroys any confidence we may have that we can satisfy the demands of morality by ourselves. In return it fosters the hope that if we do everything in our power, assistance will come from 'another source'—namely God. That is, if we make a concerted effort to do our duty, God will credit us as if we succeeded even though strictly speaking we did not.[28] Note however that if this is true, our plight is exactly like that of Sisyphus except that unlike him, we can call on the grace of God to close the gap between expectation and performance.

How do we know that a finite agent cannot fulfil the demands of the moral law? Kant's answer is that there is in all of us a propensity to subvert the moral law or what he calls *a perversity of the heart*.[29] It is clear then that Kant accepted some version of the doctrine of original sin, not that we can inherit the sin of another person, but that we cannot rise above the perversity that afflicts all people—either in this life or in any finite segment of the next.

The position he finally adopts is one in which people pervert the moral law in every action they take even though there is no internal or external force that compels them to do so. The reason there is no compulsion is that if there were, people could not be held responsible for what they do. Kant takes this to mean that the decision to act for less than pure motives is not the fault of our sensuous nature because we cannot control the fact that we have a material component. Nor is it the fault of an external devil or demon. Rather it is we ourselves

[26] Kant, *Critique of Practical Reason*, Lewis White Beck, trans. (Indianapolis: Bobbs-Merrill, 1956) 123.

[27] *Critique of Practical Reason*, 127.

[28] *Religion*, 70.

[29] *Religion*, 25.

who chose to act this way. It is as if in each thing we do, we make our own decision to fall from grace.[30] Evil then is freely chosen and taints the motives of even the most virtuous among us.

Here one is inclined to ask: If evil is chosen rather than compelled, what prevents someone from choosing to act for noble motives rather than selfish ones? Why can people not overcome the perversity of the heart by simply willing to do so? To this Kant has no answer except to say it is obvious they cannot. Accordingly: 'That such a corrupt propensity must indeed be rooted in man need not be formally proved in view of the multitude of crying examples which experience *of the actions* of men puts before our eyes.'[31] But again the question is not whether history contains ample evidence of human perversity but why, as free agents capable of choosing in a spontaneous fashion, we cannot overcome it.

There are passages where Kant comes dangerously close to answering this question by falling back on the recalcitrance of matter, as when he asks: 'How indeed can one expect something perfectly straight to be framed out of such crooked wood?'[32] But this will not do. He cannot invoke a metaphysical principle to account for a moral failing because this would mean the source of the problem is beyond our control and would exempt us from responsibility. So the question remains: Why can the perversity of the heart not be overcome?

Eventually Kant responds that the cause of this evil, which he terms *radical*, is inscrutable.[33] The only thing from which a propensity to evil could originate would be an evil maxim that serves as the grounds of all other maxims. But this would only put the question off. Why has mankind adopted such a maxim? Moreover, its adoption would conflict with the view, which Kant also accepts, that mankind is predisposed towards the good, that is, created *for* good. He concludes: 'there is for us no conceivable ground from which the moral evil in us could originally have come.'

I take this to mean that while there is no possibility of a *systematic* explanation for the propensity to pervert the moral law, and nothing that can be derived from the concept of *humanity* as such, there is no denying that all of humanity has such a propensity. As he puts it, evil can be predicated of man as a species even though it cannot be

---

[30] *Religion*, 32.   [31] *Religion*, 28.
[32] *Religion*, 92.   [33] *Religion*, 32.

inferred from the *concept* of his species.[34] It exists because each of us of his own accord wills to do it.

To this Kant adds that we often flatter ourselves about the nobility of our own character so that: 'man is never more easily deceived than in what promotes his good opinion of himself'.[35] No doubt this is true. But it does not prove the larger point: that it is impossible for human action ever to comply with the demands of morality. For if that were so, by Kant's own principles, we could not be held responsible for failing to comply. Again we can take refuge in the grace of God. Although our actions will always be defective, and prevent us from reaching the goal of complete conformity with the moral law, if we make a sustained effort to try to reach it, God will credit us not for what we are but for what we are trying to become. Such is the nature of divine grace.

Beyond the doctrine of original sin is Kant's Platonism, or what he terms Plato's 'spiritual flight' from the physical world to the architectonic ordering of it according to ends.[36] This is explained a few pages earlier, when he notes that Plato used *idea* 'in such a way as quite evidently to have meant by it something which not only can never be borrowed from the senses but far surpasses even the concepts of understanding.'[37]

For Kant, as for Plato, that fact that a perfect state had never been realized has no tendency to show that the idea of a perfect state is illegitimate or a figment of the imagination. In the same way, the fact that the moral law has not been fulfilled by a rational agent in the world of sense has no tendency to show that it is not obligatory. If philosophy were forced to deal only with the data of experience, Kant thinks, morality would be impossible. This means that complete fitness of the will to the moral law is the standard at which every action aims but to which nothing in the realm of sense will ever be adequate.

Although Cohen owes no religious allegiance to the doctrine of original sin, he accepts Kant's Platonism and the view that morality presents us with an infinite task. The idea that there is an inborn predisposition to evil in the human heart is inconsistent with God's holiness and status as creator.[38] Still Cohen is forced to say that

---

[34] *Religion*, 27.   [35] *Religion*, 62.
[36] Kant, *Critique of Pure Reason*, A318/B375.
[37] ibid A313/B370.   [38] *Religion of Reason*, 182.

human behaviour will always be inadequate on the grounds that God's holiness is infinite and thus represents an infinite standard for humans to aspire to. Schwarzschild puts this point as follows: 'Divine norms are, by definition, infinite.'[39] Because 'human beings cannot, of course, either individually or collectively, attain infinite goals', we are left with a conception of history according to which the purpose of human life is to pursue an ideal that can never fully be realized. That is why the Messiah will always *be* coming.

If the point being made here is that human behaviour as we know it is a long way from the ideal, there is no argument. Material comforts and increased standards of living have not put an end to war, violence, hatred, or mass murder. On the other hand, the crux of belief in the future is that war, violence, and hatred are not inevitable. The way things are is not the way they have to be. Kant and Cohen would certainly agree. Their point is not that history is destined to repeat itself but that if *per impossible* human beings could remove any trace of evil from their behaviour, they would cease to be human and, in effect, become divine. God then is the standard by which human behaviour is measured. While the line separating God and humans is often blurred in mythology, in a monotheistic religion of the sort envisioned by Kant and Cohen, it is sacrosanct. It follows that human behaviour will always be found wanting when measured by a divine standard and thus requires infinite time to perfect itself.

5. CONCLUSION

We are left with three ways of looking at human perfection and, by implication, three ways of looking at the idea of the future. The first is cataclysmic and looks on the idea of steady progress towards the goal of perfection as unrealistic. That is why nothing short of a cataclysm is needed to rid the world of sin and set it on a new and better course. As Scholem put it: 'The Bible and the apocalyptic writers know of no progress in history leading to the redemption.'[40] Instead they foresee a time when redemption will come from an outside source leading to a world completely unlike this one.

---

[39] *Pursuit*, 223.   [40] *The Messianic Idea*, 10.

It is along these lines that we can understand Paul's rejection of salvation through law. The law is divine. The problem is that there is something deep within the human soul that prevents us from fulfilling it (Romans 7:14-23):

> We know that the law is spiritual; but I am of the flesh, sold into slavery under sin. I do not understand my own actions. For I do not do what I want, but I do the very thing I hate . . . For I delight in the law of God in my inmost self, but I see in my members another law at war with the law of my mind.

If this is right, exhortations to obey the law, though appropriate, are insufficient.[41] The only way to hope for something better is to believe that God will not judge us on the basis of law alone. Beyond Law is Grace. Thus redemption can only come through the grace of God.

I have deliberately abbreviated Paul's position in order to highlight its similarity to the apocalyptic strand of Judaism. Though the human propensity to evil is ineradicable, on this view, it is not irredeemable. It can be redeemed by God and only by God. Anything less than a divine solution to the problem of evil ignores the gravity of the problem. There are two differences: (1) while Paul thinks the redeemer has already come, the apocalyptic strand of Judaism still awaits his arrival and (2) for Paul the redeemer is an aspect or part of God while for Judaism the redeemer will be only a messenger or servant of God. Note, however, that neither tradition believes the redeemer will come as a result of human merit; rather he was (or will be) sent because of human sinfulness and the inability to rise above it.

The problem with this view is that it stems from a peculiar theology. Why would God give humanity a law he knew they could not fulfil? Alternatively, why would he create humanity in such a way that fulfilment of the law is too difficult for it? From an ethical standpoint, the inability of humanity to live up to God's expectations appears to have more to do with God than it does with us.

The second position is Maimonidean. No fallen condition or inherited sin stands in the way of the fulfilment of the Law. According to Maimonides, it is within the power of every human being to become righteous like Moses or wicked like Jeroboam, wise or foolish, merciful or cruel, stingy or generous, and so with all other moral

---

[41] Note, however, that Paul himself resorts to exhortation at Romans 13:8-10.

virtues.[42] If the Torah has not been fulfilled, the fault lies with us, not with God. While the laws set forth in the Torah may push us to the utmost of human capacity in order to be fulfilled, they were never intended to take us beyond it.[43] Fulfilment of the Law will not turn us into a perfect being; it will simply mean we have perfected our nature as human beings. By the same token, there is nothing in the idea of the Messiah that requires divine interference.[44] Rather than God sending the Messiah, humanity will bring the Messiah; rather than a cataclysm, what will take place is a process of education leading to universal knowledge of God.

In addition to naturalism, Maimonides' view is informed by the rigours of negative theology, which holds that there is no resemblance between God and anything in the created universe. No resemblance implies no measure of comparison. There is then no possibility of putting God and us on the same scale—even an infinite one—and talk about closing the gap. While God demands ethical behaviour, in Maimonides' view, ethical behaviour does not give us a way of imitating God but rather a way of seeing to it that the consequences of our behaviour resemble the consequences of God's (*Guide* 1.54, 123–8). When it comes to God himself, Maimonides insists all attempts at praise or description fail and the only option left to us is a studied silence. More specifically, the only option left to us is to follow the lead of Rabbi Akiba. This means the gulf separating God and us is unbridgeable so that any attempt to demand superhuman effort from human beings is misguided.

The third position is that of Kant and Cohen, for whom knowledge of God is just knowledge of the ethical ideal. While the gulf separating God and us is not bridgeable in the way that a finite distance is bridgeable, we can use knowledge of God as a standard for judging human behaviour. The fact that we will forever fall short of the standard does not negate its validity or undermine the possibility of

---

[42] *MT* 1, Repentance, 5.2.

[43] *MT* 14, Kings and Wars, 12.5. cf. Aviezer Ravitzky, '"To the Utmost Human Capacity": Maimonides on the Days of the Messiah', in *Perspectives on Maimonides*, Joel L. Kraemer, ed. (Oxford: Oxford University Press, 1991) 232–3: 'Even in the future, "They will attain an understanding of their Creator according to the utmost human capacity [*kefi koah ha-adam*]" i.e. without transcending human limitations.'

[44] Menachem Kellner, *Maimonides on 'The Decline of the Generations and the Nature of Rabbinic Authority'* (Albany: SUNY Press, 1996) 75.

historical progress. On the other hand, no matter how much progress is made, humanity will still have something to strive for.

It will come as no surprise that my sympathies are with Maimonides. Not that I want to return to animal sacrifice in a rebuilt Temple but that I want to maintain a strict interpretation of the principle that *ought* implies *can*. If it is not within the power of human beings to do something, they cannot be obliged to do it. Conversely, if they have done everything that can be asked of them, it is pointless to insist on a standard that requires still more. Although I have tried to resist the tendency to have scriptural citations take the place of philosophic argument, I confess that I can resist it no longer and direct attention to the famous passage from the end of Deuteronomy (30:11–14):

> What I am commanding you today is not too difficult for you or beyond your reach. It is not up in heaven, so that you have to ask: 'Who will ascend into heaven to get it and proclaim it to us so we may obey it?' Nor is it beyond the sea, so that you have to ask: 'Who will cross the sea to get it and proclaim it to us so we may obey it?' No, the word is very near you; it is in your mouth and in your heart so you may do it.

I take this to mean that the law was never meant to impose super-human standards or to close the gap between God and us. In the days of the Messiah, humans will still have to deal with the limitations imposed by their condition, God will still be unknowable, and the gulf between them will still be unbridgeable.

Like Maimonides, I am suggesting that the end of history lies within the reach of history. This too needs clarification. By the end of history, I do not mean that time will stop, that science will run out of things to investigate, that sickness and poverty will be completely eradicated, that the state will whither away, or that conflicts will no longer arise. To stay with Maimonides, I mean that peace will prevail, that the needy will be cared for, and that people will see that material comforts are not the be all and end all of human existence. Whether this age will be brought about by a single individual, an institution, or a host of institutions, no one can know. Nor can anyone know when it will occur and how long it will last. It is possible that having been achieved, it will eventually deteriorate so that historical progress will have to begin anew. All these things are beyond the capacity of anyone to predict.

My only claim is that belief in the coming of this age is justified, if not on historical grounds, then at least on moral ones. It is not a matter of saying that if we continue doing what we are now doing, we will reach a new and better age because many of the things we are now doing are wrong. Nor is it to say that historical redemption is guaranteed. It is rather to say that it is within our power to change the path we are on, to strive for something better, and ultimately to achieve something better. In short, we should expect much more from our political leaders than what we are now getting. We should reject any claim to the effect that caring for the poor or finding alternatives to war is too difficult. By the same token, we should reject the view that the task before us is infinite. Not only is this questionable on philosophic grounds, if taken to heart, it can easily cause people to give up. If, no matter how much progress we have made, there is still an infinite amount of work to do, why bother trying? While it would be outrageous to claim that all of this is implied by the opening lines of Genesis, it is nonetheless true that the opening lines of Genesis introduce us to a world in which these questions become unavoidable.

Part II

Judaic Culture and Politics

3

Hebraism

The Third Culture

Steven Grosby

The following enquiry into the character of Hebraism, as distinct from Judaism, takes the form of an argument for the merit of 'Hebraic Culture' as a category of *Kulturgeschichte*. While the evidence for the category will obviously have to be adduced, it will not be pursued here in great detail; for the focus of this enquiry is the justification for the category itself. If this category proves useful in furthering our understanding of developments in the Occident from the sixteenth to the eighteenth centuries, and likely before and subsequently, then it will be a significant expression of the enduring presence of Jerusalem. Even though that enduring presence raises methodological considerations by necessarily exhibiting both the ambiguities of the reception of any tradition and the problems of the formation of historiographical categories, those considerations will only be referred to in passing.[1] What are the reasons for proposing this category?

---

[1] On the reception of tradition and the formation of historiographical categories, see Joachim Wach, *Das Verstehen: Grundzüge einer Geschichte der hermeneutischen Theorie im 19. Jahrhundert* (Tübingen: J.C.B. Mohr (Paul Siebeck), 1926–33). See also Edward Shils, *Tradition* (Chicago: University of Chicago Press, 1981) and Hans Freyer, *Theory of Objective Mind: An Introduction to the Philosophy of Culture*, Steven Grosby, ed. and trans. (Athens: Ohio University Press, 1998 [1928]).

I

The prima facie case for the category of Hebraic Culture is not difficult to discern. There was the explosive growth of Christian Hebraism throughout the European continent and England during the sixteenth and seventeenth centuries, as represented by such figures—to name only a few of the better known—as Johannes Reuchlin, Sebastian Münster, Paul Fagius, Michael Servetus, the two Buxtorfs, Jean Bodin, Hugo Grotius, Petrus Cunaeus, Wilhelm Surenhuis, Edward Pococke, John Lightfoot, and the quintessential example of this turn to the Hebrew Bible, John Selden.[2] The ostensible purpose of much of this Christian Hebraism was the pursuit of a more accurate understanding of the Old Testament, a pursuit that, as such, often entailed consulting the Mishnah and Talmud, both of which, in either their entirety (Mishnah) or large sections (Talmud), had been translated into Latin by the end of the seventeenth century. An accurate understanding of the Old Testament was often understood as being necessary for establishing a more secure foundation for Christianity, even if doing so meant clarifying the relation of the views of the Apostles to those of the Pharisees through examination of the Mishnah and Talmud, for example, Paul Fagius' edition and translation of the *Pirke Aboth* in 1541. While never questioning the superiority of Christianity, the works of the Christian Hebraists nonetheless often aroused the opprobrium of being 'Judaizing'.

There were many, including Luther, especially the young Luther, who insisted that a proper understanding of the Bible required a careful reading of the Old Testament in Hebrew. By the end of the sixteenth century, few in Protestant Europe doubted this requirement. However, once the priority of both the putatively miraculous translation of the Septuagint and the Vulgate had been put aside in favor of the Hebrew Old Testament, it proved impossible to arrest other investigations increasingly viewed as appropriate for a proper

---

[2] For an overview of Christian Hebraism, see Jerome Friedman, *The Most Ancient Testimony: Sixteenth-Century Christian-Hebraica in the Age of Renaissance Nostalgia* (Athens: Ohio University Press, 1983). See also, Frank Manuel, *The Broken Staff: Judaism through Christian Eyes* (Cambridge: Harvard University Press, 1992). For Selden see Jason P. Rosenblatt, *Renaissance England's Chief Rabbi: John Selden* (Oxford: Oxford University Press, 2006) and G.J. Toomer, *John Selden: A Life in Scholarship* (Oxford: Oxford University Press, 2009).

understanding of the New Testament. Thus, there were those who uncompromisingly defended the necessity for impartial investigations of not only the Hebrew Old Testament, thereby calling into question the translation of, for example, Isaiah 7:14 (see below), but also even the Talmud, for example, Reuchlin and Selden (but not Erasmus). Occasionally these investigations resulted in varying points of agreement with the conclusions of the Jewish commentaries on the Hebrew Bible, in particular those of Rashi, Maimonides, Abraham ibn Ezra, and David Kimchi, hence the accusation of 'Judaizing'.[3]

Perhaps it was this noteworthy and admirable impartiality—to anticipate further clarification of the category Hebraic Culture—that Matthew Arnold (1885: 112, 122) had in mind when he observed that the Hebraism of the Reformation contained a 'subtle Hellenic leaven', the latter referring to the idea 'to see things as they really are'. But it became all too clear that the goal of seeing things as they really are could carry a high price; for no one surely needed to be reminded of the antitrinitarian Servetus' burning at the stake in 1553 at the urging of Calvin, whose shameful complicity in this dark assault on the freedom of thought did not spare his own reputation from the accusation of Judaizing by the Lutheran Aegidius Hunnius in *Calvinus Iudaizans* (1593).[4]

As significant as this Christian Hebraism was for the Reformation, the reasons for the category of Hebraic Culture are by no means only the philological, textual, and theological clarification arising from careful examination of the Hebrew Bible still understood as the Old Testament. If they were, then one would have cause to doubt the breadth, hence utility, of the category for *Kulturgeschichte*, as it would be confined to the history of religion. However, the turn to the Hebrew Bible was also manifest in works of political theory, specifically, various understandings of the image of ancient Israel as a polity. To be sure, numerous ostensibly theological treatises conveyed implications for political theory, for example, Jean Bodin's *Colloquium heptaplomeres de rerum sublimium arcanis abditis*

---

[3] For Kimchi, see J. Baker and E.W. Nicholson, *The Commentary of Rabbi David Kimchi on Psalms CXX–CL* (Cambridge: Cambridge University Press, 1973).

[4] For Servetus, see Jerome Friedman, *The Most Ancient Testimony: Sixteenth-Century Christian-Hebraica in the Age of Renaissance Nostalgia* (Athens: Ohio University Press, 1983); for the accusation of Calvin as a Judaizer, see Sujin G. Pak, *The Judaizing Calvin: Sixteenth-Century Debates over the Messianic Pslams* (Oxford: Oxford University Press, 2010).

(Colloquium of the Seven about Secrets of the Sublime, 1588) and surely John Selden's *De Synedriis & Praefecturis Iuridicis Veterum Ebraeorum* (On the Sanhedrin and the Judicial Magistrates of the Ancient Hebrews, 1650–5). It is impossible to avoid the political implication of the former as a plea for freedom of religion and civility and that of the latter as a parallel between the Sanhedrin and the English Parliament. The political implications of many of the theological treatises during this period are impossible to ignore, just as are the theological implications of many of the works of political theory. It is often difficult to disentangle the two (surely the tumultuous history of the Dutch Republic indicates as much); and all the more so when there are individuals, for example, François Hôtman, Hugo Grotius, and Jean Bodin, whose works (respectively, *Franco-Gallia, Eucharist; De Republica Emendanda, De Veritate, Annotationes;* and *Colloquium, Methodus, Six Livres de la République*) fall into both areas. That it is so difficult suggests further the utility of the category Hebraic Culture.

In addition to those works of Bodin and Selden, political treatises that exploited the image of ancient Israel were the youthful Grotius' *De Republica Emendanda* (*On How to Emend the Dutch Polity,* 1600), Johannes Althusius' *Politica* (1603), Petrus Cunaeus' *De Republica Hebraeorum* (1617), which had explicitly acknowledged (2006: 7, 107) its debt to the earlier Corneille Bertram's *De Politica Judaica* (1574), and Carlo Sigonio's *De Republica Hebraeorum* (1582), Wilhelm Schickard's *Jus Regium Hebraeorum* (1625), and James Harrington's *The Art of Lawgiving* (1659). This is to note only a few of the more prominent examples of works of Hebraic political theory.[5] Some of the authors of these works, most notably Selden, recognized that to understand properly the political character of the Israelite and Judean state, one had to turn to the Mishnah and Talmud. And yet this reception of the image of ancient Israel could be, and was put to diverse political purposes, as is clear when one compares the monarchical absolutism, albeit Gallican, of Jacque-Bénigne Bossuet's *Politique tirée de l'Écriture sainte* (*Politics Drawn from the Very Words of Holy Scripture,* 1679) or Robert Filmer's *Patriarcha* with the federalism of Althusius' *Politica* or the Republicanism of John Milton's *Defense of the English People* (1651), the latter two falling within what

---

[5] See http://www.hpstudies.org/20/resources/bibliography.asp for a bibliography of political Hebraism and the journal *Hebraic Political Studies.*

is often described as the covenantal tradition.[6] The question is, if there is, despite this diversity, a distinctiveness in this reception for the purpose of politics that would further support the historiographical utility of the category Hebraic Culture.

In addition to these theological and political orientations of Hebraism, a third component is to be observed. J.G.A. Pocock, in *The Ancient Constitution and the Feudal Law*, commented on 'the peculiar importance of law in the history of historiography' (1967: 24), and he was right to do so. A number of Hebraists were either lawyers or Professors of Law, for example, Althusius, Cunaeus, and Selden; and in their works on legal and constitutional principles, they turned not to Roman law but to ancient Israelite and Jewish law. Thus, here too, Hebraism is to be observed. We have already noted in passing Althusius' and Cunaeus' understanding of ancient Israelite history and law for constitutional purposes, specifically as a model for the Dutch Republic, and Schickard's *Jus Regium Hebraeorum* and Harrington's *The Art of Lawgiving*. More developed and compelling examples of the turn to the Hebrew Bible and rabbinic tradition for clarifying law and its character are the works of Hugo Grotius and John Selden. Both Grotius and Selden turned to the rabbinic, Noahide laws (BT Sanhedrin 56a–b) in support of their conceptions of natural law, respectively in *De Jure Belli ac Pacis* (*On the Law of War and Peace*, 1625) and the monumental *De Jure Naturali et Gentium juxta Disciplinam Ebraeorum* (*On the Natural and Gentile Law in Comparision with Hebrew Teaching*, 1640). It is obvious enough that when Grotius and Selden did so, it was in the service of locating principles that would provide a basis for civil peace both within a national state and between states.[7] One wonders, however, if, especially in the case of Selden, the use of the past as not only a guide for contemporary law but also as presumptively binding (as can also be seen in Selden's *Uxor Ebraica* in support of laws of divorce) suggests yet another characteristic of Hebraic Culture.

The final, important reason in this cursory, introductory overview of the case for the category of Hebraic Culture is the recurrence of the

---

[6] For the covenantal tradition in politics, see Daniel J. Elazar, *Covenant Tradition in Politics* (New Brunswick: Transaction, 4 vols., 1995–8).

[7] The differences between Grotius' and Selden's understanding of natural law need not be entered into here; see Richard Tuck, *Natural Right Theories: Their Origin and Development* (Cambridge: Cambridge University Press, 1979).

self-description of a people as (the new) Israel or a (new) chosen people. During the past 20 or so years, much has been written on the Reformation's revival of the image of Israel as the chosen people in support of consolidating further a socially distinctive nation. The obvious examples are the Netherlands, England, Scotland, and the United States.[8] Here, we come across the decisive reason for positing Hebraism as a necessary, distinct category of cultural analysis, namely, socio-historical (or anthropological) development: the self-justification for the existence of a particular nation. However, it is possible to push this recognition even further, for it has long been observed that the turn to the image of ancient Israel as a nation occurred earlier and in contexts different from the 'covenantalism' of the Reformed, Calvinist tradition, for example, medieval England and France.[9] If so, we will have to consider an even broader cultural and historical significance for the category.

Such is an outline of the reasons for the merit of Hebraic Culture as a historiographical category: theological, political, legal, and socio-historical. It will already have become clear that these various reasons in support of the category are inter-connected. That they are is to be expected; for the relation between them is an indication of a symbolic centre, the implications of which are historically unfolded in varying directions. The character of that centre will have to be elucidated in the ensuing remarks; but that such a centre exists is a prerequisite for postulating any category of the *Geisteswissenschaften*.

All enquiries of this kind bear defects. By concentrating attention on a particular idea or combination of ideas—a symbolic centre—that are thought to characterize a certain period by constituting a respectively particular culture, thereby influencing both the thought and

---

[8] See Anthony D. Smith, 'Nation and Covenant: The Contribution of Ancient Israel to Modern Nationalism' *Proceedings of the British Academy* 151(2007) 213–55. See also Steven Grosby, 'The Nation of the United States and the Vision of Ancient Israel' reprinted in *Biblical Ideas of Nationality: Ancient and Modern* (Winona Lake: Eisenbrauns, 2002[1993]) 213–34.

[9] For England, see Adrian Hastings, *The Construction of Nationhood: Ethnicity, Religion and Nationalism* (Cambridge: Cambridge University Press, 1997). For France, see Joseph Strayer, 'France: the Holy Land, the Chosen People, and the Most Christian King' in John F. Benton and Thomas N. Bisson (eds), *Medieval Statecraft and the Perspectives of History* (Princeton: Princeton University Press, 1971). See also Bernd Schneidmüller, *Nomen Patriae: Die Entstehung Frankreichs in die politischgeographischen Terminologie (10.–13. Jahrhundert)* (Sigmaringen: Jan Thorbecke, 1987).

conduct of individuals, these analyses exaggerate one set of facts at the expense of another. They thus can not avoid simplifying, in the service of isolating an historiographical category, an always complicated reality, made up of temporally deep historical processes that are, in fact, usually in tension with one another. The justification for this approach, upon which rests the very concept of culture and the *Geisteswissenschaften* in general, is heuristic.

Having briefly noted these methodological concerns appropriate to *Kulturgeschichte*, let us reiterate, and by so doing clarify, the problem before us by distinguishing its point of departure from that of two outstanding books, Frank Manuel's *The Broken Staff: Judaism through Christian Eyes* and Jerome Friedman's *The Most Ancient Testimony: Sixteenth-Century Christian-Hebraica in the Age of Renaissance Nostalgia*. Manuel (1992: 11) insightfully referred to Hebraism as the 'third culture'; and it is Manuel's regrettably only passing use of the phrase 'third culture' that has served as the catalyst for the argument of this chapter. He correctly observed that 'the "third culture", the Hebrew, which alongside the Greek and the Latin was once an ornament of the trilingual gentleman-scholar, deserves a more prominent place in the history of Western thought than has been accorded to it'. Now, with this observation, Manuel has placed before us the task of determining what is distinctive of Hebraic Culture by distinguishing it from Greek, Roman, and Christian. Unfortunately, this task was not taken up by Manuel, as the focus of his book was confined to the intellectual history of the recovery of Judaism in Christendom. Our focus here, while indebted to Manuel's history of ideas, is different; for we have observed reasons—theological, political, legal, and socio-historical—for why Hebraism appears to be of greater cultural significance such that we are dealing with a heuristically productive historiographical category.

The possibility of this analytical category of the third culture of Hebraism may have been suggested by Friedman (1983: 183) when he wrote, 'one can only be astounded at the incredible influence allegedly exerted by Jewish thought . . . one might consider an entirely new classification of Renaissance-Reformation intellectual life organized according to degrees of judaization. Such a system would enable us to dispense with all traditional concepts of classification which have only served to divide historians since the sixteenth century.' This is a most provocative suggestion, one that echoes Matthew Arnold's (1885: 122) reference to the Reformation as 'a Hebraising revival' and

Max Weber's (1958: 156, 165) revealing but often ignored observations about the emphasis placed by English-Dutch Puritanism on the 'ebionitic elements of the New Testament' and the 'ethical tendency of Puritanism, especially in England, as English Hebraism'. Friedman, however, did not follow through with his own suggestion as it was deflected by his evaluation of 'Christian-Hebraica' as a nostalgic road into yesterday. In so doing, he missed the significance of the cultural transformation of—to employ Weber's (1934: 181) formulation—'Die charackterologischen Folgen der Durchdringung des Lebens mit alttestamentlichen Normen'. The reference to Weber's observations is not a consequence of an interest in his argument about the relation between Protestantism and the rise of Capitalism; rather, it is to emphasize the influence of this penetration of life with the norms of the Old Testament—a penetration surely refracted through Christian civilization and the socio-economic developments of early modern Europe—on the entire psychological conduct (as Weber put it, 'inneren Gesamthabitus') of many of the Protestants. It is this inner attitude, with its attendant allegiances, that allows us to consider the possibility of Hebraism as a cultural category of historiographical significance.

We do so with good reason. The Catholic, accusatory suspicion that Protestantism was essentially a type of Judaism should not be forgotten. Of course, the accusation was wide of the mark, for even Severtus' rejection of the Nicene creed in *De Trinitatis Erroribus* (1531) did not for a moment doubt the superiority of Christianity, however understood, over Judaism. Moreover, while a number of Christian Hebraists dramatically departed from the tradition of Christian interpretation by calling into question whether or not the prophecies of the Old Testament (for example, Isaiah 7:14; 9:6; 11:1–2; 52–3, and the so-called messianic Psalms 2, 8, 16, 22, 45, 75, 110, 118) literally referred to Jesus, none doubted that the New Testament was a fulfilment of the Old. Thus, Hebraism is certainly not Jewish; after all, if there existed the possibility that the Dutch, English, or Americans might be Israel, it was assuredly a new Israel.

Granted the Catholic characterization of Protestantism as Jewish is an inappropriate hyperbole, let us nonetheless pose this question: what is accurate about the characterization? Answering this question will open up the category of Hebraism to a more detailed examination, leading us to ascertain in what ways it is distinct from both Greek/Roman and Christian cultures. The examination will begin with the theological orientation of Hebraism and then proceed with its historical and political expressions. However, proceeding this way in no way implies sharply divergent manifestations of Hebraic culture; for, once again, the assumption of this argument is that these different orientations or manifestations achieved a configuration of relative coherence. While not being uniform, they nonetheless form a unity; for otherwise we could not speak of a culture. The point of unity remains to be clarified.

II

The theological orientation of Hebraism has forever been expressed scripturally as the problem of the relation between the Hebrew Bible and the New Testament. Adolph Harnack (1894: 88) succinctly formulated the problem in the following way:

> In the conviction that salvation is entirely bound up with faith in Jesus Christ, Christendom gained the consciousness of being a new creation of God . . . [and yet] in the conviction of being the true Israel, it claimed for itself the whole historical development recorded in the Old Testament, convinced that all the divine activity recorded there had the new community in view. The great question which was to find very different answers was how, in accordance with this view, the Jewish nation, so far as it had not recognized Jesus as Messiah, should be judged.

To this we must, of course, add 'and how the Old Testament should be understood'. We need not discuss here in any detail those different answers to the problem of the relation between, on the one hand, Christianity and, on the other, the tradition it claimed, that is, Jesus as not only Christ but also the son of God who, as such, sat at the right hand of the LORD (Psalm 110:1, 5 = Matthew 22:44, Mark 12:36, Luke 20:42, Acts 2:34–5, Ephesians 1:20, Colossians 3:1, Hebrews 1:13, 8:1, 10:12), as they have been examined often enough.[10] Our

---

[10] To cite only a few examples, W.D. Davies, *The Gospel and the Land: Early Christianity and Jewish Territorial Doctrine* (Berkeley: University of California Press, 1974). See also E.P. Sanders, *Paul and Palestinian Judaism: A Comparison of Patterns of Religion* (Philadelphia: Fortress, 1977) and Brevard S. Childs, 'The Sensus Literalis of Scripture: An Ancient and Modern Problem' in Herbert Donner, Robert Hanhart, and Rudolf Smend (eds), *Beiträge zur Alttestamentlichen Theologie* (Göttingen: Vandenhoeck & Ruprecht, 1977) 80–7.

concern here, in elucidating the conceptual lineaments of Hebraic Culture, is the response to the exegetical dilemma—a variation of the problem of the reception of tradition—posed by this relation already insisted upon in the Gospels and Paul's letters as seen above in the example of Psalm 110. Was the Hebrew Bible to be read through the lens of the 'new creation of God', the New Testament and subsequently the conclusions of the Councils of Nicea and Chalcedon, and, thus, as the Old Testament; or did the proper understanding, that is, 'the plain sense of the verse', of the Old Testament require that it be read as Rashi and other Jews had done (the latter by no means straightforward, as there were various Jewish readings, including philosophically allegorical, for example, Philo and later Joseph Karo, and, of course, mystically, for example, Moses Cordovero), and, thus, as the Hebrew Bible?[11]

This dilemma was by no means new to the Christian Hebraism of the sixteenth to the eighteenth centuries. It had already been posed point blank by Marcion's rejection of allegory in the reception of tradition. Much was at stake in this rejection of allegory in favour of a putatively literal reading or plain sense of the Old Testament, with the potential consequences being radical: not merely, in the case of Marcion, a rejection of the Old Testament but also a quite critical stance toward the Gospels themselves. Servetus may be the quintessential example of the realization of this potential for Christian Hebraism, but his interpretation of Scripture had obviously been anticipated by Arius. Thus, many of the exegetical problems of the Christian Hebraism of the Reformation parallel those of the first to the fourth centuries of early Christianity.

Justin Martyr (1963: 209), in his *Dialogue with Trypho*, written sometime after 135 CE, posed provocatively the problem of how the Old Testament should be read, 'For these words (the knowledge of Jesus Christ and the Christian baptism of the Holy Spirit) has neither been prepared by me, nor embellished by the art of man; but David sung them, Isaiah preached them, Zechariah proclaimed them, and Moses wrote them. Are you acquainted with them, Trypho? *They are contained in your scripture, or rather not yours, but ours. For we*

---

[11] This is not the place to enter into a detailed discussion of the principles of rabbinic exegesis, other than to note: 1) Rashi's emphasis on the plain sense of the verse (*peshat*), see BT Shabbat 63a, and 2) numerous Christian Hebraists, eg, Cunaeus and Selden, were careful students of Rashi's commentaries.

believe them; but you, though you read them, do not catch the spirit
that is in them' (my emphasis). Here, to expand upon Harnack's
summary of the hermeneutical problem of the Christian reception
of the Hebrew Bible, Justin, on behalf of Christianity, claimed the
Hebrew Bible as exclusively Christian scripture, hence, as the Old
Testament. As such, the now Old Testament could only be properly
understood in light of the New, which is why Trypho, a Jew, was
unable to 'catch the spirit that is in them'.

Justin was well aware that numerous difficulties existed in his
insistence on the claim of continuity between the Old and New
Testaments. To take an obvious example alluded to earlier, in response to Justin's proof that Jesus was born of a virgin as prophesized
by the Septuagint's Isaiah 7:14, where παρθένος is used, Trypho states,
'the scripture has not, "Behold, the virgin (παρθένος) shall conceive,
and bear a son", but "Behold, the young woman (Hebrew, עלמה) shall
conceive, and bear a son"... [Moreover] the whole prophecy refers to
Hezekiah' (1963: 231). The same difficulty of the proper reading of
Isaiah 7:14 was well known to the Christian Hebraists, for example, it
is addressed in the exchanges of Bodin's *Colloquium of the Seven*
about the Secrets of the Sublime (1975: 273).

We need not concern ourselves with Justin's ensuing and lengthy
defence of the Septuagint's παρθένος for the Hebrew עלמה, other than
to note, once again, that a more accurate reading of the Old Testament based upon the Hebrew Bible runs the risk of causing acute
interpretative difficulties for the Gospels, in this case, the use of the
Septuagint's Isaiah 7:14 in Matthew 1:20–25. Our immediate interest
is to see how Justin, as an early representative of an ensuing tradition
of interpretation, overcame the many difficulties of this kind. He did
so by observing that 'there were many sayings written obscurely, or
parabolically, or mysteriously, and symbolical[ly]' (1963: 232, and see
221); and that the ambiguity of these writings—an ambiguity acknowledged in the *Dialogue*—could only be properly resolved by
being hermeneutically guided by the spirit of the New Testament.
So guided, interpretative clarity emerged; thus, Justin's (1963: 211)
evaluation of Psalm 72 as referring not only to Solomon, as Trypho
had argued, but also and better to Christ. Here we have the interpretative principles of metaphor, allegory, and typology—already
explicitly evident in the New Testament itself, for example, the
allegory of Galatians 4:24–26 where, according to Paul, Hagar represents the old covenant and Sarah the new, and the typological

substitutions of Jesus for David in Psalm 110:1, 5, and for Solomon in Psalm 72, as alluded to above—that would largely hold sway within Christendom until challenged by the Christian Hebraists beginning in the sixteenth century.[12]

A glance at only a few of the many examples of the Hebraist re-evaluation of this tradition of Christian interpretation of the Hebrew Bible will allow us to draw conclusions about aspects of the character of Hebraic Culture. Evidently the only explicit Trinitarian formulation to be found in the Gospels is Matthew 28:19, if, in fact, that is what it is, 'Go therefore and make disciplines of all the nations, baptizing them in the name of the Father and of the Son and of the Holy Spirit'. Nonetheless, occasional passages in the Pentateuch were interpreted as having some kind of reference to the trinity, for example, the three visitors to Abraham as described in Genesis 18 (so Justin Martyr); but especially numerous verses in the Psalms were understood this way.

Psalm 2:7 states, 'I will tell of the decree of the LORD: He said to me, "You are my son; today I have begotten you"'. Rather than understanding the use of 'son' here as referring to David or a Davidic king (*pace* 2 Samuel 7), as would seem to be required by the verse preceding it, Psalm 2:7 was often interpreted as referring to Jesus and the trinity, for example, by Luther. However, the Christian Hebraist's 'concern for maintaining the "simple and natural sense" of the verse' forced, for example, Calvin to reject any Trinitarian implication of the verse, allowing, at most, for the possibility of both a reference to David and an anticipation of Jesus (Pak 2010: 83). Similarly, consider Psalm 16:8–10.

> I keep the LORD always before me; because he is at my right hand, I shall not be moved.
>
> Therefore my heart is glad, and my soul rejoices; my body also rests secure.
>
> For you do not give me up to Sheol, or let your faithful one see the Pit.

Rather than interpreting these verses as referring to Jesus and the resurrection, as in Acts 2:29–36, Calvin understood them as referring plainly to David (Pak 2010: 86–7).

---

[12] For a more qualified acceptance of allegory, see Augustine's discussion of Galatians 4 in Book XVII, chapter 3, *City of God*.

From the selection of only these few, but characteristic, examples of re-evaluation, one can observe that a pattern of interpretation, indicative of Christian Hebraism, had emerged. The pursuit of a more accurate understanding of the Old Testament led to a restraint of the allegorical reading insisted upon by Justin. One consequence of this restraint was that the Old Testament, no longer viewed as merely a typological anticipation of Jesus Christ, was allowed, so to say, to stand on its own feet. Perhaps the groundwork for this pattern of interpretation was laid by the 'Hellenic leaven' of the humanism of the Renaissance. It may be that the earlier, exegetical stance of a critical attitude toward Greek, Roman, and legal texts, for example, Roman law, that entailed not only philological, but also increasingly historical examination, was a factor contributing to the emergence of the interpretative orientation of Christian Hebraism. It is difficult to imagine that this earlier, humanistic and legal exegesis was not an influence on the development of the thought of, for example, Grotius (influenced by the classicist Scaliger at Leiden), Cunaeus, and Selden.[13] Be that as it may, it is certain that the attention paid to Jewish scholarship (especially Rashi, Maimonides, and Kimchi) by the Christian Hebraists was a factor contributing to this shift in interpretation.[14] More will have to be said about the significance of this interpretative shift; but, for now, we note from just these few, above examples that the image of David himself, rather than being obscured as a prefigurement of Jesus Christ, became an example for Christianity even to the point where 'it can appear to some that (for example) Calvin elevates the example of David where he should be promoting Christ' (Pak 2010: 98). There are other consequences of this interpretative shift.

Verses like Psalm 68:18 were long understood as clearly referring to Christ's ascension, 'You ascended the high mount, leading captives in your train and receiving gifts from people, even from those who rebel against the Lord God's abiding there.' The ascension was the prerequisite for Christ's gift of grace that frees humanity from the slavery of this world, so Ephesians 4:8–13. However, the focus on the 'plain

---

[13] Martha A. Ziskind, 'John Selden: Criticism and Affirmation of the Common Law Tradition', *The American Journal of Legal History* 19/1(1975) 22–39, is useful here.

[14] See, e.g., Jerome Friedman, *The Most Ancient Testimony: Sixteenth-Century Christian-Hebraica in the Age of Renaissance Nostalgia* (Athens: Ohio University Press, 1983).

sense of the verse', when taken within the context of Psalm 68 in its entirety, was, so argued the Christian Hebraists, not the other-worldly ascension to heaven, but rather the this-worldly order that God brings to his people Israel in the land of Israel. This Hebraist shift of understanding, as in the previous example of David for Psalms 2 and 16, redirects the previous, Christian focus from the pursuit of eternal life in heaven and the faith required for that pursuit to this world and, thus, potentially the law (or 'works') required to live properly there. We are now in a position to clarify the significance of this Christian Hebraist, interpretative shift for Hebraic Culture.

One consequence of this shift was to assert the possibility of a continuity different from that which Justin had insisted upon. Rather than the Old Testament being interpreted as only the precursor of the New—an interpretation requiring the hermeneutical techniques of allegory and typology—a new continuity emerged, as the Old Testament was now understood as also offering directly a model for life in this world. Of course, the New Testament remained primary, as the goal was to establish a true Christianity; nonetheless, the Old Testament achieved a different significance for Christendom. Previously, the life of Jesus was to be imitated (as commanded in, for example, John 3:16, 15:12–13, and Ephesians 2:4–8); however, now the new hermeneutical approach, requiring a critical, historical exegesis, had, if you will, freed both David to become an appropriate example of Christian piety and Israel to become an example of how Christians should organize themselves in this world.

The pursuit of an accurate understanding of the Old Testament posed anew the old interpretative problem of the theological disputes of early Christianity: were, for example, the so-called messianic Psalms literally, hence, only, prophecies of Jesus Christ? To be sure, the responses to this question varied; but the exegetical requirement of taking into account a particular verse's historical context resulted in a more complicated answer to the question, including occasionally 'no'. A new spirit—Hebraism—had emerged, different from the one that Justin Martyr had insisted upon. No longer Jesus but now also David was worthy of imitation. No longer were the heavenly Jerusalem and the new Israel of the New Testament the sole objects of contemplation; but now also were the this-worldly Jerusalem and Israel of the Old Testament. Properly appreciating the latter, so it was believed, was necessary for a Christian life in this world.

The Hebraism of this 'Old Testament Christianity' revivified the image of the earthly Jerusalem and Israel, an image whose original content had previously been, if not emptied then obviously deflected by the hermeneutical techniques of allegory and typology. The re-animation of these symbols is one manifestation of the continuing presence, albeit modified, of Jerusalem for the Occident, but with this important Hebraic development: now, both Jerusalems—the earthly and the heavenly—and both Israels—the this-worldly territorial polity and the Church, however differently understood—were significant. Here we have a central, conceptual lineament of Hebraic Culture: a this-worldly orientation—the problem of how to organize life in this world—that drew upon the models of the Old Testament within the otherwise other-worldly orientation of Christianity. The hermeneutical approach that made possible the theological expression of this conceptual lineament was the historical perspective as a prerequisite for an accurate reading of the Old Testament.

If Israelite and even Jewish experience (for example, the Sanhedrin and the Noahide laws) were worthy of reception and imitation, then other consequences followed. An understanding of law different from that of Paul, as expressed in Galatians 5:17–18 and Romans 7:15–23, could not be avoided; for if Israel was to serve as an example as to how Christians should organize themselves in this world, then the law of the polity achieves significance. Thus, the Pauline (and Augustinian) contrast between faith and works was examined anew, with responses ranging from Luther's Pauline reaffirmation, including casting aspersion on the 'ebionitic' Epistle of James, to Paul Fagius' and clearly John Selden's mollification of the contrast. Above all, the this-worldly orientation of Christian Hebraism posed point blank the question of how to understand, in the world of early modern Europe and, subsequently, the Old Testament category of 'chosen people'; for it, too, had been reanimated. The image having been given new content, various Protestant nations understood themselves as the chosen people; after all, they understood themselves as attempting to live their lives in this world according to Israel's law (more accurately, a part of the law), thereby according significance to both the civil polity and nationality. If, as was to be the case, the reanimation of the significance of attachment to the nation, through the law and the image of a people chosen by God to dwell in a land promised to them, within doctrinally universal Christianity, resulted in a conceptually richly productive, however tension ridden, combination of the this-worldly particular and the other-worldly universal, then the merit of Roman Catholicism's hyperbolic accusation of Protestantism as a variant of Judaism exists in its implicit recognition of Hebraism as a category of *Kulturgeschichte*.

III

We gain some insight into the significance of the combination of particular and universal of Hebraic Culture by again turning to Adolf Harnack's *History of Dogma*, but this time to his examination of the Jewish Christianity (or Ebionitism) of the first and second centuries CE (1894: 287–317). The purpose of doing so does not arise out of an interest in Harnack's analysis per se. We turn to his examination because it will prove useful for our clarification of the conceptual centre of Hebraic Culture, thereby allowing us to ascertain the distinctiveness of that culture.

Harnack (1894: 287) began his examination by observing that the 'original Christianity was in appearance Christian Judaism, the creation of universal religion on Old Testament soil'. Today we take for granted the merit of Harnack's observation about the nature of the movement around the Apostles (for example, Vermes 1981; Sanders 1985), but it was not always so. Despite the merit of Harnack's characterization about the origins of Christianity, it is nonetheless skewed; for Judaism clearly contains a universal orientation, both biblically, for example, Amos 9:7, Isaiah 2:2–4, 42:6–7, 49:6, etc., and subsequent to the Tanakh, for example, the Noahide laws.[15] The distinction between Judaism and Christianity does not exist in whether or not Judaism is a universal, world monotheistic religion; rather, it is a question of the precise expression of the universalism. The image of Jerusalem of both the Hebrew Bible for Judaism and the Old Testament for the early Christian Jews and later for many Christian Hebraists bears a universal orientation, but it also contains a national orientation. This combination indicates that participation in the universal is through the nation, as is manifestly clear in those

---

[15] Of the enormous literature on this point, I cite here only H.M. Orlinsky, 'Nationalism-Universalism and Internationalism in Ancient Israel', reprinted in *Essays in Biblical Culture and Bible Translation* (New York: KTAV, 1974).

above examples, for example, Isaiah 49:6b, 'I will also give you [Israel] as a light to the nations, that my salvation may reach the end of the earth'. In contrast, the development of Christianity during its first several centuries swept away as obstacles what I have, in other places, characterized as the primordial attachments to territory and kinship (Grosby 1996, 2001). This difference, crucial to Hebraism, should be obvious, and it has been observed before (see, for example, Davies 1974). We can, however, see what is at stake in this difference and, thus, the consolidation of the conceptual lineament of Hebraic Culture by ascertaining the implications of Harnack's analysis of the earlier Christian Judaism.

In his effort to clarify the character of early Christianity by delimiting the scope of the category of Jewish Christianity, Harnack (1894: 288) insisted that 'we are *not* justified in speaking of Jewish Christianity, where a Christian community, even one of Gentile birth [!], calls itself the true Israel' (my emphasis). Now, this is a very curious insistence, for it appears unnecessary. Given the obviousness of Harnack's point, one wonders what he had in mind. It surely cannot be simply the self-description of Christians as being the 'true Israel'; for Harnack was correct, as that is how Christendom has often referred to itself, albeit with the symbol, Israel, now referring to the Church (of the elect or otherwise), for example, already in Irenaeus' *Against Heresies*, Justin's *Dialogue with Trypho*, and later in Augustine's *City of God*. We perhaps get a clearer idea of what was likely Harnack's concern when he (1894: 291-2) continued by mentioning the 'reproach of Judaizing' against those in the early Church who had turned to the Old Testament for 'regulations and statutory enactments' necessary for their existence as an organization in this world.[16] Here, too, Harnack brushed aside the accusation as illegitimate. Thus, according to Harnack, one is *not* justified in understanding the early Christians, who described themselves as the 'true Israel' and who had turned to the laws of the Old Testament, as Jewish Christians; rather, they were firmly in the developing tradition of Christianity. There is nothing so far in Harnack's argument with which to take issue, although it is difficult to shake off the impression that more than just clarifying the category of Jewish Christianity in

---

[16] Adolph Harnack, *History of Dogma* (London: Williams and Norgate, 1894) 291-2s, n. 3, continued by assuming that these Christians accused of being Judaizers had objected to the allegorical interpretation of the Old Testament.

the early history of Christianity was on Harnack's mind. Could it be that the inclusion of the qualifying phrase 'even one of Gentile birth' indicates that Harnack was implicitly defending the Lutheran Church against such a characterization?

Harnack (1894: 288) insisted that it was a most arbitrary view of history that looked upon the Christian appropriation of the Old Testament, after any point (for example, the use of the term 'true Israel' or Old Testament law for civil legislation), as no longer Christian, but Jewish Christian. Thus, Harnack would have objected to the direction of the argument of this chapter, and specifically the conclusion of the previous section. In contrast, he (1894: 289) thought that what was decisive for distinguishing Christianity from Jewish Christianity is that 'wherever the universalism of Christianity is not violated in favor the Jewish nation, we have to recognize every appropriation of the Old Testament as Christian'. But here is where we find our problem. Whatever the merits of Harnack's analysis for distinguishing the early Christians from the Ebionites, his criterion for the distinction fails for the historical period of early modern Europe. It is abundantly clear that the arguments of the Christian Hebraists were not in favour of the Jewish nation per se. However, do we not have a different, animating spirit of a culture when the universalism of Christianity is, in fact, 'violated' in favour of, for example, the Dutch, English, or American nation as the newly chosen people of the now true Israel?

An objection to this conclusion about the failure of Harnack's criterion can be raised because it takes his observation about what is distinctive in the differentiation between Jewish Christianity and Christianity out of its historical context. After all, the new or true Israel of the Dutch, English, or American nation did not claim to be Jewish, as did the Ebionites. Furthermore, it is obvious that early Christianity carried out the implications of Paul's orientation of a universalism through the individual and not the nation, the political corollary of which, insofar as there is one, was and perhaps can only be empire. However, if our point of departure is the utility of Hebraism as a category of *Kulturgeschichte*, then we must modify Harnack's criterion by observing that whenever the (individualistic) universalism of Christianity is qualified by the introduction of nationality, as in the case of not only the Israel of the early Jewish Christians but also the 'Israels' of early modern Europe, we have Hebraic Culture.

There are, I think, compelling historical reasons, as there must be to justify the utility of the category of Hebraic Culture, for this different point of departure. We have already observed how Hebraism, by allowing us 'to dispense with the traditional concepts of classification', as Friedman (1983: 183) put it, may provide a more accurate understanding of theological developments during the first and second centuries CE; and surely there are striking similarities between those developments and the Christian Hebraism of the sixteenth to the eighteenth centuries. However, there are other reasons.

The qualification, or complication, of Christian universalism through recognition of the significance of nationality took place in contexts different from those of the Reformation and its aftermath. We know that the reanimation of the image of ancient Israel was a factor in the emergence of the self-understanding of England as a nation during the eleventh to the fourteenth centuries (Hastings 1997: 35–56; Grosby 2003). We also know of similar developments (for example, the conflict between Boniface VIII and Philip the Fair, or the origins of Gallicanism) in fourteenth-century France (Strayer 1971, Schneidmüller 1987). And there are the religious, political, and legal developments of the transformation of the *corpus mysticum* of the universal Church to that of the nation, exemplified by the idea of *pro patria mori*, described so well by Ernst Kantorowicz (1957: 193–272).

In these examples, we find ideas of a new chosen people and a new promised land through the reception of the Old Testament. Should we not seek to group together these historically earlier developments with those of the Reformation and its aftermath? Are we not entitled to observe here a distinctive cultural pattern of this uneasy but conceptually fruitful combination of nationality and universal, Christian monotheism, the further significance of which is precisely that it is not confined to one historical period?[17] The pattern of this third, Hebraic Culture is not Greek, which never developed fully a national perspective. Moreover, its emphasis on tradition and history distinguishes it from the rationalism that is usually associated with the

---

[17] A similar pattern—the qualification of an otherwise universal civilization by the significance attributed to nationality—is also to be observed in both Buddhism, specifically, Sri Lanka, and Islam, specifically, Persia/Iran; nonetheless, Hebraism should be restricted to European civilization as its heuristic utility exists in comparison to Greek/Roman and Christian cultures.

category 'Greek Culture'. It certainly is different from Hellenism; and it is a stark alternative to Roman, imperial ambition.

One might entertain the possibility of 'Protestantism' as a category of *Kulturegeschichte* that encompasses the characteristics presented in this argument. However, to do so is heuristically unproductive on two counts. First, a proposed historiographical category of Protestantism would only obscure the important pre-Reformation examples of Hebraism, as described above. Secondly, there were significant currents within Protestantism that were not Hebraic, for example, the Anabaptists or individuals like Roger Williams, who rejected the nation of Israel as a model as is clear from his 'Queries of Highest Consideration' and 'The Bloody Tenet of Persecution for Cause of Conscience'.

It is to be taken for granted that there were numerous factors contributing to the emergence and consolidation of the nations referred to above. The intention of this argument is not that the Hebraic reception of the Old Testament, specifically the reanimation of the image of Israel, was a primary, causal factor in that emergence and consolidation. It is merely to observe that this image was and remains a symbolic resource for the Occident. Few today would disagree with this observation. The disagreement may arise over the significance of this continuing presence of Jerusalem such that the symbol of Israel represents the potential for an alternative, cultural pattern. The revival of that image of Israel (the political autonomy of the territorially bounded land of a people chosen to be distinctive for the sake of an other-worldly purpose) or more accurately, the actualization of its potential, irrespective of how opportunistic it may have been in the service of any number of interests, can indicate the specific pattern of Hebraic Culture. The theological underpinning of the this-worldly orientation of Hebraic Culture's conception of a chosen people of (a new) Israel was expressed by the idea, so prevalent especially in the Reformed Church, of carrying out God's work in this world, an idea anticipated by the rabbinic conception of Israel's partnership with God (BT Shabbat 10a): both stand in contrast to the Islamic total submission to God and the Christian tradition of *imitatio dei*.

The political manifestation of that actualization does not simply consist of the use of any number of quotations from the Old Testament in support of a particular political stance. The reanimation of the image of Israel for political purposes also does not consist in whether or not 'the Bible was "correctly" read, but whether biblical ideas of a theoretical nature, on top of biblical examples, figures of speech, and quotable verses informed political thought' (Oz-Salzburger 2008). It clearly did so for Filmer, Grotius, Althusius, Cunaeus, Selden, Milton, Harrington, Locke, Bodin, and John Cotton to name only a few; and I think it continues to do so today, although less obviously so.[18]

It may be that political Hebraism should be understood as primarily the same as the orientation found in the literature of the *Respublica Hebraeorum*, so prevalent during the sixteenth to the eighteenth centuries.[19] If so, then political Hebraism would be the conceptual vehicle for a free and just society of republican form, where the understanding of the Old Testament was used in support of the primacy of Parliament, the subordination of the sovereign to the law in contrast to Roman law, and occasionally a federalist structure. There is much to commend this view, for the majority of the works of Hebraic political thought runs in this direction. Nonetheless, two cautionary observations are required.

The first and less pressingly relevant for the purposes of this chapter is to note that the emergence of a liberal *Rechtsstaat* in early modern Europe is historically a most complicated matter. Numerous traditions, including those of canon and medieval law, contributed to that emergence, as described, for example, by Gierke (1939). This is not to gainsay the fact that the Hebraic political tradition has made an important contribution to the Western conception of liberty (Oz-Salzberger 2002). Certainly, the rule of law is manifest in the biblical and rabbinic tradition, but it is not unique to them. The more pressingly relevant question is, whether or not Hebraic Culture, as a category of *Kulturgeschichte*, must be understood as the bearer of this particular political orientation? After all, even though distinctly less influential, the Hebraism of this period also contained arguments in favour of absolutism. Perhaps this question need not be definitively answered; for what is surely decisive for Hebraic Culture, in contrast to Hellenism and Roman culture, and

---

[18] For Cotton, see Shira Wolosky, 'Biblical Republicanism: John Cotton's "Moses His Judicials" and American Hebraism' *Hebraic Political Studies* 4/2 (2009) 104–27.

[19] For an overview of this literature, see Manuel (1992: 115–27); Adam Sutcliffe, *Judaism and the Enlightenment* (Cambridge: Cambridge University Press, 2003) 42–57, and Eric Nelson, *The Hebrew Republic: Jewish Sources and the Transformation of European Political Thought* (Cambridge: Harvard University Press, 2010).

what encompasses all of the currents of Hebraic political thought is the political autonomy of a particular nation in opposition to empire.

There is, however, a further consideration. The religion of ancient Israel had, in a way not done previously, shattered the asserted harmony between this world and the other world, by recognizing a chasm between these two worlds—a chasm that was bridged only uneasily and uncertainly through the covenantal relation (see Nicholson 1986: 191–217). Much of the Tanakh bears witness to this unease and uncertainty. This chasm is characteristic of the religions of the so-called axial age (Eisenstadt 1986); but it is especially acute for the religion of ancient Israel and Judaism given the latter's refusal to flee from this world, for example, its attachments to kinship and territory. One consequence of this uncertainty, heightened by the unequivocal transcendence of God modified only by his word—the law—present in this world, was to foster *discussion* about the character of the covenantal relation between God and humanity, if for no other reason than the word had to be properly interpreted (the interpretation of history is another reason).[20] Although it may appear counter-intuitive, there are numerous examples of this discussion in Scripture, some of the more obvious examples of which are Genesis 18:23–5, Exodus 32:11–14, 1 Samuel 8, Jeremiah 28 and 44, and Job, to which should be added the less obvious commentary on the Bible within the Bible (see Fishbane 1985). And as is well known, the place of discussion in the developing determination of the relation between the human and divine is central to the rabbinic corpus and its understanding of law, especially the Mishnah and Talmud, as is obvious from just the often cited Mishnah Rosh Hashanah 2:9 and BT Bava Metzia 59b.

Now, our concern here is not primarily the significance of the conception of God transcending the state for the rule of law and liberty conveyed by Hebraic political thought, as crucially important as that conception is. And it would be foolish to suggest that the tradition of discussion about the character of law, politics, and even the truth or God's will is due exclusively to the influence of Hebraism. But what does historically seem to be justified is that some Hebraists, notably Selden, turned to Israelite and especially Jewish experience as the classic example of this developing determination of the relation

---

[20] Perhaps this uncertainty is also expressed in the arresting question, 'Can there be doubt in Heaven?' BT Berakhot 3b.

between the human and divine through discussion, that is, as common, national law with a universal reference. That reference was
provided by the Noahide laws, used by the Hebraists in support of
liberty; for their existence indicated that not all law had its source in
the sovereign as postulated by Roman law. Certainly such a support
could be and was found elsewhere than in the rabbinic legal tradition,
for example, the 'light of reason'. But what was distinctively Hebraic
was not Grotius' understanding of natural law as innate as a consequence of reason, but as a conception of a body of law that did and
had to develop through the reflective process of an evolving tradition
through which universal principles became manifest and embodied
(Haivry 2010; Stone 2007). It was precisely the interpretative problem
of this reflective process that led S.N. Eisenstadt (2004: 216–37) to
characterize this Jewish tradition not as the rule of law but as the rule
of the court. In the rabbinic legal tradition, a Hebraist like Selden
found an example that informed his own understanding of English
common law. It allowed him to understand better how a humane
universalism was borne by and refracted through the history of a
particular nation, or, formulated in a different idiom, not merely
liberty but ordered liberty.

IV

The coherence of the category Hebraic Culture would be greater if
this legal tradition of a combination of common and universal law
were integral to it. Such a conception of law entails the characteristics
of Hebraic Culture: the elevation of tradition, a critical historical
perspective, a significance accorded to nationality, and, yet, maintaining a universal reference. As such, this understanding of law, or at
least especially Selden's understanding, confirms Pocock's observation about the peculiar importance of law in the history of historiography: it indicates a category of *Kulturgeschichte*.

The various aspects—theological, socio-historical, political, and
legal—of Hebraic Culture having been observed, the argument,
albeit more of an outline, for its usefulness as a category of *Kulturgeschichte* has been made. To the extent to which these characteristics
cohere, then one is entitled to speak of Hebraic Culture. Doing so, allows
for a better understanding of a number of significant historical

developments that are otherwise obscured by historiographical categories such as 'modernity', for example, the continued importance of tradition, nationality, historical perspective, common law, and self-government. One final problem should be introduced, not to be answered but for future consideration.

It is sometimes the case that the investigations of the *Geisteswissenschaften* entertain the question of perennial human orientations: tendencies that, despite necessarily exhibiting wide historical variation, are nonetheless persistent expressions of the spirit or mind. Perhaps questions of this kind cannot be avoided, indicating that the pursuits of the *Geisteswissenschaften*, including *Kulturgeschicthe*, sooner or later stumble into the problems of philosophical anthropology. This question has been lurking in the background of this enquiry. A number of years ago I (Grosby 1996) observed that there was a dogmatic and historical irony at play; for rather than finding the New Testament in the Old, it is the Old Testament, with its beliefs in a promised land and chosen people, that haunts the New. One vehicle for this irony was Christian Hebraism. However, rather than being content with the historical examination of the different ways the image of Israel has been reanimated, as an example of the continuing presence of Jerusalem, one would like to know just why is it that the symbol of Israel has proven to be so fruitful and resilient?

4

The Political Thought of the Biblical History

Genesis–Kings

Yoram Hazony*

My purpose in this essay is to suggest that the central historical narrative of the Hebrew Bible, beginning with Genesis and ending with the book of Kings, presents its readers with a coherent political teaching. In the course of this discussion, I will argue that the advancement of a particular set of political ideas is one of the purposes of the biblical text, and give a preliminary account of a few principal aspects of these political ideas.

1. THE BIBLICAL HISTORY, GENESIS–KINGS

Does it make sense to speak of 'the political teaching of the Hebrew Bible'? Anyone who knows the Bible well will immediately recognize that to speak in this fashion is to engage in a reduction. The Bible is not, after all, one book by one author. As a consequence, it does not have a single point of view on the matters of concern to it, politics included. For example, one would have a hard time reconciling the political understanding of the book of Daniel, in which faith in God is virtually all one needs to gain political salvation; with that of the book

* I would like to thank Joshua Berman, Matt Goldish, Ari Gontownik, Steven Grosby, Ofir Haivry, Joseph Isaac Lifshitz, and Menachem Lorberbaum for their comments on drafts of this chapter.

of Esther, which comes closer to the view that in politics, God tends to help those who help themselves.[1] This divergence in political teachings is endemic to the part of the Hebrew Bible known as the 'Writings' or Hagiographa, the last one-quarter of the Bible, and is apparently a reflection of the fact that these were collected with the intention of establishing a broad Jewish tradition, embracing a diversity of viewpoints.[2]

But this is not the case for the earlier parts of the Bible. The first half of the biblical text comprises a single, largely unbroken narrative, which begins with the creation of the world, but whose focus is the emergence of the Israelites as a people and the rise and fall of the independent state established by this people. The completed narrative, extending from Genesis until the destruction of the kingdom of Judah at the end of the book of Kings, was assembled not long after the fall of this Israelite state. And regardless of what one may think were the origins of the sources used in constructing this history, it is clear that the author or editor of this unbroken narrative intended for it to be read as a coherent whole, with a coherent purpose: namely, to provide an account of why the Israelite state rose and why it declined.[3]

This unbroken narrative is the core of what we call the Hebrew Bible. It is followed by the orations of the prophets, which make up the third quarter of the Bible and provide us with an evaluation of the events recounted in the history. The prophetic orations, too, represent a tradition and a school of thought with an evident internal integrity. But unlike the main historical narrative, they present

[1] For the divergent treatments of politics in Daniel, Esther, and Nehemia, see Yoram Hazony, *The Dawn: Political Teachings of the Book of Esther* (Jerusalem: Shalem, 2000) esp. 89–92, 135–43.

[2] Sid Z. Leiman, *The Canonization of Hebrew Scripture* (New Haven: Connecticut Academy of Arts and Sciences, 1991) 28.

[3] A systematic treatment of the question of the coherence of the historical narrative from Genesis to Kings appears in Donald Harman Akenson, *Surpassing Wonder: The Invention of the Bible and the Talmuds* (New York: Harcourt, Brace, 1998). A variation of this view places the compilation of most of the narrative before the final destruction of the state, during the restoration under the Judean king Josiah. See, e.g., William M. Schniedwind, *How the Bible Became a Book* (New York: Cambridge University Press, 2004). The difference between these two positions is not significant, however, to the present argument. Both views can be seen as the consummation of the theory of a single author for the entire 'Deuteronomistic history' proposed by Martin Noth. See *The Deuteronomistic History* (Sheffield, England: Journal for the Study of the Old Testament, 1943) esp. 24–6, 128.

themselves as the teachings of individuals, with all this implies. As the rabbis pointed out, Ezekiel does not necessarily see things as Isaiah does, even when they are the same things. Thus the presumption that we are approaching matters from a single, unified perspective gives way, in this part of the Bible, to a certain pluralism of voices. Finally, when we reach the last quarter of the Bible—the Psalms, Proverbs, *megilot,* and so forth—we find ourselves in a much looser compendium of different kinds of works, written in different periods and with different purposes in view.

It is therefore certainly correct to speak of the Bible as containing different political teachings. But this in no way diminishes the fact that the Bible does advance a central, unified political teaching: that which is expressed in the story of the rise and decline of the Israelite people and their state—as told in the unbroken narrative from Genesis to Kings, and interpreted by the prophetic writings. It is this core political teaching to which we refer in speaking of the political teaching, or of the political theory, of the Hebrew Bible.

What, then, is the content of this political teaching? I will here restrict myself to four points, which I hope will suffice to give a sense of what future generations were to learn from the biblical narrative. Each of these can easily be associated with one of four pivotal developments in the narrative: (i) the exodus from Egypt; (ii) the concubine in Geva; (iii) the founding of the Israelite state in the time of Samuel; and (iv) the division of the kingdom of Solomon.

2. EXODUS AND REVOLUTION

As was emphasized long ago by the great medieval commentator Isaac Abravanel, the Hebrew Bible is fundamentally suspicious of worldly power, and particularly of the state.[4] There are intimations of this from the outset, as when the establishment of the first city is attributed to Cain, who is also the first murderer.[5] But this biblical aversion to the state is presented in a much more direct fashion in the story of the tower of Babel:

---

[4] Isaac Abravanel, commentary on I Samuel 8.
[5] Genesis 4:17. For an extended treatment of this subject, see Leon R. Kass, *The Beginning of Wisdom: Reading Genesis* (New York: Free Press, 2003).

The whole earth was of one language and of one speech ... And they said to one another, 'Come, let us make bricks and fire them thoroughly ... ' And they said, 'Come let us build us a city and a tower, whose top may reach to heaven. And let make us a name, lest we be scattered abroad the face of the whole earth.' And the Lord came down to see the city and the tower, which mankind were building. And the Lord said, Behold, they are one people and they all have one speech, and this they begin to do. Now nothing that they scheme to do will be withheld from them. Come, let us go down and confound their language, that man may not understand the language of his neighbor. And the Lord scattered them from there across the face of the earth, and they stopped building the city.[6]

In this account, we have the biblical suspicion of the state in its distilled form: When men see themselves as a single people and live together in a single state, their ambition knows no bounds. By virtue of ruling the earth they come to believe they can rule heaven; by virtue of making themselves a great name they come to believe they can be eternal. They come to think, in other words, that they are themselves God. And indeed, it is in this way that the great emperors of the Bible are portrayed: Pharaoh, Sanherib, Nebuhadnezzar, and Ahashverosh are all men whose self-worship is such that there is no limit to the evil they may be moved to do.[7] Nor is this impression limited to emperors. Petty kings, too, are depicted as being of this same kind: 'Seventy kings, having had their thumbs and their big toes cut off, gathered food at my table,' boasts the Canaanite king Adoni-bezek.[8] Even lesser kings, it seems, would extend their rule over all the earth and heaven as well, if only they could. The evil they do is limited by nothing other than the strength of their arms.

Now, the Hebrews, from the first moment they are presented to us in the narrative, appear as rebels against the hubris and self-worship of kings and their states. God takes Abraham out of the great metropolitan centres of Mesopotamia and leads him into a veritable wilderness, Canaan, where he lives his life as a nomad, making his home in a herdsman's tent. The point of this ideal is evidently to be free from the rule of men, so that one may properly turn one's heart

---

[6] Genesis 11:1–9.

[7] Even Darius, the best-loved of the imperial rulers in the Bible, who issues the decree to rebuild Jerusalem, is presented as accepting the idea that supplication before God should be forbidden for 30 days, so that all requests in the empire should be directed to him alone. Daniel 6:8–10.

[8] Judges 1:7.

to God. There is, in other words, a palpably anarchic tendency at work here.[9]

The Hebrew Bible, however, is no utopia and the idyll of the herdsman's life is spoiled time and again by the kings that keep reappearing in it, and by the terrible deeds they do: trying to purloin one's wife, kidnapping one's kinsman, stealing one's wells, raping one's daughter.[10] Moreover, it is not the violence that puts an end to this experiment in living beyond the state. It is the economics of the thing. Canaan is on the verge of famine in every generation from the time Abraham arrives there, and this threat of starvation forces the Hebrews to turn to the Egyptian state for help time after time.[11] And each time, Egypt does indeed save them. Like any crime family, it offers protection—but at the price of one's freedom.[12]

As we have seen, the God of the Hebrew Bible does not much like the state. When he cares for someone, as he does for Abraham, his inclination is to tell him to get out. But in the case of Israel in Egypt, we have an entire people enslaved. They cannot just walk away. What then?

---

[9] On the anarchic tendency in the biblical political teaching, see Yoram Hazony, 'The Jewish Source of the Western Disobedience Teaching,' *Azure* 4 (Summer 1998); John W. Flight, 'The Nomadic Ideal in the Old Testament' *Journal of Biblical Literature* 42 (1923) 158–226, esp. 213f.

[10] Genesis 12:15, 20:2; 26:17–18; 14:11–12; 34:1–2.

[11] This pattern is already established in Abraham's time. See Genesis 12:10.

[12] It is important to note that as a consequence of this economic argument, a powerful dissent is registered against the anarchic ideal within the text of Genesis itself. This dissent is represented in Genesis by Joseph, a Hebrew herdsman, who, as a boy, dreams of harvesting grain and ruling the heavens. Genesis 37:9. By the time he emerges as Pharaoh's minister, Joseph appears to have been won over to the view that man cannot survive without the state, and that God himself wishes men to be saved by it. See, e.g., Genesis 45:5–8. For discussion of Joseph's politics of engagement with the state and its subsequent treatment in the Hebrew Bible, see Aaron Wildavsky, *Assimilation Versus Separation: Joseph the Administrator and the Politics of Religion in Biblical Israel* (New Brunswick: Transaction, 1993); and Yoram Hazony, *The Dawn*, esp. 83–92, 127–43.

For this reason, I am unable to accept the argument of Moshe Weinfeld and others, to the effect that the establishment of the Israelite state 'contradicts' the earlier traditions of Israel. The critique of anarchy within the biblical narrative is immanent in the very first presentation of the anarchic vision, in Genesis. Neither the violence nor the economic dependence on Egyptian agriculture represented by Joseph permits us to accept anarchy as a simple and unalloyed ideal. The rejection of the preferences of Gideon and Samuel represents the conclusion of the biblical narrative that Joseph's critique of anarchy is in large measure correct. For Weinfeld's view, see his essay, 'The Transition from Tribal Republic to Monarchy in Ancient Israel' in Daniel J. Elazar (ed.), *Kinship and Consent: The Jewish Political Tradition and Its Contemporary Uses* (New Brunswick: Transaction, 1997) 216–32.

To this, the biblical answer is breathtakingly bold, and in line, once again, with its tendency towards anarchism: The answer, we are told, is resistance and revolution.[13] Indeed, the book of Exodus, which tells the story of the departure of the Israelites from Egypt, opens with three consecutive scenes of resistance against the state. In the first, Pharaoh instructs the Hebrew midwives to murder all the male children born to the slaves; but the midwives refuse the order of the king.[14] In the second, a Hebrew woman hides her infant son from Pharaoh's men, and Pharaoh's own daughter conspires with her to save the boy, again in direct contravention of the order of the king.[15] In the third, this child of disobedience, Moses, is introduced to us as a grown man. Here is what we are told about him:

> And the child grew ... and he became her son. And she called his name Moses.... And it came to pass that when Moses was grown, he went out to his brothers and saw their suffering; and he saw an Egyptian beating a Hebrew man, one of his brothers. He looked this way and that, and when he saw that there was no man, he slew the Egyptian and buried him in the sand.[16]

In this scene, as in the others, there is no pretence of being bound to obey Pharaoh, his law, or the agents of his state. There is not even some kind of divine intervention to justify rebellion against the state. On the contrary, in all three scenes, women and men violate the law of the state simply because they think it is the right thing to do. And the Bible evidently considers it the right thing to do, as well. For as a direct result of these acts of disobedience, the Hebrews are given Moses, the man who will deliver them out of Egypt. Not until Moses has slain an Egyptian, fled Egypt, and reverted to the life of a herdsman—all on his own accord—does God reveal himself to him.[17]

The message here is unequivocal: God loves those who resist the state and its injustice. It is to those that he reveals himself, and those whom he is willing to help. True, the Hebrews are depicted as being largely passive, and it is God who delivered them 'with a mighty hand and an outstretched arm.' But the story of the exodus does not reach its climax until each Hebrew family has obeyed God's command to

---

[13] See Aaron Wildavsky, *Moses as Political Leader* (Jerusalem: Shalem Press, 2005 [1984]); Michael Walzer, *Exodus and Revolution* (New York: Basic Books, 1985).

[14] Exodus 1:15–21.   [15] Exodus 1:22–2:10.

[16] Exodus 2:11–12.   [17] Exodus 3:1f.

slaughter and eat a lamb, smearing the blood on their doorposts. God asks them, in other words, to attest publicly to having killed and consumed the god of the Egyptians.[18] An act of public disobedience and contempt towards Egypt is, as it were, the minimum price one had to pay to be delivered from the 'house of bondage'[19] and to freedom in the promised land.

3. THE CONCUBINE IN GEVA

To this point, the choice between anarchy and the state is rather straightforward. Although marred by violence and hunger, there can be no doubt that enslavement in Egypt is far worse than anything experienced by the patriarchs in Canaan. For this reason, it is to a condition of anarchic liberty—and not to subjugation under the heel of a king—that the Israelites hope to return in Canaan. As this hope is famously expressed by Gideon after the defeat of the Midianites:

> I will not rule over you, nor will my son rule over you. But God will rule over you.[20]

Similar sentiments are given powerful expression by Yotam, Gideon's son, after the death of his father; and by Samuel, the greatest of the judges, who repeatedly inveighs against the establishment of a permanent state.[21]

---

[18] Exodus 12:3–11, 21–3. Amon, the god of the Egyptian capital of Thebes, was represented as a ram. By the time of the enslavement of the Jews, Amon had become the most powerful and prominent god in the pantheon, under whose standard the Egyptian armies waged war.

[19] Exodus 13:3, 14, 20:2; Deuteronomy 5:6, 6:12, 7:8, 8:14, 13:6, 11; Joshua 24:17; Judges 6:8; Jeremiah 34:13.

[20] Judges 8:23.

[21] Judges 9:7–15; I Samuel 8:10–20. See in particular I Samuel 12:1–25, in which Samuel presents an interpretation of history contrary to that favoured by the narrative itself. On Samuel's view, the judges Gideon, Jeftah, and Samuel are listed in one breath as having 'delivered you out of the hand of your enemies round about, and you dwelled secure' (12:11). Moreover, Samuel insists that although 'I am old and grey-headed,' nevertheless 'my sons are with you' (12:2); against the narrative's determination that the sons of Samuel had taken bribes, Samuel makes his famous speech, without precedent in the annals of Israelite leadership: 'Whose ox have I taken? Whose ass have I taken? Whom have I defrauded?' (12:3) In addition, as a

But much as the narrative evidences sympathy for the dream of an anarchic order, its verdict is not for anarchy. It is for a state. And the reason is simple: anarchy just does not work out as one might have hoped. Indeed, the entire book of Judges is one long indictment of anarchy, making it the pivot on which the political teaching of the Hebrew Bible turns.

The book of Judges describes the aftermath of the Israelite invasion of Canaan under Joshua. The conquest under Joshua is depicted as being—in one sense, anyway—a kind of ideal, in which the Israelites act virtually as one man, almost with one heart, in their common effort to conquer the land and cleanse it of abominable practices of its inhabitants.[22] But men, it seems, cannot maintain such unity of purpose indefinitely, 'and there arose another generation after them, which knew not the Lord, nor what he had done for Israel.'[23]

The book of Judges consists of eight episodes, arranged in such a way as to describe the gradual dissolution of all the Israelites had been fighting for:[24]

demonstration of Israel's vulnerability, now that they have followed after the ways of Joseph, choosing an earthly ruler and becoming dependent on agriculture, Samuel threatens (with God's help) to destroy the wheat harvest and bring all Israel to starvation (12:17–19). And yet the narrative, while sympathetic to Samuel's longing for anarchy, does not support him in his views: Both the continual violence in the land and the corruption of his own sons testify against his view of anarchy.

[22] See especially Joshua 1:16–18; 24:16–21, 31.

[23] Judges 2:7, 10. These words are intended to invoke the opening passage of the book of Exodus, in which the Hebrews are enslaved in Egypt. Exodus 1:8. This parallel between Exodus and Judges sets up the twin dangers of empire and anarchy. It is worth noting the additional message that is packed into this matter of politial forgetfulness. Indeed, the subject of the *transmission* of wisdom may be said to be one of the most pressing political questions raised by the biblical narrative.

[24] On this progression as representing a decline in civic virtue, see Daniel J. Elazar, *Covenant and Polity in Biblical Israel* (New Brunswick: Transaction, 1995) 290–1. See also Noth, *Deuteronomistic History*, 72–6, 122–3; D.W. Gooding, 'The Composition of the Book of Judges', *Eretz-Israel* 16 (Jerusalem: Israel Exploration Society, 1982) 70–9; and J.P.U. Lilley, 'A Literary Appreciation of the Book of Judges', *Tyndale Bulletin* (1967) 94–102. This view is opposed by Martin Buber, who recognizes no such decline, and sees in the last two episodes 'a monarchical book appear[ing] at the side of the anti-monarchical book of Judges, or rather, in opposition to it.' Buber, *Kingship of God*, Richard Scheimann, trans. (Atlantic Highlands, N.J.: Humanities, 1967) 77–84. It remains difficult to see how this view can be reconciled with the plain meaning of the text. An updated reading that sees the book of Judges as a struggle among competing voices can be found in the essays in Michael Walzer, Menachem Lorberbaum, and Noam J. Zohar (eds.), *The Jewish Political Tradition* (New Haven: Yale, 2000). See in particular Michael Walzer's introduction to the chapter on 'Kings', 109–16; and Moshe Halbertal's essay on 'God's Kingship', 128–32.

3.1. Otniel, Ehud, and Deborah

The stories of Otniel, Ehud, and Deborah continue to reflect some of the cohesion and moral strength that characterized the period of Joshua. In these tales, the leadership belongs to the most significant tribes—Judah, Efraim, and Benjamin—and the judges themselves are, so far as we can tell, individuals of exceptional character. Each of these results in a dramatic and complete victory over the enemies of Israel, and we are told that 'the land was quiet for forty years'.[25]

Already in the third episode, however, the tribal alliance begins to show signs of cracking.[26] The song of Deborah the prophetess explicitly names four tribes—Reuben, Gad, Dan, and Asher—that refuse her summons to go to war against Yavin, king of Canaan. 'Why did you sit among the sheepfolds', she cries, 'to hear the bleating of flocks?'[27]

3.2. Gideon

In the fourth episode, Gideon, himself from a minor tribe,[28] is followed only by four of the lesser tribes. He does not really exercise leadership over any of the greater tribes, and indeed, he nearly comes to blows with the leaders of Efraim.[29] Moreover, the tribe of Gad has such contempt for him that they will not even give his men bread in the midst of battle.[30] Later, Gideon returns and kills the men of Gad in revenge, marking him as the first judge of Israel to turn his sword

---

[25] Judges 3.11, 30; 5:31. At 3:30, the land was quiet for not 40 but 80 years. The fourth episode, concerning Gideon, likewise ends with the claim that 'the land was quiet for forty years.' Judges 8:28.

[26] When Deborah asks the northern strong-man Barak to muster for battle, he responds, rather cryptically: 'If you will go with me, then I will go. But if you will not go with me, then I will not go. And she said: I will surely go with you.' Judges 4:8–9.

[27] Judges 5:14–18.

[28] For the first time a judge in Israel is explicitly described as the son of a man who owns an altar to Ba'al. Judges 6:25.

[29] The narrative, however, leaves open the possibility that Efraim would have followed Gideon had he summoned him at the outset of the war. Instead, he only calls on Efraim after victory is already at hand. It is apparently his own fear of the greater tribes that prevented him from issuing the summons. See Judges 7:23–8:1.

[30] The tribes that go with him are Menasheh, Zevulun, Naftali, and Asher. Judges 6:34–6. His troubles with Efraim and Gad are described at 8:1–9.

against his own people.[31] As if this is not enough, it transpires that Gideon has a weakness for idols. He fashions himself a fetish, which he displays in Ofra, and we are told that 'all Israel went astray after it, and it became a snare to Gideon and to his house'.[32] When Gideon dies, his son Avimelech massacres the rest of Gideon's sons and declares himself king, only to die himself in a bloody altercation after a falling out with his followers.[33]

3.3. Jeftah[34]

In the fifth episode, Jeftah is depicted as leading only the Giladites, which is to say, at most the two and a half tribes of Transjordan alone. The son of a prostitute, we are told that he has gathered about him a band of *anashim reikim*—'worthless men',[35] and that he speaks of Kemosh, the god of the Moabites, as though he were a living being and comparable to the God of Israel.[36] In order to gain victory over the Ammonites, he sacrifices his own daughter as a burnt offering to the God of Israel.[37] And he does not bring peace to

---

[31] Judges 8:16–17.   [32] Judges 8:24–8.   [33] Judges 9:1–57.

[34] Until the end of the Gideon episode, the narrative had begun each time with 'the children of Israel cried up to the Lord'; and each time, God heeded their cries by raising up a judge to deliver them from their enemies. Judges 3:9, 3:15; 4:3; 6:6. But in the fifth episode, when the children of Israel cry up to the Lord, they are met with despair. As God tells them: 'You have forsaken me and served other gods. Therefore I will deliver you no more. Go and cry to the gods that you have chosen. Let them deliver you in the hour of your troubles.' Judges 4:8–9. And indeed, the last two of Israel's judges are not precisely redeemers.

[35] Judges 11:3.

[36] Jeftah's discourse on Kemosh appears in Judges 11:23–4. Compare to Joshua's prohibition on speaking the names of the gods of Canaan: 'Brace yourselves, therefore, very much … that you come not among these nations that remain among you. Neither make mention of the names of their gods, nor swear by them, nor serve them', Joshua 23:7. See also Exodus 23:13; Hosea 2:19; Psalms 16:4. It is noteworthy that the narrative describes the followers of Kemosh as continuing to sacrifice their children to him. II Kings 3:26–7.

[37] Jeftah's sacrifice of his daughter to the God of Israel is described in Judges 11:30–1, 34–9. On the 'Molochization' of the God of Israel implicit in his act, see Martin Buber, *Kingship of God*, 68, 116. Precisely such an act was envisioned and proscribed by Moses: 'Take heed of yourselves, that you not be ensnared into following them, after they are destroyed before you. And that you do not inquire after their gods, saying "How did these nations serve their gods? I too will do likewise". You will not do likewise on behalf of the Lord. For every abomination to the Lord, which he hates, have they done for their gods. Even their sons and their daughters have they burned in the fire to their gods.' Deuteronomy 12:30–1. Similarly: 'There must not be

the land:[38] Indeed, Jeftah deepens the rift with Efraim to the point of open civil war between that tribe and the men of the East Bank, in which he massacres tens of thousands.[39]

3.4. Samson

In the sixth, Samson is even more deeply immersed in the ways of the idolaters than his predecessors. He is depicted as associating with Philistine men, marrying a Philistine woman, sleeping with Philistine prostitutes. And these betray him time and again until his eyes are put out and he is put on display, a freak-show in Gaza.[40] He delivers no one, not even himself; he dies a suicide in the land of the enemy.

3.5. Micha's idol

In the seventh episode, there appears to be no judge in Israel at all, and 'every man did that which was right in his own eyes'.[41] The Danites, unable to defeat the enemy that God has judged deserving of

found among you anyone that makes his son or his daughter to pass through the fire. . . . Because of these abominations the Lord thy God drives them out before you.' Deuteronomy 18:9–10.

[38] The first four episodes explicitly speak of peace having been returned to the land. The last four, beginning with Jeftah, do not describe peace as having been returned to the land.

[39] Judges 12:1–7. The bloodshed between Gad and Efraim finally brings to a head an internal tension between Israel and the tribes east of the Jordan, which both Moses and Joshua struggled to subdue. In particular, Joshua had insisted that the men of the east bank remain with the Israelite armies until the west bank had been subdued, and only then retired to their own homes. Joshua 1:12–18. They are released from their pledge, after years of war, in Joshua 22:1–6. Already in Joshua's day, there had been a move by the tribes of the west bank to wage war against the east, but it had been defused. Joshua 22:9–34. Particularly important is to compare Jeftah's failure in this regard to Gideon's successful defusing of a similar situation in Judges 7:23–8:3.

[40] Judges 16:20–1, 25. The passage that dominates the entire Samson episode is the proscription of Joshua: 'For if you should at all turn back to attach yourselves to the remnant of these nations, these that remain among you, and shall make marriages with them, and go in unto them, and they to you . . . they shall be snares and traps to you, and a scourge in your sides, and pricks in your eyes, until you perish from off the good land which the Lord your God has given you.' Joshua 23:12–13. Note in particular the chilling foreshadowing of Samson's eyes being put out.

[41] Judges 17:6. Compare 18:1.

destruction,[42] find a weaker, innocent people on the northern border of Israel, and fall upon them and destroy them instead.[43] Their priest is a feckless man, a Levite who ministers to a statue fashioned from silver, which becomes the idol of the tribe of Dan.[44] The name of this purveyor of idolatry before a desperate tribe, we are told, is Yehonathan, son of Gershon—the grandson of Moses.[45]

3.6. The Concubine in Geva

One might think that Israel could sink no lower. But the people can, and they do. In the last episode, we meet a Levite returning with his concubine to his home in Efraim. Along the way, he stops in the Benjaminite town of Geva for the night. There, the traveller is discovered by an old man who begs him to not to spend the night in the street, as he had intended. It transpires that the old man has good reason:

> They turned aside there to go in and to lodge in Geva. . . . And behold, there came an old man out of his field at evening, who was also of mount Efraim, and he sojourned in Geva . . . And he lifted up his eyes, and saw a traveler in the open place of the city . . .
>
> And the old man said, 'Peace be with you. Only let all your wants lie upon me, but lodge not here in the street.' So he brought them into his house, and gave fodder to the asses, and they washed their feet, and they did eat and drink.
>
> Now, as they were gladdening their hearts, behold, the men of the city, worthless men, beset the house round about, and beat at the door, and spoke to the master of the house, the old man, saying, 'Bring out the man that came into your house, that we may know him.'

---

[42] Tellingly, Dan's enemies are defeated in battle by the Efraimites, who choose to make them tributaries, rather than giving Dan its land. Judges 1:34–5. Thus the Efraimites come directly to profit by the suffering of Dan—and this despite the explicit prohibition on making covenants with the peoples of the land. Judges 2:2.

[43] Judges 18:5–10, 27–8.

[44] Compare this episode with Moses' exhortations: 'Neither shall you bring an abomination into your house, least you become accursed like it, but you shall utterly detest it, and utterly abhor it.' Deuteronomy 7:26. 'Take heed of yourself that you forsake not the Levite as long as you live upon the earth.' Deuteronomy 12:19.

[45] Judges 18:30. Look at the Hebrew version of the verse, in which the letter *nun* in the name 'Menasheh' is suspended above the rest of the word; if this letter is ignored, the text reads 'Moshe'—Moses. That this is the intention is clear because Moses' son was Gershon, a Levite; whereas Menasheh has no such son, and is not a Levite.

And the man, the master of the house, said to them, 'No, my brothers, no, I prey you, do not so wickedly. Seeing that this man is come into my house, do not carry out this vileness. Behold, here is my daughter, a virgin, and his concubine. I will bring them out now. Ravish them, and do to them what is good in your eyes. Only to this man do not such a vile thing.'

But the men would not hearken to him, so the man seized his concubine, and brought her out to them. And they had their desire of her and abused her all the night until morning. And when the day began to break, they let her go. Then came the woman in the dawning of the day, and fell down at the door of the man's house, where her lord was, until it was light. And her lord rose up in the morning, and opened the doors of the house, and her hands were upon the threshold.

And he said to her, 'Up, and let us go.'[46]

But there was no answer.

The Levite carries his concubine's body back to Efraim with him. There, he takes a knife and cuts her into twelve pieces, and sends one to the elders of each of the twelve tribes. Outraged, the tribes muster and demand that the Benjaminites hand over the responsible men. When the Benjaminites refuse, there ensues a civil war involving virtually all of Israel, with horrendous casualties on both sides. But Israel has the upper hand, and in the end they manage to destroy nearly every man, woman, and child in Benjamin. Only at verge of the annihilation of the entire tribe do they pull back, leaving only six hundred young men.[47]

Now, this episode, with which the book of Judges closes, carries a very powerful, and very specific message. For the story of the Concubine in Geva is a re-enactment of another scene much earlier in the biblical narrative. It is a re-enactment of the destruction of Sodom:

There came two angels to Sodom that evening, and Lot sat in the gate of Sodom. And Lot, seeing them, rose up to meet them.

And he bowed himself with his face to the ground and said, 'Behold, now, my lords. Turn in, I pray you, into your servant's house . . .

And they said, "No, but we will abide in the street all night.'

---

[46] Judges 19:15–28.

[47] Judges 20:1–21:25. In the aftermath, Israel goes up to the settlement of Yavesh Gilead in Gad, which again had been remiss in participating, and conducts an additional massacre there. Judges 21:8–12.

And he pressed upon them greatly, and they turned in to him, and entered into his house. And he made them a feast, and baked unleavened bread, and they did eat.

But before they lay down, the men of the city, the men of Sodom, compassed the house around, both old and young, all the people from every quarter. And they called to Lot, and said to him, 'Where are the men who came in to you this night? Bring them out to us, that we may know them.'

And Lot went out at the door to them, and shut the door after him, and said, 'I pray you, brothers, do not so wickedly. Behold now, I have two daughters who have not known man. Let me, I pray you, bring them out to you, and do to them as is good in your eyes. Only to these men do nothing, seeing that they have come under the shadow of my roof.'

And they said, 'Stand back.' And they said again, 'This fellow came in to sojourn, and he needs be a judge...' And they strongly urged the man, Lot, and came near to break down the door.

But the men put out their hand... and they smote the men that were at the door of the house with blindness... And the men said to Lot, 'Have you any here besides?... Bring them out of this place, for we will destroy this place.'[48]

Now, it is immediately clear from a comparison of the two texts that the story of the Concubine in Geva is the story of Sodom.[49] It was composed in such a way that the parallel could not be missed. But coming as the capstone of the slide into barbarism described in the book of Judges—in which each generation, as we are told, 'became more corrupt than their fathers'[50]—it is intended to teach a very specific lesson: that while enslavement to the Egyptian state was an evil of unfathomable proportions, so too is anarchy in which 'every man did that which was right in his own eyes.' For what happened in Benjamin, could as easily happen anywhere—or everywhere. No obstacle remained to prevent all Israel from descending to the level

---

[48] Genesis 19:1–13.

[49] C.F. Burney, *The Book of Judges* (Eugene, Oregon: Wipf and Stock, 2004 [1918]) 444–5. See also Susan Niditch, 'The 'Sodomite' Theme in Judges 19–20: Family, Community, and Social Disintegration', *Catholic Bible Quarterly* 44 (1982) 365–78. Like Sodom, Geva becomes a byword for sin in the Bible. See Hosea 10:9.

[50] Judges 2:19. Noth suggests that this is likewise the meaning of the expression *veyosifu l'asot hara* at Judges 3:12, 4:1, 10:6, and 13:1, which is then read 'And they did even worse in God's eyes'. *Deuteronomistic History* 72.

of Sodom. And Sodom, of course, was judged so perverse that it was destroyed from the face of the earth.[51]

4. THE FOUNDING OF THE ISRAELITE STATE

On four occasions, the narrative refers to the period of rising barbarism depicted in the book of Judges as one in which 'there was no king in Israel'. Twice we are told explicitly that 'there was no king in Israel, and every man did that which was right in his own eyes.'[52] Indeed, it is the revulsion against every man doing 'that which was right in his own eyes' that is the central theme of the Bible's account of the period of the Judges. In the end, it becomes clear that anarchy is unlivable. And the Hebrew Bible knows of no alternative to anarchy other than the establishment of a state—and of a king.

The establishment of the Israelite state is described in I Samuel 8, in a scene that apparently served as the inspiration for the Enlightenment idea that the establishment of the state takes place on the basis of a social contract that ends the violence and terror of the preceding 'state of nature'. The Jews turn to Samuel, the judge in their day, and demand a king—that is, a permanent and united sovereignty that will be able properly to defend the people in war and to judge them in peace. Samuel is appalled, but God, whose wisdom is greater, acquiesces. The Jews are to have their state.

Significantly, the man chosen to be the first king of Israel is Saul of Geva, a youth from the very town in which the infamous atrocity occurred, and apparently one of the 600 young men spared death in

[51] Of course, there is an important difference between the two cases. In Geva, it is man that judges and punishes, and not God. Like much else in the book of Judges, this matter is ambiguous. On the one hand, we have to see the attempt to restore justice in an unjust land as being praiseworthy. In this sense, man is expected to emulate God. On the other hand, the Israelites do not really succeed in this effort. For in Sodom, God is depicted as sparing the righteous, whereas the righteous of Benjamin die together with the wicked. Moreover, the subsequent slaughter of the men of Gad seems utterly gratuitous. We are pressed to draw the conclusion that under conditions of anarchy, even the effort to bring justice to the land must end in mob rule and injustice.

[52] Judges 17:6; 21:25. Also 18:1; 19:1 Compare: 'You shall not do after "All the things we do here this day," each man what is right in his own eyes.' Deuteronomy 12:8.

the war against Benjamin.[53] The fact that Israel is able to accept a king from among the Benjaminites is the ultimate sign of the tribes' contrition over what they had done. Saul's very election, then, must be seen as a symbol of the new era of brotherhood and internal integrity that the kingdom was to bring about. And, indeed, the narrative in Samuel portrays the election of the Israelite king as the repair of the chaos and civil strife that had characterized the life of the tribes in Judges.[54] When the Ammonites threaten to enslave Yavesh Gilead and put out the eyes of its inhabitants—the very same Gadites who had been in open rebellion against Israel under the judges—Saul raises an army from all Israel to save them:

> And Saul said, 'What troubles the people that they weep?' And they told him of the message of the men of Yavesh. And the spirit of God came upon Saul when he heard these things, and his anger burned greatly. And he took a yoke of oxen and cut them up in pieces, and sent them throughout the land of Israel by the hands of messengers, saying, 'Whoever does not come forth after Saul and Samuel, so shall be done to his oxen.' And the fear of the Lord fell on the people, and went out as one man . . . And entered the [Ammonite] camp during the morning watch, and they smote Ammon until the heat of day, so that those that survived were scattered, and no two of them remained together.[55]

Saul wins a great victory by uniting all of Israel 'as one man'. But how was this great victory achieved? The division of the oxen and their dispatch throughout Israel is intended to remind the Jews of the chilling events surrounding the death of the concubine in Geva. To be sure, by dividing oxen rather than a human being, Saul makes it clear that his rule will be tempered by humanity; even the accompanying threat ('Whoever does not come forth after Saul and Samuel, so shall be done to his oxen') is aimed at property, not at the lives of his subjects, marking a significant improvement over the methods introduced by Gideon and Jeftah. But there can be no mistaking the fact that the unity of the tribes is achieved—as was never the case in the time of the judges—through the introduction of a universal threat of sanction, as a result of which 'the fear of the Lord fell on the people'. Saul is perhaps more humane than some of his predecessors, but he

---

[53] I Samuel 10:21–6.

[54] I am indebted to Ari Gontownik for his insightful remarks concerning this passage.

[55] I Samuel 11:1–14.

ultimately achieves the unification of the people through the imposition of a regime of fear of retribution.

But have we not now come full circle? Does not Saul's recourse to a threat of violence against the Israelites' property (and by implication, against their lives) not make of him a king just like those of the hated imperial states of antiquity? Is not the Israelite state to be just like Egypt or Babylonia, an imperial state in embryo? Will it not continually build up its might at the expense of its people until the moment when it, too, can make a bid for world empire? What is to prevent it?

It is here that the establishment of the biblical state differs from that of the social-contract state of Enlightenment thought. The social contract of the Enlightenment is concluded among the individual members of a people;[56] whereas the agreement that establishes the biblical state is an agreement between the people, on the one side, and God on the other. Moreover, God is here portrayed as a reluctant party to the agreement. And it is precisely this supposition of God's reluctance to enter into the agreement that provides the theological underpinning for the most important aspect of the Hebraic political theory, which is the *conditional* nature of the contract that brings the state into being. A king may be established because of the needs of his people. But his legitimacy cannot derive from the consent of the people alone—for what if the people consent to evil? This is the problem posed, for instance, by the example of Weimar Germany, where the consent of the people gave birth to one of the most vicious tyrannies mankind has known.

In order to win over a reluctant God, the contract that establishes the state includes a clause that the king must rule not only in fashion that is (i) consonant with the consent of the people that established the state[57], but also (ii) in manner that is in keeping with what Samuel here calls *haderech ha-tova vehayeshara*—'the way that is

---

[56] Thomas Hobbes, *Leviathan* (New York: Penguin, 1985 [1651]) 228; Jean-Jacques Rousseau, *On the Social Contract*, Roger D. Masters, ed., Judith R. Masters, trans. (New York: St. Martins Press, 1978) 53–4.

[57] Interestingly, the text is emphatic on this point, with God himself being depicted as telling Samuel: 'Listen to the people in all that they say to you.' I Samuel 8:7. This passage is parallel to Genesis 21:12, in which Abraham does not want to drive out Hagar and Ishmael, but God tells him, 'In all that Sarah says to you, listen to her voice.' The implication is that, here too, God acquiesces in what is necessary, although in some sense also obviously wrong.

good and right.'[58] That is, his rule must be in keeping with an independent standard of justice and goodness, without which the consent of the people will never suffice. As Samuel tells the people upon Saul's coronation:

> Behold the king whom you have chosen, and whom you have desired! Behold, the Lord has set a king over you—if you will fear the Lord and serve him, and obey his voice, and not rebel against the commandment of the Lord, if both you and the king that reigns over you will follow the Lord your God. . . . I will teach you the way that is good and right. . . . But if you shall do wickedly, both you and your king shall perish.[59]

We have, therefore, a system of *dual legitimacy*, which responds both to the desires of the people, and to a standard of right that is ultimately independent of these desires.[60]

But what is the content of this independent standard of right? The biblical narrative tells us much about what the Israelite king must do if he is to be judged to have ruled in a manner that is 'good and right', and it is not possible to make a full study of the matter here. But I would like to draw attention to the fact that the biblical standard of right is not only concerned with driving idolatry from the land, nor even with elementary moral concerns such as the defence of the widow and the orphan. Perhaps the most important principles describing what it means for the king to follow the right path are those found in the 'Law of the King' articulated in the books of Moses.[61] Here, the Israelite king is bound by the following *political* principles:

> You may appoint a king over you, whom the Lord your God will choose. One from among your brothers shall you set as a king over you. You

[58] The standard of 'the way that is good and right' is the standard that is used to judge the kings of Judah and Israel throughout the rest of the narrative. In the book of Kings, especially, the term 'right' apparently refers to the achievement of a minimally decent society; whereas the 'good' refers to the attempt to serve God with a whole heart. A discussion appears in Ofir Haivry, 'The Way of the World', *Azure* 5 (Autumn 1998) 44–53.

[59] I Samuel 12:13–14, 23, 25.

[60] The institution of prophecy is properly understood as the expression of this system of dual legitimacy in the political understanding of ancient Israel, and in the political theory of the Bible.

[61] The Mosaic 'Law of the King' is not to be confused with the speech of the prophet in I Samuel 8, which is known by the same name. In this essay, I use this term exclusively to refer to the Mosaic law in Deuteronomy.

may not set a stranger who is not your brother over you.[62] But he shall not multiply horses to himself, nor cause the people to return to Egypt to the end that he should multiply in horses. . . . Neither shall he multiply wives to himself, that his heart not turn away. Neither shall he greatly multiply to himself silver and gold. And it shall be, when he sits upon the throne of his kingdom, that he shall write himself a copy of this Torah . . . and he shall read therein all the days of his life, that he may learn to fear the Lord his God, to keep all the words of this Torah and these statutes to do them, that his heart not be lifted above his brothers . . . to the end that he may prolong his days in his kingdom.[63]

Thus we find that the king is forbidden to amass large quantities of horses; that he is to avoid having many wives; and that he is not to accumulate large quantities of gold. And upon consideration, it becomes clear that these three proscriptions of the Law of the King are really one: For the warning against horses is clearly aimed against maintaining very large standing armies. The warning against multiple wives is similarly aimed to preclude too great an involvement in foreign alliances, of which the accumulation of high-born foreign wives was an important instrument. And warning against the hoarding of gold was aimed against a regime of heavy taxation, impressments, and conquest, such as would be necessary to pay for many horses and many wives.

If we are to state this simply, the Law of the King was set against the life of the imperial state. Instead, it proposes what we might today call a *limited state*:[64] one headed by a king whose life is not consumed in the unending quest for ever greater power.

In a similar vein, the narrative insists that the state be limited territorially as well. Thus the books of Moses and Joshua include clear boundaries for the land, instructing the Israelites that they are to:

Come to the mountain of the Emorites, and to all the places near it, in the plain, in the hills, and in the lowland, and in the Negev, and by the

---

[62] Although there were foreign prophets, it is to prophets from among the people of Israel that the Jews were to take heed. Deuteronomy 18:15, 18.

[63] Deuteronomy 17:14–20.

[64] This may be seen as the basis of constitutional government. See Daniel J. Elazar, *Covenant and Polity in Biblical Israel* 313. The theological implications of such a state are discussed by Alan L. Mittleman, *The Scepter Shall Not Depart from Judah: Perspectives on the Persistence of the Political in Judaism* (Lanham, Maryland: Lexington, 2000) 95ff.

seaside, the land of the Cana'anites and the Lebanon, as far as the great river, the river Perat.[65]

Perhaps in comparison to the borders of the present Jewish state, the borders stipulated by Moses and Joshua seem generous. But if we compare Israel's ambitions to those of Egypt and Mesopotamia, we see that the biblical narrative is laying down as law the idea that Israel is to be limited in terms of the territories it may seek.[66]

This impression is borne out, too, by God's command that Israel is to keep its hands off of the territories of its neighbors to the east, Edom, Moav, and Ammon. As Moses tells the Israelites before they enter Canaan:

> You are to pass through the border of your brothers the children of Esau. . . . Take good heed of yourselves therefore. Meddle not with them, for I will not give you of their land. No, not so much a foot's breadth. Because I have given Mt. Seir to Esau for a possession. . . . Do not harass Moav, nor contend with them in battle, for I will not give you of their land for a possession, because I have given Ar to the children of Lot for a possession. . . . And when you come near, opposite the children of Ammon, harass them not, nor contend with them, for I will not give you of the land of the children of Ammon any possession, for I have given it to the children of Lot for a possession.[67]

Taken together, the Law of the King, the limitation of Israel's borders generally, and the proscription of conquest on Israel's eastern border in particular, afford a clear understanding that Israel is to be a state different from its neighbours in that it is to be limited in its aspirations—perhaps the first state in the world to have been limited in its might by decree of its own God.

5. SOLOMON AND THE DECLINE OF THE STATE

The Mosaic Law of the King has been called minimalistic. But I think such a view underestimates the difficulty of what is being asked. For just as the laws of sexual purity, dietary restrictions, and Sabbath

---

[65] Deuteronomy 1:7. cf. Deuteronomy 11:24, 32:8; Joshua 1:4.

[66] See Steven Grosby, *Biblical Ideas of Nationality: Ancient and Modern* (Winona Lake, Ind.: Eisenbrauns, 2002).

[67] Deuteronomy 2:4–6, 9, 19.

observance impose a regime of systematic moderation of the appetites in the individual, so too does the Law of the King—which seeks to limit the accumulation of gold, wives, and horses—impose a regime of systematic moderation of the appetites of the state. And for a similar reason: It is the appetites of the state, as expressed in the profligate accumulation of gold, wives, and horses, that is seen as the cause of much of the violence, oppression, and even idolatry that had characterized the states of neighboring peoples. If one could some-how restrain these appetites, space might be cleared for a regime that would win the consent not only of men, but also of God.[68]

Of course, restraining the appetites of the state means restraining the appetites of the rulers, and the narrative emphasizes that this problem is not one that is intrinsic to monarchy, but haunts all political leadership. Trouble in this vein goes back to Gideon, judge of Israel, who nobly refuses his followers' demand that he make himself king, but who nevertheless exhibits a pronounced taste for quantities of gold and wives—precisely that which the Law of the King proscribes. Neither of these do him much good. The gold permits him to fashion the aforementioned fetish at Ofra, and there-fore to lead the Israelites straight into the idolatrous ways of the Canaanites. His many wives, on the other hand, give him 70 sons.[69] As tends to happen in the Bible, these sons and their mothers imme-diately begin conniving for succession, and when Gideon dies, they go about declaring themselves king and murdering one another—a political horror that goes on for several years until the last of the pretenders to the throne is killed and the whole story brought to an end in a bloodbath.[70]

Even this, however, does not quite end the story. For the heritage of Gideon to Israel includes an entire tradition of incontinence on the part of subsequent judges, who continued multiplying their own wives, horses, and wealth;[71] David's house, too, is plagued with

---

[68] It is relevant that in the rabbinic retelling, the first kingdom of the Israelites was destroyed as a result of idolatry, bloodshed, and sexual impropriety—an account that seems to parallel the biblical categories of gold, horses, and wives. See Yoma 9b. I am indebted to Ofir Haivry for this observation.

[69] 'He had many wives', at Judges 8:30, follows precisely the language of the proscription in Deuteronomy.

[70] Judges 8:30–9:57.

[71] Thus the judge Yair the Giladite has 30 sons who ride 30 horses and lived in 30 cities. Judges 10:3–4. Ivtzan of Bethlehem has 30 sons, whom he married off to

intrigue and bloodshed arising from his commitments to multiple wives and their children.[72]

All of this, however, is small potatoes in comparison with what is to come in the kingdom of David's son, Solomon. Under Solomon, the Israelite state reaches the apex of what man can achieve on this earth. Israel has won its wars and now has peace on all sides; it has power and wealth, and is honoured among the nations; it has reached its prescribed borders; its ruler is wise, and he brings justice to the state; he is pious, and builds a great Temple to God; under his leadership science and art flourish; and the people are happy.[73] Indeed, it is the success of the early stages of Solomon's reign that serves the prophets as a model of the messianic vision.

Nevertheless, even as Solomon's kingdom reaches the pinnacle of what the state can hope to be, the seeds of its destruction are sewn through its incontinence. The state grows ever more distant from the Law of the King:

> Now, the weight of the gold that came to Solomon in one year was 666 talents of gold, besides what he had of the merchantmen, and of the traffic of the merchants, and of the kings of Arabia, and of the governors of the country. And king Solomon made two hundred targets of beaten gold; 600 shekels of gold went to one target. And he made three hundred shields of beaten gold.... Moreover, the king made a great throne of ivory, and overlaid it with the best gold.... And all king Solomon's drinking vessels were of gold, and all the vessels of the house of the forest of Lebanon were of pure gold; none were silver, for that was considered as nothing in the days of Solomon....
>
> And Solomon gathered together chariots and horsemen. He had 1,400 chariots, and 12,000 horsemen, whom he placed in the cities for chariots.... And Solomon had horses brought from Egypt and from Keve. The king's merchants took the horses from Keve at a fixed price. And a chariot coming out of Egypt would cost 600 shekels of silver, and a horse 150, and so by their hand were they exported to the kings of Hittim and the kings of Aram.
>
> And King Solomon loved many foreign women. Together with the daughter of Pharaoh, there were Moabite, Edomite, Sidonian, and

---

30 foreign women, and 30 daughters whom he married off to 30 foreign men. Judges 13:8–9. And Avdon of Piraton had 40 sons and 30 grandsons who rode on 70 horses. Judges 13:13–19.

[72] The succession of Solomon is described in just this manner. I Kings 1:5f.

[73] I Kings 3:3–28; 4:20–5:22.

Hittite women—from the nations concerning which the Lord had said to the children of Israel, You shall not go into them, nor shall they come into you, for they shall surely turn your heart away after their gods. To these, Solomon attached himself in love. And he had 700 wives, princesses, and 300 concubines, and his wives turned away his heart.[74]

Now, attention has often been directed particularly to the matter of Solomon's wives, who 'turned away his heart' towards foreign gods. This is in keeping with the text that immediately follows, which emphasizes that Solomon built temples in Jerusalem to the gods of all of his foreign wives.[75] But it is also clear that the narrative is not concerned exclusively with the establishment of idolatry in Jerusalem. Rather, there is here a systematic rejection of the Mosaic Law of the King on all three counts—with respect to gold, horses, and wives. It is the influence of the wives, we are told, that turns his heart; but as in the case of Gideon before him, the gold is what permits Solomon to engage in excesses—the establishment of the temples to Kemosh, Molech, and others in Jerusalem—he might otherwise not have committed.

But the Law of the King does not aim only to keep the king's heart turned towards God. It has an additional purpose, which is to keep the king loyal to his people and sympathetic to them: 'That his heart not be lifted above his brothers.'[76]

With regard to Solomon, we are not told that his heart was 'lifted above his brothers'—although one can only wonder what a king who will not drink from a silver vessel because it is too lowly might have understood concerning the sufferings of his people. But when the king dies, and his son Rehavam takes the throne, it is precisely the sense that the heart of the king is 'lifted above his brothers' that is depicted as leading to the downfall of the state. A popular leader rises against the state, who seeks to remind the new king that his wives

[74] I Kings 10:14–11:4.
[75] 'Then Solomon did build a high place for Kemosh, the abomination of Moav, on the hill that is before Jerusalem, and for Molech, the abomination of the children of Ammon. And he did likewise for all his foreign wives, who burned incense and sacrificed to their gods. And the Lord was angry with Solomon, because his heart was turned from the Lord, God of Israel, who had . . . commanded him concerning this thing, that he should not go after other gods. But he kept not that which the Lord commanded.' I Kings 11:7–10.
[76] Deuteronomy 17:20. It is particularly important that study of the Torah is supposed not only to turn the king towards God but also to prevent the evil of his feeling too high above his brothers.

and chariots and vessels of gold are paid for by impressment and taxation[77]—and to demand a reduction in the burden imposed by this burgeoning state:

> Yarovam and all the congregation of Israel came, and spoke to Rehavam, saying, 'Thy father made our yoke hard. Now therefore make the hard service of your father, and they heavy yoke which he put upon us, lighter, and we will serve you.'[78]

The young king retires to consider what to do. The young men around the king swell his head.

> The young men who had grown up with him spoke to him, saying, 'Thus shall you speak to this people, that has spoken to you saying, your father made our yoke heavy, but you make it lighter for us. Thus shall you speak to them: My little finger shall be thicker than my father's loins. Whereas my father did burden you with a heavy yoke, I will add to your yoke. My father chastised you with whips, but I will chastise you with scorpions.'[79]

In the assurance that Rehavam's 'little finger' shall be 'thicker than my father's loins' we find precisely that imperial arrogance that characterized the imperial state in the story of Babel—and, apparently, the soaring of the heart above the people that is proscribed in the Law of the King.

> And the king answered the people harshly . . . and spoke to them after the counsel of the young men. . . . And the king hearkened not to the people . . .
>
> And all Israel saw that the king hearkened not to them. And the people answered the king, saying, 'What portion do we have in David? We have no inheritance in the son of Jesse. To your tents, Israel. Now tend to your own house, David' . . .
>
> Then Rehavam sent Adoram, who was over the tribute, and Israel stoned him with stones, so that he died. And the king Rehavam made haste to mount his chariot, and to flee to Jerusalem. Thus Israel rebelled against the house of David, to this day.[80]

---

[77] As Aaron Wildavsky points out, there is a point at which impressment and taxation begin to look like slavery, and kingship like the idolatry of Egypt. Wildavsky, *Moses as Political Leader* 257–8.

[78] I Kings 12:3–4.   [79] ibid 12:10–11.   [80] ibid 12:13–17.

When the young king delivers this message to the tribes north of Judah, they rise against him, kill the tax collector, and tear the north of the kingdom away from Judah.[81]

In this sequence of events, we are permitted a clear view of the manner in which the violation of the Law of the King brings about the downfall of the state. Solomon hoarded wives, gold, and chariots. It was his wives and gold that brought about the establishment of idolatry in the land. It was the taxation and servitude that brought resentment and rebellion. And it was the arrogance of a ruler whose 'heart was lifted above his brothers' that brought precipitous decline to a kingdom that only a few years earlier had been the envy of all mankind.

But the limited state is not the only political lesson here. It cannot escape notice that the rending of the kingdom of David and Solomon in two is treated by the biblical narrative as a terrible tragedy. This is not an intuition that is original to the book of Kings. It already appears in Genesis, which reaches its climax with the hatred spilled between Joseph and his brothers. In Joshua and Judges this same theme appears in the form of the recurring threat of civil war. It is the united state of Saul, David, and Solomon that lays this threat to rest for a time. And it is Solomon's violation of the Law of the King that is depicted in bringing about the resurgence of this fratricidal warfare in the time of his son, Rehavam. Henceforth, the treachery of one Israelite state against another is always possible, and sometimes a reality. It is a nightmare that will only be alleviated one day when, according to the visions of the prophets, the Israelites will again be united, under a king of their own, one ruler over all Israel.[82]

6. CONCLUSION

As I have attempted to show, the principal narrative sequence of the Hebrew Bible—spanning half of its length—is constructed with political lessons in mind. And while later generations may have seen fit to emphasize different parts of this teaching, this is no reason for an

---

[81] ibid 12:18.   [82] Ezekiel 37:15–24.

impartial observer to miss the fact that a coherent and more or less clear teaching can nonetheless be discerned.

The most significant step in seeking the biblical political teaching is to recognize that in this central biblical history, the Israelites are delivered not once, but twice. They are delivered once in Exodus, and once again in Samuel. Their first deliverer is Moses, who redeems them from the tyranny of the state; their second deliverer is David, who redeems them from anarchy. It is in the early stages of his son Solomon's reign that we find the political condition the Bible depicts as the best that can be achieved by man—an achievement that is at once both fleeting and real.

With this in mind, it is not difficult to recognize the political understanding that the narrative was written to teach. The biblical history sees the political order as oscillating between the imperial state, as represented by Egypt of the Pharaohs; and anarchy, as represented by Israel in the period of the judges. The first road leads to bondage; the second, to dissolution and civil war. Neither alternative, then, can serve as the basis for the freedom of a people. The question with which the biblical narrative wrestles is whether there is a third option, which can secure a life of freedom for Israel in the face of these two mortal threats.

On the political theory advanced by the Hebrew Bible, there is such an alternative. If one wishes for political betterment, there is no choice but to establish a state. Yet this state cannot be unlimited in principle, like the states of 'all the nations'[83] in the ancient Near East. Rather, it must be a state that will steer a course between the two extremes, seeking 'the good and the right'. For this, one must have rulers who understand that virtue emerges from limitation of the state: from the limitation of the borders of the state; from the limitation of the size of the armed forces and of what one is willing to do in the name of foreign alliances; from the limitation of the income of the state; and from the limitation of the degree to which the king sees himself as being raised above his own people. It is within the framework of these constraints that the both the people and their king are to find the love of justice and of God that characterized the herdsmen who were their forefathers.

---

[83] I Samuel 8:5, 20.

The biblical history thus endorses the integrity of a single, limited state as preferable both to anarchical order and to the imperial state. This limited national state, in which the king will be chosen from among the people and will be one of them in spirit, is in fact the biblical ideal. Yet this is an ideal suspended at the mid-point between two competing evils, and perpetually threatens to decline in the one direction or the other. In the eyes of the author who laboured to assemble the core biblical text in the shadow of the destruction of the Judean state, it was clear that the political mission of man is to steer the state between these twin threats, thereby assuring the sympathies of both man and God, and therefore the political longevity of the kingdom.

Part III

Fundamental Elements of Morality and Moral Psychology

5

Tradition, Rationality, and Moral Life: Medieval Judaism's Insight

Jonathan A. Jacobs

Judaism is a crucial source of ideas of the intrinsic dignity and value of the human individual, the concern for justice, compassion for the unfortunate and the downtrodden (the 'lowly in spirit'), and the importance of integrity and moral responsibility, among other moral principles and ideals. This is clear even if many such ideas with roots in Judaism became detached from it and even from the notion of a divine covenant. This discussion explicates some key insights in medieval Jewish philosophy bearing on enduring issues of moral thought and moral life. Rather than focusing directly on substantive moral notions I will sketch out how Jewish thought provides resources for an illuminating conception of tradition, one in which there is both a pronounced rationalistic element and a kind of rational humility.[1]

The key figures here are Saadia Gaon, Bahya ibn Pakuda, and Maimonides. Saadia is important for having set a (broadly) rationalist agenda for medieval Jewish philosophy. Bahya is important for the moral psychology he elaborated, and for his astute appreciation of

---

[1] Some of themes and issues discussed in this essay are also discussed in my *Law, Reason, and Morality in Medieval Jewish Philosophy* (Oxford: Oxford University Press, 2010). In particular, in that work I go into depth concerning differences between medieval Jewish moral thought and the practical wisdom approach to morality and the natural law approach. In addition, some of my claims about tradition are discussed in my 'The Epistemology of Moral Tradition: A Defense of a Maimonidean Thesis', *The Review of Metaphysics*, September 2010. I am grateful to the editors of that journal for permitting me to borrow from that article in the present essay.

how we use the intellect to deceive ourselves. Maimonides articulated a powerful, subtle, integrated account of the relation between intellectual virtue and ethical excellence and the complex role of reason in it. These three thinkers provide the elements for a distinctive and plausible rationalist conception of tradition.

I will sketch the contours of a conception of tradition that takes seriously the aspiration to attain rational justifications for moral requirements while acknowledging significant limits on how rationally evident those justifications are likely to be. The central insight of the view is an important one, indicative of a sophisticated appreciation of the epistemological role of tradition. Moreover, its relevance is not contextually confined to the medieval world.

1. MEDIEVAL JEWEISH RATIONALISM

At numerous points in the discussion contrasts with Aristotle's thought will be highlighted. There are a couple of reasons for this. First, some of medieval Jewish philosophy appropriated Aristotelian philosophical categories and idiom, but often with significant revision, and the differences matter a great deal. Second, Aristotle's ethical thought has a pronounced presence in *contemporary* philosophy and we will see how that fact supports the claim of relevance for medieval Jewish thought. Also, Aristotle and Jewish thinkers recognized the significance of habit and the social world in regard to the acquisition of virtue yet there are important differences in how they interpreted and explicated that significance.

The view to be discussed is what we might regard as a rationalist conception of tradition. This is not Cartesian or Spinozist rationalism. It is not a structure of a priori principles or truths from which others are derived, the whole being claimed to comprehend the intelligible structure of the world. It is rationalism consistent with an important role for tradition. In this view: (i) reason and revelation are complementary and mutually reinforcing; (ii) fulfilling the requirements of tradition enables a person to more fully understand the rationales for the requirements; (iii) seeking rational comprehension of Torah, which is the key to walking in God's ways, is among the things commanded. We are to employ our intellects in order to understand the world and Torah, and to lead lives of righteous activity. That activity involves a complex interpenetration of understanding and practice, to which tradition is vitally important.

Saadia, Bahya, and Maimonides all contributed to this conception of tradition. In distinguishing 'laws of reason' and 'laws of revelation' Saadia argued that commandments in neither class are merely arbitrary tests of obedience. Even for the least evidently justified commandments we can discern some general utility. The commandments as shaped by divine wisdom and not just will. And both Bahya and Maimonides had a powerful sense of the unity of the intellectual and the ethical. Bahya wrote, 'Whoever ascends from this stage [performing the commandments without fail] to obedience by way of the mind's persuasion reaches the stage of the prophets and the saints chosen by God.'[2] Berkovits says of him, 'Bahya declares it to be man's duty to study God's creation in order to come nearer to God's wisdom. In another passage, elaborating the idea further, he practically develops a plan for the scientific study of nature, inspired by the purely religious motivation of coming closer to God.'[3] Twersky writes of Maimonides, 'Spiritualization and intellectualization are firmly allied.'[4] And in discussing Maimonides' interpretation of biblical history, with reference to matters such as the abolition of idolatry, Twersky remarks, 'We see again how the reciprocity of action and knowledge, of moral virtue and intellectual virtue, appears in Maimonidean writing with the emphatic regularity of a poetic refrain.'[5] This is a rationalism in which comprehension is attained through investigation and reflection, and to which acting in certain ways is crucial to the ability to understand.

The medievals held that both reason and revelation help liberate human beings from idolatry, a corrupt and corrupting orientation to specious authority. Idolatry reflects an erroneous view of the world (the point of Maimonides' critique of Sabeanism). It involves a corruption of what is best in us (illustrated by Bahya's extensive treatment of the ways in which we trick and misguide ourselves

---

[2] Bahya ibn Pakuda, *The Book of Direction to the Duties of the Heart*, Menahem Mansoor, trans. (Oxford: Littman Library of Jewish Civilization, 2000) 187.

[3] Eliezer Berkovits, *Essential Essays in Judaism*, David Hazony, ed. (Jerusalem: Shalem Press, 2002) 240–1.

[4] Isadore Twersky, *Introduction to the Code of Maimonides* (New Haven: Yale University Press, 1980) 481.

[5] ibid 478.

through the sophistical employment of intellect).[6] The more perfect our understanding, the less susceptible we are to specious authority and false values. The more righteous our way of life, the better positioned we are to understand and appreciate the true and the good. There is some likeness here to Aristotle's view of the relation between habits on the one hand, and ethical virtue and practical wisdom on the other. There are also some important differences between the two views and they will be indicated as we proceed.

The general character of the medieval Jewish view contrasts with some important currents of modern moral thought. One of those currents maintains that an agent need not (indeed, should not) regard a moral claim as obligating unless its justification is rationally compelling. This is true of some of the most influential early modern conceptions of natural law and it is true of Kant's theory and Kant-inspired approaches. Jewish thinkers articulated a conception of tradition such that its requirements are rational but in ways that come into view *through* living in accord with the practices, perspectives, and commitments constitutive of the tradition. They argued that in some cases we are to uphold tradition even if we cannot explicate fully the justifications for some of its elements. Though some of the justifications are not, and will not become, fully evident to us, that does not imply that they lack rational justifications. We will see the significance of this below.

In a good deal of modern moral (and political) thought the agent's grasp and endorsement of the rationality of values, principles, and ideals has a key role in their bindingness. The notion has been formulated in diverse ways. Many formulations hold that morality concerns what an agent recognizes as universally endorsable from the standpoint of rational agency. In some versions, morality is responsive not only to what is rationally objective, but it also reflects rational *self-legislation.*[7] Whether the focus is on rational endorsement or rational self-legislation, the central point is that one answers to the authority of one's own

---

[6] Maimonides states that the abolition of idolatry is the purpose of the Law. See *Guide of the Perplexed*, Part III, chapter 29, 517, Shlomo Pines, trans. (Chicago: University of Chicago Press, 1963).

[7] Different figures in the natural law tradition illustrate this. Despite their diverse accounts of the rational evidence of fundamental principles they agree that those principles are evident to reason, whether we arrive at them through careful reflection or construct them from a priori resources. Consider, for instance, Hobbes, Locke, and Kant.

reason. (Compare, for example, Kant, Hobbes, Locke, and Spinoza. In all cases, the authority of one's reason is crucial.) Diverse views insist that unless the rationale of requirements is evident to me, I need not regard (or should not regard) them as obligating me. Tradition is regarded with suspicion because it introduces (allegedly) less than rational elements into morality. In much modern thought there is an explicit or implicit emphasis on a conception of epistemic responsibility in which the authority of one's own reason, and the clarity and distinctness of what reason discerns, replaces other possible authorities, whether traditional, theological, or something else.

There is another highly influential approach to ethics in modern thought, this one involving a conception of tradition, but one different from the Jewish view. In this modern view tradition sustains moral dispositions and moral orientation and this is important because they are *not* underwritten by rational justification. Reason does not supply moral substance and form but tradition does. To a large extent, this is a perspective born out of reflective critique of the modern insistence on the role of the rationally evident. If one believes that there are strong reasons *against* an objectivist conception of moral considerations, this conception of tradition might be highly attractive. This is because tradition can supply valuative commitments and conceptions and tradition can maintain realist-seeming features of ethical judgement and practice even though the metaphysics of morals does not underwrite realist value. (In both that view and the medieval Jewish view tradition is important for the cultivation of virtue, including the development of fluency of judgement, a discerning sensibility, and moral motivation.) This is *not* the view that, while there are universal moral principles, they are taught and sustained through the traditions of different societies and cultures. It is an antirealist view maintaining that there are no objective values. Different cultures, societies or communities have different moralities but within each of them tradition is important as a way of maintaining coherence, transmitting values and practices, and shaping moral perspective and rationales.

The view to be explicated here is rationalistic in a way that distances it from the antirealist conception of tradition. Yet, the way it involves tradition also distances it from the modern insistence on rational transparency. How it differs from both of those are the bases of its interest and its plausibility. Maimonides and other medieval Jewish thinkers regarded tradition as an ethical and intellectual resource keeping reason directed rightly. A key feature of the view is that it has a place for rationalist aspiration *and* rational humility.

2. SOME CONTRASTS WITH ARISTOTLE

Saadia's *The Book of Beliefs and Opinions* opens with an extensive treatment of epistemological matters, essentially a project of showing how Judaism is a religion of reason. He argued that reason, sense, scripture, and tradition are all appropriate sources of evidence and that tradition is actually important to the reliability of the others. (When we consider how extensively our knowledge-claims depend upon testimony, even in regard to a priori matters, we see what Saadia meant.) The 'Introductory Treatise' to *The Book of Beliefs and Opinions* shows how, with regard to one major concern after another, Judaism can be interpreted in terms of rational considerations. Saadia was not wholly assimilating Judaism to what is rationally evident. But he sought to show that there are no fundamental conflicts or tensions between Judaism and rationality, and that Jewish tradition can be explicated rationally.

The employment of reason shows that divine wisdom informs the world and the commandments. Created in the divine image, our proper task is to be as like God as possible, largely through attaining as complete comprehension as possible and through informing action with that understanding. The giving of Torah and, for that matter, creation of the world, is an act of divine graciousness. God helped mankind by giving a Law through the fulfilment of which human beings can be perfected. Perfection is a *task* for human beings, and much of the work involved is intellectual work. Saadia wrote:

> Moreover, in support of the validity of these laws, His messengers executed certain signs and wondrous miracles, with the result that we observed and carried out these laws immediately. Afterwards we discovered the rational basis for the necessity of their prescription so that we might not be left to roam at large without guidance.[8]

---

[8] Saadia Gaon, *The Book of Beliefs and Opinions*, Samuel Rosenblatt, trans. (New Haven: Yale University Press, 1976) 138.

The interpenetration of the intellectual and the ethical is evident in Bahya's thought also. Bahya wrote, 'Is meditation upon creation our obligation? Meditation upon creation as a demonstration of God's wisdom is made obligatory upon us by reason, Scriptures, and tradition alike.'[9] We are to attain the fullest measure of understanding we can, and the intellect is the capacity through the exercise of which we are able to walk in God's ways.

Finally, in Maimonides' thought we find even more pronounced rationalism, along with intellectualist perfectionism. It is distinguished from other forms of rationalism by the way in which it acknowledges that our rational comprehension needs to develop over time, through practices required by tradition. Knowledge is required for holiness, and excellent activity is required as well, and those are mutually supporting and motivating in the life of a person aspiring to holiness.

Saadia's distinction between 'laws of reason' and 'laws of revelation' with regard to the commandments is a key distinction in Jewish thought. The distinction has been articulated in different formulations reflecting the different philosophical commitments of various thinkers. Saadia's distinction registered the notion that the commandments are requirements *for rational beings* and that striving to understand them is itself one of the commandments. Deuteronomy 4: 5–8 is quoted repeatedly by Jewish thinkers as the statement of the wisdom of the commandments and of the obligation to seek that wisdom.

> Behold, I have taught you statutes and ordinances, even as the LORD my God commanded me, that ye should do so in the midst of the land whither ye go in to possess it. Observe therefore and do them; for this is your wisdom and your understanding in the sight of the peoples, that, when they hear all these statutes, shall say: 'Surely this great nation is a wise and understanding people.' For what great nation is there, that hath God so nigh to them, as the LORD our God is whensoever we call upon Him? And what great nation is there, that hath statutes and ordinances so righteous as all this law, which I set before you this day?

The passage points to the fact that understanding what is commanded is vitally important to the covenant with Israel. Striving to be like God and close to God can succeed only through enlarged and

---

[9] ibid 154.

deepened understanding. Even the most obviously moral elements of the commandments are connected with understanding. Study of the Law motivates strengthened devotion to it through appreciating its wisdom. The more devoutly and fully we fulfil the requirements of the Law the better able we are to walk in God's ways and to take delight in closeness to God. The project of fulfilling the Law also improves the world and relations between human beings. There is a complex spiral of mutual reinforcement between understanding and ethically virtuous activity.

The medieval Jewish understanding of tradition involves some counterparts to Aristotle's view that good habits and good dispositions are necessary for attaining sound ethical understanding. Aristotle wrote of the student of politics:

> It does not matter whether he is young in years or immature in character, since the deficiency does not depend on age, but results from following his feelings in his life and in a given pursuit; for an immature person, like an incontinent person, gets no benefit from his knowledge. But for those who accord with reason in forming their desires and their actions, knowledge of political science will be of great benefit.[10]

Without good habits, the agent will not be able to acquire sound understanding. A poorly disposed second nature will orient the person to apparent, rather than genuine goods. The individual's valuations and pleasures will not agree with what reason understands to be good. That is a significant impediment to ever attaining right understanding. What an agent enjoys can make a difference to his conception of what is good. If an agent becomes habituated to take pleasure in apparent, rather than genuine goods, he may become unable to recognize genuine goods. The pleasures he enjoys are bad pleasures.

Aristotle held that practical wisdom includes knowledge of what is good and bad for human beings. The *phronimos* is, so to speak, a living norm. Someone lacking the virtues of the *phronimos* will not acquire right understanding of (objective) ethical considerations. Certain moral-psychological features are needed for the agent to acquire a sound grasp of those considerations. To understand the

---

[10] Aristotle, *Nicomachean Ethics*, T. Irwin, trans. (2nd edn, Indianapolis: Hackett Publishing Company, Inc., 1999) *NE*, 1095a 6–11.

good and to be attracted to it in the way the practically wise person understands and is drawn to it requires dispositions that are not 'purely' cognitive. This is not a type of knowledge that the agent can acquire *regardless* of dispositions constitutive of character, dispositions of the agent's sensibility and appetites.

Despite important likenesses between them, the Jewish view differs from Aristotle's in some key respects. One difference concerns the relations between understanding the world on the one hand, and excellent ethical practice on the other. I will comment on this shortly. In addition, the Jewish view has a historical and communal dimension not present in Aristotle's thought. The enlargement of understanding is a process occurring in the history of a people and not just in the maturing of an individual and the development of the agent's reflective sophistication. Individuals are to see their relation to God through being members of a community with a covenantal bond with God, who has promised redemption. That helps explain some of the difference between the transmission of habits and the nature of tradition. It is also a basis for the objection that Jewish moral thought is particularist in ways that are impediments to objectivity. We will consider the force of that objection below. We will find that the view acknowledges the significance of particular practices and commitments to the cultivation of virtues, while the virtues are informed by understanding of objective values.

Unlike Aristotle, medieval Jewish moral thought, including some that was strongly influenced by Aristotle, did not maintain that there is a virtue of practical wisdom—an action-guiding *intellectual* virtue—in Aristotle's sense. It involves a different account of the relations between understanding, on the one hand, and ethical dispositions and activity, on the other. It is *less* optimistic, in not sharing Aristotle's conviction that nature supplies a fully adequate basis for ethical realism, and *more* optimistic in maintaining that human beings receive aid in the form of guidance to perfection. Understanding of the world is important to the Jewish rationalists' conception of moral requirements but that understanding does not constitute a distinct intellectual virtue, namely, practical wisdom.

Knowledge of God and an understanding of the Law are ways a person is engaged to reality and is perfected. We do not have direct, positive knowledge of the divine nature but we can come to understand much about it through comprehension of the created order, including Torah. Thereby we can attain insight into the divine nature through knowledge of divine activity. Throughout the created order there is evidence of God's wisdom and loving kindness, and the Law itself is a compelling demonstration of God's graciousness. Thus, even though we cannot have a positive, substantive comprehension of the divine nature we can know fundamentally important things about God. That, in conjunction with comprehension of the created order, is the counterpart to Aristotelian practical wisdom. Through knowledge of God's graciousness and the goodness of the created order we attain the understanding informing and guiding ethical thought.

There is an intersection of science, philosophy, and revelation, which offers human beings guidance to perfection. Of Bahya's conception of this fundamental matter, Eliezer Berkovits writes:

> It is worth noting that even Bahya ibn Pakuda, whose *Duties of the Heart* is highly valued in the yeshivot as a work of moral wisdom, adopts a position very similar to that of Maimonides. As he states in the work's 'Examination of Creation' (*sha'ar habehina*), it is through our meditations that we come to appreciate 'the manifestations of God's wisdom in all created things . . . For all wisdom is one;'[11]

Berkovits takes this to be a crucial likeness between Maimonides and Bahya, despite their many differences. They have

> prepared the ground for us for a religious approach to a scientific investigation of all reality and to the evaluation of the truth that it may reveal. The basic principle is that this world is God's world—and all truth has its source in God. The laws of nature are God's laws; and the wisdom in the creation is of his wisdom. The truth revealed in God's creation and the truth revealed in the Torah are alike: Both have their origin in the same 'highest truth' (*emet elyona*), to use the terminology of Maimonides.[12]

Maimonides' negative theology enabled him to elaborate the most sophisticated version of this type of view, but numerous medieval Jewish thinkers held such a view. Bahya wrote: 'I realized then that it would be impossible for us to conceive of Him by way of His essence and I saw that we must know Him and conceive of His existence by way of His creatures.'[13] And, 'The greatest favor God has done us is to give us a mind and the power of discrimination, by which He

---

[11] Berkovits, 240.   [12] ibid 241.   [13] Bahya, 103.

distinguished us from the rest of living creatures.'[14] 'The second pillar of wisdom is manifested in the human species. Which is the microcosmos that brings to perfection all the order, beauty, loveliness, and completeness of the macrocosmos, as it is said (Ps. 8:2): "O Lord, our Lord, How glorious is thy name in all the earth!" etc.'[15]

Divine wisdom and goodness are recognizable throughout the created order, both in the natures of individual beings and the organization of the cosmos overall. Maimonides wrote:

> If you consider the divine actions—I mean to say the natural actions— the deity's wily graciousness and wisdom, as shown in the creation of living beings, in the gradation of the motions of the limbs, and the proximity of some of the latter to others, will through them become clear to you. Similarly His wisdom and wily graciousness, as shown in the gradual succession of the various states of the whole individual, will become clear to you.[16]

The same 'wily graciousness' is in evidence in the Law, inasmuch as what it requires of people is practicable, not only in the abstract sense, given basic human capacities, but in a more concrete sense, having to do with what actual people can actually accomplish in actual historical conditions. The achievement of the monotheistic revolution requires disciplined, sustained effort. Revealed commandments are suited to the ability of the recipients to fulfil them, and that fulfilment can perfect them without requiring a change in their nature. There is an important role for tradition, which both maintains the wisdom that has been achieved, and carries on a process of enquiry, reflection, and elaboration essential to enlarging wisdom, and progressively informing practice.

It would be too simplistic to just say that, for Jewish thinkers, Torah fills the space and the role filled by practical wisdom in Aristotle's thought. Rather, the Jewish thinkers held that, to the extent that human beings attain ethical understanding, it is through comprehension of divine wisdom and benevolence, reflected in the created order, including the gift of Torah. There is an anchoring for tradition and for the understanding attained by fulfilling the requirements of tradition. Given the nature of that anchor, both tradition and that understanding are informed by true value. A dichotomy of

[14] ibid 166.   [15] ibid 158.
[16] Moses Maimonides, *Guide of the Perplexed*, Shlomo Pines, trans. (Chicago: University of Chicago Press, 1963) III, 32, 525.

'objective good' and 'divine volition as the basis of value' would be a
false dichotomy for these thinkers.

3. THE ROLE OF TRADITION IN
ETHICAL UNDERSTANDING

In Judaism there is less presence of voluntarism of the sort prominent
in medieval Islamic thought and in some currents of Christian
thought.[17] The thinkers referred to here emphasized divine wisdom
along with divine will and power, and emphasized rational understanding in explicating submission to God and God's commands.
Revelation is where the tradition begins yet tradition is expansive
through calling for extending understanding and an ongoing articulation of the application of the commandments. Divine wisdom informs the Law, and the more fully we live in accord with the Law, and
the more fully we study it, the more completely we will understand
the wisdom in it. It is a law for rational beings, not a test of unques-
tioning, uncritical obedience.[18]

The issue of the 'reasons of the commandments' illuminates fundamental issues of moral epistemology and the nature and significance of tradition. It connects the rationalism of medieval Jewish
thought to its commitment to tradition through the project of articulating and elaborating the understanding of rational justifications
of the commandments. A distinction such as Saadia's, between laws
of reason and laws of revelation, indicates awareness that some of the
commandments (especially, many of those in the Decalogue) are (or
plausibly can be claimed to be) rationally evident.[19] Or, if they are

---

[17] See Michael Harris, *Divine Command Ethics* (London: Routledge Curzon, 2003)
for discussion of the various positions on divine command in Jewish thought. The
discussion is especially helpful because it includes coverage of philosophical issues,
textual issues, and the rabbinic tradition, as well as contrasting Jewish views with
Christian views.

[18] The caricature of Judaism as brittle legalism is altogether at odds with the
tradition's articulation of the nature of the Law and what it is to fulfil it. For an
example of the caricature see Kant's references to Judaism in *Religion Within the
Limits of Reason Alone*.

[19] Compare Scotus, who held that some of the Decalogue registered rational truths
about God and what we owe to God. This was a basic component of his view of
natural law.

not self-evident, they are at least ascertainable by reason without the aid of revelation. Human reasonableness could arrive at them. With respect to all the others, which are the vast majority of the 613 commandments, there is the difficult question of whether, and to what extent, they are rationally justified. Then there is also the issue of *why* laws are revealed if they *can* be ascertained by unaided reason.

With regard to the epistemology of the commandments Saadia held that, in some cases, the reasons of the commandments were sufficiently evident as to count as rational knowledge. For instance, he held that it is fully evident to reason that a benefactor is owed gratitude, and that one who labours for another is owed compensation. He had an account of why these matters are included in the revelation but he took them to be unproblematically accessible to reason. Revelation supplies a great deal of specification, obviating the need for some of the immense effort of elaborating how principles apply and preempting what could become a great deal of disagreement and friction.[20] Revelation also ensures that there is knowledge of fundamental ethical requirements. One might not employ reason ambitiously but there is no excuse for ignorance of many ethical requirements.

Maimonides criticized Saadia for his claims about the rational evidence of some requirements, insisting that even where the reasons for commandments were most clear the justifications did not have the status of rational self-evidence. Maimonides argued that *no* ethical matters are demonstrated or self-evident. Ethics does not include rational knowledge in the narrow, technical sense of 'rational'. Yet, he also insisted that there are reasons for each and every commandment. There are many matters that are 'generally accepted' in the sense that reason can ascertain grounds for them but they are not rationally self-evident, a status Maimonides reserved for certain theoretical truths. Saadia held that only a small number of basic requirements are rationally evident, but even in the case of commandments whose rationales were least clear he thought that we could see that they have *some sort of utility* in a general sense. Maimonides was emphatic that God commanded nothing without reason, though in

---

[20] See Saadia Gaon, *The Book of Beliefs and Opinions*, Chapter III of Treatise Three for his explanation of why even rational laws needed to be revealed. Chief among the reasons is that revelation supplies specificity human beings might not attain otherwise.

many cases, we could not ascertain the specific rationales, and in some cases, God simply must choose what the detail is to be, for example, whether a sacrifice is to be a lamb or a ram.[21]

Still, it is appropriate to regard Maimonides' view as a form of rationalism because the view holds that there are rational justifications—justifications not dependent upon norms that people just happen to accept or commitments that could be explained in relativist terms. They are justifications that figure in an *integrated system* of requirements rather than justifications for what is just a collection of requirements without any principles of coherence. And, as noted above, part of what Maimonides called God's 'wily graciousness' is divine knowledge of just what sorts of practices and actions would lead to the acquisition of ethical perfections in the actual circumstances, considering the practices and perspectives to which people were accustomed.[22]

We noted above that while there is some affinity between practical wisdom and comprehension of 'the reasons of the commandments' they are distinct. The Jewish view holds that ethical understanding adequate for perfection is not attainable without guidance, which is the anchor of tradition. The understanding of human nature informs ethical thought but the former is not accurately described as an independently sufficient action-guiding portion of the latter, as in Aristotelian practical wisdom. The understanding of nature affords insight into divine wisdom, which also informs the Law. As we enlarge our understanding of the world, we enlarge understanding of the discipline of perfection, shaped (including in quite unobvious ways) to actualize human good.

---

[21] See, e.g., *Guide*, Part III, Chapter 26, 509. Maimonides observes that we will not ascertain why this sacrifice consists in a lamb and that consists in a ram, or why each is the particular number it is. Still, as he insists in Chapter 31, at 524, there is a reason for every commandment. Every commandment has a *telos*, even if there is some measure of discretion in God determining the precise particulars of some of the details.

[22] In the *Guide* Maimonides explains God's 'wily graciousness', one aspect of which is in making the commandments such that fulfilling them will lead people to genuine moral and intellectual perfection and will utterly abolish idolatry. But the commandments do not require so radical and abrupt a change in people's practices that people might regard the commandments as strange, inscrutable or beyond any recognizable purpose. Thus, ritual practices (such as sacrifice) are retained though, in the context of the commandments overall, an entirely new meaning is discernible in them. See especially *Guide*, III, Chapter 32.

The view in question can be distinguished as well from natural law approaches.[23] We might think that the fact that there are reasons for the commandments would be in favour of a natural law interpretation of them or at least in favour of those of them concerning basic moral requirements. Certainly the Noahide commandments seem amenable to being regarded as natural law, both because of their content and because they are meant to apply universally, not just to a covenanted people. Nonetheless, there are reasons not to interpret Jewish moral thought as reflecting natural law. It involves a meta-ethics that preserves universality and objectivity without invoking natural law. It does not include the Thomistic notion of *synderesis*, habitual knowledge of fundamental principles of practical reason, though it does maintain that reason enables us to attain correct ethical understanding. Tradition, rather than natural law, is the chief mode of access to sound ethical comprehension.

In this current of Jewish thought moral understanding and practice are transmitted *and enlarged* through tradition. Though Torah is given to humanity via revelation, it, and the created order overall, are to be studied in depth by generation after generation. The combination of fulfilling the commandments along with the knowledge attained by doing so is crucial to perfection (and redemption).

Human beings can be at home in the world through understanding but we cannot attain understanding without practice, and practice needs to be guided by Torah and tradition. We cannot grasp the rationality of some of the commandments without leading lives in accord with them.[24] Lenn Goodman describes the Law's role in facilitating human perfection as follows:

> right actions facilitate right choices by forming good habits; virtues promote right actions, since a virtue is, by definition, a disposition toward appropriate action. The commandments nurture certain kinds of choices, both for the life those choices foster for the individual and the community. Neither virtuous actions nor the virtues themselves are valued solely for their intrinsic worth. Both contribute to the good life materially, morally, and intellectually.[25]

---

[23] See my 'Judaism and Natural Law', *The Heythrop Journal* Vol. 50, No. 6, November 2009, 930–47, and also *Law, Reason, and Morality in Medieval Jewish Philosophy*.

[24] With the possible exception of Moses, who, according to Maimonides, had exceptional intellectual capacity.

[25] Lenn Goodman, *God of Abraham* (New York: Oxford University Press, 1996) 192.

Much that is included in tradition is not evident to reason and for
much of what is required as proper observance and practice the
justification is not at all clear. Still, Maimonides argued that each
commandment has a role in shaping human perfections, either concerning moral life, the social and political order, the intellect or
relations between these.[26] He also insisted that it is not for us to
exercise discretion over which of the commandments to fulfil, as if
our wisdom is the relevant authority to determine which of them are
necessary or *really* required. He feared that conceit of that sort, and
the endeavour to fulfil the Law only selectively, would undermine
devotion and distract from the true and the good. We can be certain
of God's goodness and wisdom—throughout the created order and
throughout the Law—and we do not have the superior knowledge to
judge divine wisdom on our own authority. This is clearly at odds
with the modern insistence on accepting only what is rationally
evident. It is also at odds with the interpretation of tradition that
sees tradition as a replacement for rational justification, because the
latter cannot be supplied.

The significance of ritual and ceremony is not reducible to
mechanical compliance and none of the commandments is rationally
capricious. Within the life shaped by all of the commandments one is
able to see how that life is integrally related to the good (to God).
Writing of Saadia's appreciation of ritual, Goodman says that for
Saadia:

> observance enhances our reward *and* our being, lightening and bright-
> ening the soul. His synthesis springs from the recognition that our
> reward is not an extrinsic response to arbitrary acts but the very
> purification that observance effects. This idea is no radical innovation
> of Saadiah's. It is the nisus of the Torah itself.[27]

---

[26] See Part III, Chapter 54 in the *Guide of the Perplexed*, for Maimonides' identification of the various human perfections. And in III, 31 he says:

> every *commandment* from among these *six hundred and thirteen commandments*
> exists either with a view to communicating a correct opinion, or to putting an end
> to an unhealthy opinion, or to communicating a rule of justice, or to warding off an
> injustice, or to endowing men with a noble moral quality, or to warning them
> against an evil moral quality. Thus all [the commandments] are bound up with
> three things: opinions, moral qualities, and political civic actions. (524)

[27] Goodman, 189.

Revelation does not displace rationality's central role. It supplies a framework of conceptualization, emphasis, foci of attention, and integration of practice and understanding so that human beings can strive for perfection in an integrated manner, addressing their nature in all of its aspects (natural, social, ethical, intellectual).

By upholding tradition, by fulfilling the commandments, people can acquire understanding, take delight in fulfilling requirements, share commitments, values, and practices with others, and have a sense of continuity with those who came before and those who will follow. Tradition's normative authority exhibits the full texture of those diverse aspects, and does so in an integrated way. Practice helps in the acquisition of understanding. Understanding can be enjoyed and can motivate gratitude to God. The gratitude can strengthen the disposition to sustain traditional practices, and so on.

According to Aristotle, habituation is the process by which our non-rational capacities are shaped such that we are able to understand what makes certain dispositions virtues (and what makes others vices). Habituation is crucial to the acquisition and transmission of practical wisdom. Not all habit is *mere* habit, and there are *rational* habits.[28] Habituation shapes the non-rational capacities that are partly constitutive of human nature in a manner making the habituated person capable of acquiring a sound understanding of good action.

In addition to habituation and one's own reason, (as one matures) law is also important to shaping dispositions to act. Aristotle discussed law briefly at the conclusion of *Nicomachean Ethics*, making the transition to politics. Law is important because of how it can guide and regulate the behaviour of those who have not acquired the virtues. Law reflects reason, and if agents are lacking in practical wisdom, it is important that they should live in a social world governed by practical wisdom, at least through its laws.

> It is difficult, however, for someone to be trained correctly for virtue from his youth if he has not been brought up under correct laws; for the many, especially the young, do not find it pleasant to live in a temperate

---

[28] See my *Choosing Character: Responsibility for Virtue and Vice* (Ithaca: Cornell University Press, 2001) esp. Chapter 1 for a discussion of how many of the habits we acquire are rational habits. They can lead to dispositions to act for certain sorts of reasons without our having to give much thought to what we are doing in many cases, though we act deliberately and could say why we are doing what we do.

and resistant way. That is why laws must prescribe their upbringing and practices; for they will not find these things painful when they get used to them. For the many yield to compulsion more than to argument, and to sanctions more than to the fine.[29]

We could contrast Torah with Greek law by saying that the former has a much more comprehensive scope and addressed many aspects left unaddressed by Greek law. Of course, in the societies Aristotle would have had in mind there were religious practices, courts, arts, educational institutions, and a complex texture of practices and activities concerning all aspects of life. There were diverse modes of normative governance even if it was not in the form of law. But Torah concerns many matters that are not included in the laws governing a *polis*. The *point* of the Law is different and thus the way it addresses people is different. People are to *fulfil* the Law and do not simply live 'under' it or obey it. Leading life guided by the Law is meant to make a difference to what sort of person one becomes and is not only a matter of regulating behaviour.

Habits can be crucial to preserving tradition, and tradition can be a crucially important context and orientation for habituation. But tradition (in the presently relevant sense) is a thicker, more substantive notion than that of habit. It is a way of seeing things as well as a matter of doing certain things regularly. It involves a certain understanding of the world and it includes the recognition of actions as having certain kinds of significance and meaning. Living in accord with tradition makes it possible to acquire understanding, which is essential for perfection, as well as sustaining the community's moral life in a way that realizes justice, ethical excellence, and the well-being of the people generally.

4. TRADITION AS ACCESS TO OBJECTIVE VALUES

It is part of the view that living in accord with tradition is the way people learn universal values and principles.[30] The particularism of

---

[29] Aristotle, *Nicomachean Ethics*, 1179b 31–1180a 5. See also *NE* XIII, Book 1, for his discussion of how some of the non-rational parts of the soul can be responsive to reason.

[30] I discuss this topic further in 'Particularism, Pluralism, and Liberty' in Daniel Frank (ed.), *On Liberty: Jewish Philosophical Perspectives* (Richmond, Surrey: Curzon,

revelation and tradition is not essentially at odds with moral universality or objectivity. The values learned are not values only for the particular community though a great deal of the form of life and activity through which they are learned reflects the particularity of the community. The covenanted community has a vital place in how commitments, ideals, and principles are acquired and transmitted. Tradition supplies a specific architecture of moral life through which individuals and the community engage with objective valuative considerations and come to understand them.

The view combines a rationalist disposition with a kind of epistemic humility. One reason tradition is to be respected is that it sustains the project of seeking improved understanding. Hence, even when the justification of what is required is obscure we still have a tether to it in a way that connects it with the understanding we have achieved so far. That way, the requirement's meaningful connections with our overall understanding can be more effectively realized. Were we to abandon those connections by discretionary commitment to tradition we would subvert the integrity of the Law. What we already understand can be fitted into an enlarged understanding, which grows over time. The coherence of the wisdom of the Law is assurance that what is now justified will not be rendered obsolete and will not fail to cohere with advancing comprehension.

The particularism of tradition does not imply that the basic values and ideals realized by it are less than universally applicable or are not objective. Maimonides, for example, argued that the perfection to which Torah guides people is *human* perfection, not something limited to the Jewish people as having a distinct nature.[31] The commandments constitute a unique form of living through which human perfection is realizable. The virtues cultivated by fidelity to tradition are human virtues and are not merely 'local' excellences.

Moreover, even some of the ritual commandments are related to deep and basic values. 'The biblical prohibitions of blasphemy, idolatry, and incest are all ritual commandments in that they seek to

---

1999) 82–97, and in 'Torah and Political Power; Judaism and the Liberal Polity', in *Trumah*, Winter, 2010, pp. 26–44.

[31] Judah Halevi is an example of a medieval Jewish thinker who saw the issue quite differently. He argued that the Jewish people and the Land of Israel had a nature distinct from that of other peoples and other lands. See Halevi's *The Kuzari* for his presentation of his view.

regulate our use of symbolism by assigning cosmic significances to elemental human actions and relations. But that makes them central thematically to the Torah; its normative scheme would be inconceivable without them.'[32] Some values may be such that without specific practices for representing them, reminding ourselves of them, and visibly introducing them into the patterns of our lives we might become detached from them or they might not figure in our lives in effective ways, our attention not having been directed to them. While symbols (including ritual behaviour) 'cannot replace what they represent, they can structure our very reality by their representations of it, and of the values it portends.'[33] Precisely those commandments that seem to have significance only within the life of a particular community, and which seem idiosyncratic to it, are conducive to dispositions it would be good for anyone to acquire.

The view acknowledges the significance for human beings of specific, concrete practices and commitments, while maintaining that moral life is shaped by requirements suited to rational beings whose action is *intelligent* action. This conception of how objective values are learned invites us to take seriously the possibility that different traditions can realize universal values *and* that human beings may be such as to become strongly devoted to those values by leading lives shaped by particular commitments. This is not a summary endorsement of tradition as the centrepiece of morality. It is a claim about what may be a thick, complex relation between moral psychology and moral epistemology.

It recognizes that more than moral requirements—if defined in a highly specific, narrow sense, setting them apart from the rest of practical life—can be vitally important to ethical life and to human excellence. The tradition in which ethical life is anchored concerns all aspects of our nature, as individuals and as social beings. That does not mean that the Law stifles individuality and imposes upon us in a way that smothers self-determination. Instead, it is alive to how integrated is the fabric of human life, and to the fact that ethical requirements cannot be compartmentalized and treated in a standalone manner, as though their rationality could be separated out from interest, excellence, aspiration, and activity more broadly construed.

---

[32] Goodman, 188.   [33] ibid 208.

Some of the features of a faith-tradition that are often regarded as impediments to its teaching universal, objective values and inculcating disinterested moral concern, may actually reflect wisdom regarding human nature. It is wisdom about how those values and that concern can become crucial to the sense of one's self as a being to whom moral life is essential to a well-led life, and is grounded in reality rather than being a construction of our own. It is also wisdom about a way in which leading a certain kind of life may be necessary for coming to understand the rightness of commitments, dispositions, and practices constitutive of that life. (That is recognizable as a broadly Aristotelian point, though that is not to say that it can only have its origin in Aristotle.)

The relevant notion of tradition includes reflection upon values and practices, and it involves the articulation of the former through the elaboration and enactment of the latter. Practice is not without a reflective dimension, and reflection is connected with the concrete details of the business of living. As Goodman remarks, 'Even revelation, no matter how explicit, gives no guidance unless we know how to evaluate its aims.'[34] For any given commandment, we need to consider what are the values at issue, and how doing *that* (whatever it is that is commanded) is related to those values. That is part of how the behaviour can make a difference to what people become.

An important respect in which tradition has epistemic authority is that it supplies access to the truth rather than occluding our vision of it or being just one among an indefinite number of valuative conceptions none of which reflects objective truth. The ambitious employment of reason shows that this is so, and shows the ways in which it is so. That 'showing' is an important part of what is involved in living in accord with tradition. In this case, it is a crucial part of the people of Israel becoming a wise and understanding people. Thus, there is a fundamental respect in which tradition reflects rationality rather than distancing people from the universal and objective. Tradition can provide a particularist approach to objective values, the rational comprehension of which depends, in large part, upon honouring what tradition requires.

At a highly abstract level we can put the point in the following terms: (a) while human beings are capable of moral excellence

---

[34] ibid 186.

reflecting the grasp of objective values, many of those values are not rationally evident except to persons who have acquired certain dispositions, habits, and sensibility; (b) grasping the rational justification of moral requirements can reinforce moral concern and the disposition to realize those values; (c) human beings are liable to error and valuative disorientation in basic ways, and without the guidance supplied by tradition—in this case, rooted in an authority and agency that transcends human nature—they would be much less able to acquire virtues (and to realize the perfection proper to them, if that is also an important part of the philosophical anthropology).

Points (a), (b), and (c) are at odds with some powerful currents of modern thought. The critic might dismiss the view altogether because of the place of revelation in it. But summary dismissal on that basis would blind us to the merits of the epistemology and moral psychology in it. It presents a view of moral requirements as including the obligation to consider, reflect upon, and study those requirements themselves in order to understand their truth and their bindingness. The notion that tradition, when studied and articulated, might reveal considerable rationality, and well-serve moral life even if people do not grasp many of the justifications of requirements, could be quite important. It indicates how ethical wisdom can be preserved and transmitted and how there is a historical dimension to moral wisdom. It can grow and deepen and become more complete. It is a transgenerational, shared project, reflecting awareness of the possibility of increased moral understanding and more perfect virtue.

5. THE ENDURING RELEVANCE OF ANCIENT TRADITION

Study of medieval Jewish moral epistemology suggests ways in which the widely endorsed modern insistence on 'no obligation without evident justification' may be exaggerated in ways detrimental to ethical life. At the same time, it suggests that another current of modern thought—one that regards tradition as a rival to rational justification—is also exaggerated in unhelpful and distorting ways. Tradition can keep people engaged to values and ideals supplying a stable basis for elaboration of the content of those values and ideals.

But, what of the objection that this conception depends upon a faith-tradition, a set of theistic commitments inseparable from the moral epistemology and moral psychology? There are two points to make in response to this. The first is that, whether or not one shares Judaism's faith-commitments it is still possible to see the ethical wisdom in much of the content of the tradition. One might utterly reject the claim for a divine origin of Torah but find truth and insight in the moral anthropology it portrays and the moral tradition to which it gave rise. Second, it is worth reflecting upon the way Jewish moral thought is alert to the joint significance of the individual's understanding and responsibility on the one hand, and the role of community and tradition in preserving, transmitting, and enlarging understanding and moral commitment, on the other. Tradition is not to be upheld thoughtlessly or uncritically but we should have faith in what it transmits, as long as transmission includes the hard, ongoing work of explicating what is required and improving our understanding. Tradition is not an alternative to, or a rival to, rational objectivity. It can be a mode of commitment to the aspiration to attain objective understanding and rational justification.

There are some important respects in which the metaphysics of morals bears on moral psychology. For example, the relevant faith-commitments (concerning revelation and providence) can be interpreted as reflecting the appropriateness of a deep humility on the part of human beings. Medieval Jewish thinkers insisted that we are not altogether self-sufficient in regard to moral life and that the gift of Torah is God's graciously given help. Creation is also strongly relevant. When God rested and looked upon the created order he saw that it was very good. Creation is a basis for believing that we can be at home in the world and that through study of the world we can achieve a growing appreciation of objective value, worth, and significance.[35] Value is not an expressively grounded reflection of *valuing*. The aspiration of intelligent beings to acquire an *understanding* of good is an appropriate and realizable aspiration. The realism of value helps explain the importance of both humility and gratitude as basic dispositions in regard

---

[35] This is a claim I develop more fully in *Normative Realism and Freedom of the Will in the Bible*, an unpublished manuscript. See also 'The Durability of Goodness' by Alan Mittleman, in this volume. There are several substantial points of contact between the argument he develops and the account of moral objectivity articulated in my contribution to the present volume.

to God. We are to be humble before the reality of good and its transcendent cause. We are to be grateful for that reality and for our aptitude to be intelligently responsive to it and its cause.

These are precisely the sorts of faith-commitments that critics of revealed religion find deeply problematic—or worse. The non-theist might argue that moral realism can share the combination of humility and aspiration of Judaism without any commitments to anything transcendent. At the very least, the conception of tradition explored here points to ways in which there are highly important relations between the metaphysics of morals, moral epistemology, and moral psychology. It can help us think through some of the most fundamental implications of claims about the reality of value, the possibility of moral knowledge, and the nature of moral agents.

In recent philosophy, Alisdair Macintyre's discussion of tradition is especially relevant to the present account. In his explication of what is required in order for a tradition to be carried on and to develop when it encounters issues that are difficulties arising internally or from rival traditions he writes:

> For such a tradition, if it is to flourish at all, as we have already learned, has to be embodied in a set of texts which function as the authoritative point of departure for tradition-constituted enquiry and which remain as essential points of reference for enquiry and activity, for argument, debate, and conflict within that tradition.[36]

With respect to the principles:

> The kind of rational justification which they receive is at once dialectical and historical. They are justified insofar as in the history of this tradition they have, by surviving the process of dialectical questioning, vindicated themselves as superior to their historical predecessors. Hence such first principles are not self-sufficient, self-justifying epistemological first principles.[37]

In a number of respects that seems to fit the tradition I have discussed. Jewish moral thought includes a rich, textured history of elaboration, argumentation, extension to new types of cases, revisiting of hard cases as guides to new circumstances, and, to a varying extent, interaction with other traditions.

---

[36] Alisdair MacIntyre, *Whose Justice? Which Rationality?* (Notre Dame: University of Notre Dame Press, 1988) 383.

[37] ibid 360.

For a number of complicated historical, political, and theological reasons Judaism developed in a way such that study, dialectic, and tradition-anchored elaboration are jointly centrepieces of much Jewish moral thought. That helps explain *both* why Judaism is an example of many of MacIntyre's main claims about the role of tradition *and* why one must take care to minimize ambiguity in speaking of 'the Jewish tradition'. There are a number of significantly different currents of Jewish thought and modes of practice, each with its own conception of its authenticity and often highly self-aware in regard to its differences from others. Additionally, there are diverse (plausible) ways to distinguish different Jewish traditions. The level of description and generalization can be very important. I have focused on one important current of thought in that overall complex of tradition(s).

The thinkers discussed here appropriated much from the Greek heritage in ways that illustrate some of MacIntyre's claims about how a tradition can be maintained, developed, and educated by dialectical friction with other traditions and by coming to grips with internally motivated difficulties. They did not believe that 'Athens' and 'Jerusalem' were different, irreconcilable worlds, and they saw philosophy and religion as complementing each other in the unified task of ascertaining truth and leading a virtuous life. These thinkers regarded the grasp of truth as an *elevating knowledge of the real*, crucial to good activity as well as understanding.[38] At the same time there are ways in which their thought highlights respects in which Athens' project is different from Jerusalem's. The mere mention of creation, providence, and redemption signals crucial differences. Likeness and difference regarding Athens and Jerusalem can be presented in a number of different ways. Nonetheless, several important medieval Jewish thinkers held that Greek philosophy is enormously valuable in the pursuit of truth and comprehension, and they understood both philosophy and religion as modes of access to one body of truth.

Despite the complexities of distinguishing and tracking the continuity of a tradition it is fair to say that there is a tradition of Jewish

---

[38] I discuss the 'Athens and Jerusalem' issue in 'Reasons, Commandments, and the Common Project', *Hebraic Political Studies*, Summer 2008, Vol. 3, No. 3, and in *Law, Reason, and Morality in Medieval Jewish Philosophy* (Oxford: Oxford University Press, 2010) Chapter 1. In both places I argue that an important current of thought (not just medieval) regards Athens and Jerusalem as contributing in mutually reinforcing ways to a realist conception of the world and a conception of human perfection as an elevating knowledge of the real.

thought to which the notion of the rationality of that tradition itself is central. Because of the way in which those who expounded the view understood rationality there is scope for development of the tradition. Intellectual and moral aspiration are vitally important features of it. And despite the particularities essential to the identity of the tradition and the self-understanding of those faithful to it, it is concerned with values, principles, and ideals it takes to have universal validity. There is much worth considering in medieval Jewish moral thought, and much that is not confined to the boundaries of the Jewish people or to Jewish tradition or pre-modern times. Wider study of its central insights concerning moral rationality, moral psychology and their relations would enable us to better understand a crucial source of Western moral thought. It would also enable us to deploy some of its subtlety and depth in our own thought—both theoretical and practical—concerning morality.

6

Natural Law and Jewish Philosophy

David Novak

1. IS NATURAL LAW JEWISH?

In order for 'natural law' to be of appropriate concern to a Jewish thinker, that thinker should question whether it has been of genuine Jewish concern in the past, and question whether it ought to be of genuine Jewish concern in the present. The first question is historical; the second philosophical.[1]

The philosophical question has priority inasmuch as philosophy is a discipline that is normative and contemporary, whereas history is a discipline that is descriptive of the past. As theory philosophy prescribes what we ought now to affirm because it is true; as praxis philosophy prescribes what one ought to do because it is right. Natural law is primarily a concern of practical philosophy and it is not hard to show that that has always been the case. Yet practical philosophy also has a necessary theoretical dimension, being concerned with issues of truth as well as issues of right. One always acts and thinks in the present of what is now to be done as right and what is now to be thought as true. Certainly when something is done by a human person as a right requirement of his or her human nature, it is

---

[1] This essay reworks a number of points previously made in my historical treatment of natural law and the Jewish tradition: *The Image of the Non-Jew in Judaism* (New York and Toronto: The Edwin Mellen Press, 1983), 2nd edn (Matthew Labrone ed. Oxford: Littman Library of Jewish Civilization, 2011), and in two of my philosophical treatments of the same question: *Natural Law in Judaism* (Cambridge: Cambridge University Press, 1998), and 'Judaism and Natural Law', *American Journal of Jurisprudence* 43 (1998) 117–34.

thereby an affirmation of what is true of his or her human nature. One only looks to past action and past thought retrospectively for normative precedents. That normative contemporaneity gives philosophy its existential priority over history. But why does philosophy need to look back for normative precedents, for what people in the past thought to be true and thought to be right? Why does philosophy need history at all?

Philosophers, like all thinkers, think within traditions of praxis and discourse, within cultures broadly speaking, whether they admit it or not.[2] Judaism surely being such a tradition means that self-identified *Jewish* philosophers need to find precedents within *their own* Jewish tradition for their present normative concerns. If not, what makes their thinking on their philosophical concerns 'Jewish'? How is such thinking continuing the tradition in which it is now taking place? Surely without some solid precedence, one could not truly call any idea 'Jewish' at all?[3]

Past precedence, nevertheless, does not tell us why a normative idea like natural law ought to be of present concern. Hume was correct when he taught that an 'ought' cannot be derived from an 'is' (in this case, from a 'was').[4] That is so even when the past being consulted is a normative past, viz., what was done as imperative action in the past. Because an act was done imperatively in the past does not automatically mean it must be done imperatively in the present.

Precedence is only a necessary condition for present concern to be truly *within* any ongoing tradition, but precedence is not sufficient to provide a norm having authority in the present. If it can be shown that natural law thinking *never was* authentically Jewish in the past, it

---

[2] See Alasdair MacIntyre, *Whose Justice? Which Rationality?* (Notre Dame, IN: University of Notre Dame Press, 1988); also, Michael Walzer, *Thick and Thin* (Notre Dame, IN: University of Notre Dame Press, 1994) 7. Walzer's critique of the amorphousness of much modern political thought is influenced by the cultural anthropologist Clifford Geertz's *The Interpretation of Culture* (New York: Basic Books, 1973).

[3] This is best expressed by the following dictum in the *Palestinian Talmud*: Peah 2.6/17a: 'Whatever a venerable student expounds before his teacher has already been said to Moses at Sinai.' One could paraphrase his dictum as follows: If your point has never been entertained in the Jewish tradition originally, then it does not belong here now. There are, however, points that were of Jewish concern in the past that cannot and should not be treated as live issues in the present. See, eg, *Babylonian Talmud* [hereafter 'B.']: Zevahim 44b–45a.

[4] See L.A. Selby-Bigge (ed.), *A Treatise of Human Nature* (Oxford: Clarendon Press, 1888) 3.1.1.

would then lack the necessary condition for its Jewish authenticity in the present.

When it can be shown that an idea like natural law has been of authentic Jewish normative concern in the past, it is not hard to show that it *still ought to be* of concern in the present, that is, when it can be shown that the normative issues involved in natural law are still urgently with us as Jews (and being universal in scope, these questions are with all morally earnest human beings). Since these issues cannot be ignored without making the tradition in which they are asked morally irrelevant, the burden of proof is on those who would argue otherwise. Therefore, if the issues involved in natural law were as urgent in the past as they are now in the present, why presume that we Jews have to step out of our tradition when dealing with natural law? Indeed, one does not have to make any such either/or choice; one can be a philosopher within the Jewish tradition. Indeed, philosophical discussion of natural law can take place in Jerusalem and her tradition *since* (but not *because*) it has already taken place there. A Jew need not move (figuratively) to Athens to deal philosophically with the perennial concern with natural law.

Consideration of the precedents from normative Jewish tradition by a Jewish philosopher is most urgent when the need to answer a practical question (*halakhah le-ma`aseh*) includes the need to provide an answer with the most theoretically satisfying reason.[5] It would seem that practical questions that are of concern to any morally earnest human being are most likely to look to the idea of natural law as developed in the tradition of the person seeking that answer. Only natural law would have the necessary universal scope to deal with such universal questions. And unlike the other areas of *halakhah* (law) that are taken to apply only to Jews (collectively and individually), when Jews do advocate what could be taken to be a natural law position, they are advocating *halakhah* that applies to everybody (collectively and individually).[6] It would seem that Jewish discussions of natural law have more than Jewish significance when they are concerned with certain practices Jews ought to advocate be done by every human being and every human society (including themselves) when confronted by perennial moral questions. Such questions are truly *universal*, having both a vertical and horizontal dimension:

---

[5] See B. Baba Batra 130b.   [6] See B. Sanhedrin 59a.

relevant *everywhere* and *everytime*. These questions are ubiquitous and omnipresent.

That normative universality is essential to the idea of natural law, even for those Jewish thinkers who might argue that if there is any natural law in Judaism, the word 'natural' only means that some norms Judaism teaches have universal scope (that is, applying to all those who are human by nature), even though these norms have no moral validity unless they are derived from particularly Jewish revelation rather than being readily discovered by unaided human reason. And, for them, these norms only have moral authority when they are actually prescribed by Jewish revelation as transmitted by authoritative Jewish tradition.[7] Nevertheless, it is only when the 'natural' in 'natural law' is not only a legal concept but also an epistemological and ontological concept, having precedence in the Jewish past, that it is a proper concern for Jewish philosophy. In fact, one could locate the most significant point of dissension between pro-philosophical and anti-philosophical Jewish thinkers to be on the epistemological and ontological issues raised when moral questions that seem to be universal are asked. These are the questions with which natural law has always been involved. The ontological question is why God reveals natural law to its human subjects. The epistemological question is how natural law is known by its human subjects.

I would argue that natural law is a question of political philosophy, because of its inherent public practicality, and political philosophy is where Jewish philosophers today should locate their most serious reflection and discussion, both among themselves and among other politically earnest people in the multicultural world where all Jewish philosophers live and work. And that political philosophy, in order to be philosophy in the strongest sense, must deal with the epistemological and ontological issues that politics as the most comprehensive arena of human interaction necessarily raises, especially when politics raises the question of natural law. When dealing with the question of natural law, political philosophy becomes ethics insofar as it deals with what ought to be done by humans as inherently political beings.[8]

---

[7] The most cogent formulation of this position is by Marvin Fox, 'Maimonides and Aquinas on Natural Law', in *Interpreting Maimonides* (Chicago: University of Chicago Press, 1990) 124–51. For a critique of Fox, see David Novak, *Jewish Social Ethics* (New York: Oxford University Press, 1992) 25–9.

[8] See Aristotle, *Nicomachean Ethics*, I.1/1094b1–11.

2. CONTRA NATURAL LAW IN JUDAISM

There are two basic presumptions about natural law that have prevented many from seeing natural law to be an authentic (though arguable) idea within the Jewish tradition. Because of these presumptions, many have concluded that Jewish thinkers who had been concerned with natural law were not really engaged with Judaism at all. These presumptions must first be challenged (even if never fully overcome) before the search for historical precedents of natural law thinking in Judaism can be more than just an antiquarian quibble, and before one can represent natural law in the ongoing Jewish tradition with philosophical *gravitas*.

The first presumption about natural law and Judaism that must be challenged is the opinion that the idea of natural law is only cogent when seen as the idea of 'natural right' (*dikē*) in classical Greek thought, especially in the philosophy of Plato, Aristotle, and the Stoics. This opinion was most famously put forth by Leo Strauss, who wrote:

> The idea of natural right must be unknown as long as the idea of nature is unknown. The discovery of nature is the work of philosophy. Where there is no philosophy, there is no knowledge of natural right as such. The Old Testament, whose basic premise may be said to be the implicit rejection of philosophy, does not know 'nature'.[9]

---

[9] *Natural Right and History* (Chicago: University of Chicago Press, 1953) 81. Strauss uses 'natural right' in the sense of the German *Naturrecht*, viz., a normative order (eg, *Rechtsordnung*) as distinct from any actually promulgated norm. 'Right' for him is thus *ius* rather than *nomos* or *lex* or *Gesetz*, i.e., it is *ius naturale* rather than *lex naturalis*. It is *dikē* in the classical Greek sense (see, e.g., Sophocles, *Antigone*, 369; Plato, Laws, 631B-D, 887B; Aristotle, *Nicomachean Ethics* V.7/1134b20–35). There is little V/1134b20–35). There is little doubt that Strauss was trying to avoid the theological notion of natural law as universal law proclaimed by the Creator God (see *Natural Right and History*, 7; cf. Thomas Aquinas, *Summa Theologiae*, II.1, q. 90, a. 4 ad obj. 1, and q. 94, a. 4 ad obj. 1). And even more so, he was distinguishing 'classical' natural right from the 'natural rights' proposed by modern thinkers beginning with Hobbes (see *Natural Right and History*, 165–202). For two critiques of Strauss' understanding of natural right as being an idea essentially apart from Judaism, see Novak, *Jewish Social Ethics*, 29–33, and 'Philosophy and the Possibility of Revelation: A Theological Response to the Challenge of Leo Strauss', in David Novak (ed.), *Leo Strauss and Judaism* (Lanham, MD: Rowman and Littlefield, 1996) 173–92. See also n. 12 below.

If Strauss is right (and I think he is wrong), natural law thinking can only take place in Judaism disingenuously, since Judaism bases all it claims one way or another on the 'Old Testament' or Hebrew Bible, that is, on the Torah. If Strauss is right, then there is no such basis for natural law in Judaism, and philosophy as the best way to think about natural law is undercut before it ever gets off the ground when Jews try to do it as a Jewish enterprise.

The way to counter Strauss' charge about the absence of the term and the concept 'nature' in the Bible is to show there is a concept in the Bible that functions quite similarly to what Strauss thinks is the function of 'nature' that is bespoken by classical philosophy. That concept is termed *mishpat*, best translated as *Justice*.[10] Like *dikē* ('natural right') in Greek thought, *mishpat* denotes an intelligible order within the world we experience, especially the social world of interpersonal transactions. This is best seen in the earliest mention of *mishpat* in the Bible, when God challenges Abraham to question Him as to whether God plans to act according to the *just order* God has created within the world, and which humans are to imitate in their own dealings with one another in order to actively participate in this *cosmic justice*. As Abraham famously asks: 'Will the Judge of the whole earth not do justice [*mishpat*]?!' (Genesis 18:25) Is not this *cosmic justice* what is meant by *natural right*, understanding 'nature' to be the *created order* of the world, and 'right' to be the *law* or *commandment* by which God rules the world?

It is not that this justice is something like a Platonic Form to which even God is beholden. That would make *mishpat* transcendent and God immanent, which would reverse the roles of Creator and creature. Instead, this justice too is the creation of the transcendent God. But this justice seems to be revealed generally to humans in their interpersonal experience so that if God wants humans to imitate God's action immanently in their interpersonal world, then God has to assure us that He operates according to a consistent and intelligible standard (even though we often do not see its full results in this world anyway). That is why the human exercise of justice is considered to be part of a process far greater than the ordinary administration of humanly devised procedures. 'For justice [*mishpat*] is God's' (Deuteronomy 1:17).

---

[10] See David Novak, *The Election of Israel* (Cambridge: Cambridge University Press, 1995) 120–38.

Furthermore, in the sequence of the biblical narrative, it is assumed that Abraham already knows what is 'the way [*derekh*] of the Lord, to do what is just [*mishpat*] and what is right [*tsedaqah*]' (Genesis 18:19) before God reveals to Abraham God's proposal for the judgement of Sodom and Gomorrah. And, in the same sense, it is assumed that the people of Israel have some general knowledge of what this justice is before they arrive at Mount Sinai to receive the Torah; indeed, it could be said that without this knowledge they would have been in no position to accept the full Mosaic Torah intelligently and freely.[11]

The rabbis developed this biblical idea of *mishpat* in their distinction between laws that can be inferred by human reason and laws that require direct divine revelation in order to be known by humans. Both kinds of laws are originally commanded by God. Nevertheless, laws that can be inferred by human reason are universally applicable, whereas laws that require direct divine revelation only apply to the particular people to whom God has revealed them in history.

To be sure, laws that can be inferred by human reason are also inferred to be from God too, but their status as divine law is not directly revealed as is the case with the laws not inferred by human reason. The former laws are *taken by* humans; the latter laws are *given to* humans, that is, to the particular human community who are the recipients of direct revelation, viz., the people of Israel at Sinai. This distinction comes out in the following rabbinic text:

> Our Rabbis taught [based on Scripture]: 'You shall perform My just laws [*mishpetai*]' (Leviticus 18:4), which means that had they not been written [in Scripture], it stands to reason [*din hu*] they would have had to be written. They are [the prohibitions of]: idolatry, and sexual license, and murder, and robbery, and blasphemy. 'And My decrees [*huqqotai*] you shall keep' (ibid.), these are the matters that Satan taunts [the Jews] about. They are [the prohibitions of]: eating pork, etc. . . . And lest you say they are absurd [*ma'aseh tohu*], Scriptures states there, 'I am the Lord': I am the Lord who decreed it [*haqqaqtiv*], and you are not permitted to challenge them.[12]

It is important to note here that those laws or commandments (*mitsvot*) that are considered to be inherently rational comprise the bulk of the Noahide laws (*mitsvot bnei Noah*) that the rabbis

---

[11] See Novak, *Natural Law in Judaism*, 55–60.
[12] B. Yoma, 67b (my translation). See *Sifra* re Lev. 18:4, ed. Weiss, 86a.

determined apply to all humankind. In other words, *mishpatim* are *just* laws because their comportment with *mishpat* as justice per se is immediately evident to any rational, morally earnest person. For the rabbis, a 'Noahide' (*ben Noah*) is such a person. Hence the examples of *mishpatim* show that Noahide law is knowable or discoverable as natural law, and what is not knowable or discoverable as natural law requires direct revelation from God. And, whereas all God's commandments have reasons, only some of those commandments have reasons so universally evident that their applicability to all humankind seems equally evident. Here we clearly see natural law thinking from rabbinic sages who are unlikely ever to have read Plato, Aristotle, or the Stoics, even though they were thinking of issues that certainly concerned these Greek philosophers, especially the issue of justice. There is also evidence that natural law theory was developed in Hellenistic Judaism by what could be called a carefully thought out 'judaizing' of the Hellenic idea of nature (*physis*) by the Hebraic idea of God as simultaneously the Creator of both the world and the Torah (*nomos*) in tandem.[13]

The second presumption to be rejected for the sake of an authetically Jewish natural law theory is the opinion that natural law thinking can only be done, or can only be done thoroughly and persuasively, within Roman Catholic moral theology. That is because natural law has been discussed more explicitly and extensively by Catholic theologians than anywhere else. Unlike the first presumption, here it is thought that philosophy can be taken into theology without damage to either one. In this view, philosophy loses none of its autonomy when philosophy does not let theology dictate its methods of enquiry, but when philosophy only lets theology take the results of that enquiry and give them religious authority. Yet like the first presumption, here too it is thought that natural law's historical matrix lies in classical Greek philosophy, only connected to theology when Christian (and, earlier, Jewish) theology came into

---

[13] See Helmut Koester, 'NOMOS PHUSEOS: The Concept of Natural Law in Greek Thought', in J. Neusner (ed.), *Religions of Antiquity: Essays in Memory of Erwin Ramsdell Goodenough* (Leiden: Brill, 1968) 521–41, esp. 540 where he writes: 'Philo has to be considered as the crucial and most important contributor to the development of the theory of natural law ... Only a philosophical and theological setting in which the Greek concept of nature was fused with the belief in a divine legislator ... could the Greek dichotomy of the two realms of law and nature be overcome.' See also n. 8 above.

intellectual contact with philosophically saturated Hellenistic and Graeco-Roman culture and began appropriating its wisdom for its own apologetic programme. And, if one sees that matrix to be most specifically the ethical-political philosophy of Aristotle, the best appropriation and development of that Aristotelian philosophy is thought to be found in the moral theology of Thomas Aquinas, whom the Roman Catholic Church has called *Doctor Angelicus*, its most authoritative theologian.

All of this is correct only *if* we accept the opinion that natural law finds its best expression when employing Aristotelian teleology. And there is good evidence to think that no one explained and developed Aristotle's philosophy better and more thoroughly than did Aquinas. But the fact that Aquinas did this so well for Aristotle does not require one to believe this is the only way one can think of natural law or even the best way to think of it, especially as a Jew (and probably as a Christian too) beholden to the Bible. In fact, when one thinks of the precepts of natural law that Judaism affirms, such as the equal claim to life of all human beings from conception to natural death (and thus not to be killed when innocent at any stage of human life), or the exclusively heterosexual marital claim on human sexuality, is not Aristotle (and Plato even more so) quite problematic? His views on both human personhood and human community are often at odds with biblical teaching. Also, at the ontological level, the God imagined by Aristotle does not look very much like the God revealed in the Bible as Creator/Lawgiver.

That is the theological problem with making Aristotle the key philosophical authority for any ethical theory that must be theologically correct in order to be religiously acceptable to the community for whom this ethical theory is being appropriated.

There are also big philosophical problems with Aristotelian ethical-political philosophy, which seems to presuppose a by now irretrievable teleological metaphysics, built as it is on the back of an even more irretrievable teleological natural science, especially on that natural science's cosmology or astrophysics. That being the case, even Roman Catholic moral theology might have to divest itself of Aristotelian metaphysics in order to be philosophically cogent now.[14] Furthermore, even if teleology is inherent in natural law thinking,

---

[14] See John Finnis, *Natural Law and Natural Rights* (Oxford: Clarendon Press, 1980) 52.

why does it have to be Aristotelian teleology? In fact, Kant's ethical teleology (at least as set forth in the second formulation of the categorical imperative), which designates persons as 'ends-in-themselves', is an ethical teleology that does not depend on a teleological cosmology.[15] As such, it is closer to the more personalist anthropology of the Bible and the rabbis, and it is closer to biblical-rabbinic ontology that sees humans to be God's most exalted creation and non-human nature (even that of the heavens) to be secondary to human communal nature in the divine ordering of the cosmos.[16] This is contrary to Aristotle, for whom human communal nature is only a part, and not even the most exalted part, of cosmic Nature.

As for Judaism, though some Jewish thinkers adopted Aristotelian premises, since the Jewish tradition did not give their thought the same kind of dogmatic authority, that divestment is easier to make. Thus it could be said that Jewish natural law theory and Catholic natural law theory are in the same boat so to speak. Natural law theory here and now requires profound rethinking from within a tradition that has seriously taken it to be a legitimate pursuit for its adherents.

3. FIVE PROPOSITIONS ABOUT NATURAL LAW AND JEWISH PHILOSOPHY

What follows are five propositions about natural law and its relation to Jewish philosophy. The first three deal with natural law as an issue within the Jewish tradition. The last two deal with natural law as an issue for Jewish moral advocacy in the non-Jewish world.

3.1. Natural Law is the Ethical Thrust of the Doctrine of Creation

The doctrine of creation (*beri'at ha'olam*) is not primarily an answer to the questions: 'When did the world begin?' or 'How did the world begin?' It is much more an answer to the question: 'Why does the

---

[15] See *Groundwork of the Metaphysic of Morals*, A427–31, H.J. Paton, trans. (New York: Harper and Row, 1964) 95–8.
[16] See Ps. 8:2–10; M. Sanhedrin 4.5; B. Pesahim 68b re Jer. 33:25.

world exist at all?' But since the world itself does not ask this question, it can only be asked by a person in the world who questions: 'Why do I exist at all?' Now a *why* question looks to a certain purpose or end for its answer, that is, '*For what* do I exist?' Purposes or ends are what *action* intends; action is the means or way to these ends. Thus 'Why do I exist at all?' becomes 'What am I to do that correctly intends the ends for which I exist in the world?' The existential question to which the doctrine of creation is directed is an essentially practical question that can only be asked by humans as active beings. And with the exception of persons faced with mortal danger, the answer to the existential-practical question 'Why do I exist at all?' is not survival, not existence for its own sake.[17] Active existence is for the sake of something beyond its own biological confines. Doing something without teleological intention is behaviour, not action.

The practicality of human existence, that human personhood is essentially lived actively, also means that human practical existence is communal. Human action is not the *agency* of a lone actor but, rather, it is always interaction with other humans.[18] Even a lone individual making something for himself is not just involved in a dual relation between himself and an impersonal object; his technical skills were learned from other persons, and most often, he is making something for himself to use or enjoy with other persons. And even a lone individual thinking by herself is thinking in language learned from her hearing others speak and her speaking back to them, and her thought most often will eventually be brought back to the speech she addresses to other persons. Thus the existential-practical question is in fact the existential-practical-communal question: Why do *we* actively exist or live together? The human actions with which ethics-politics is concerned are all human *interactions* of which each and every human person is both subject and object, both means and end. Minimally, that means not harming anybody else just as nobody else is to harm you.[19] Maximally, that means benefiting whoever requests your aid (without entailing great harm to yourself) just as you have the right to be aided similarly by somebody else.[20] The minimal

---

[17] At times, these purposes require that one fulfil them by dying rather than violating them. See B. Sanhedrin 74a.

[18] See Aristotle, *Politics*, 1.1/1253a1–30.

[19] See B. Shabbat 31a.

[20] See Maimonides, *Sefer ha-Mitsvot*, pos. no. 206.

relationship involves justice as the criterion of restraint; the maximal relationship involves peace (*shalom*) as the criterion of beneficence.[21] These mutual interactions, especially the minimal ones, are governed by natural law.

Finally, the existential-practical-communal question becomes theological when one asks: *Why* are these human persons to be actively engaged, to be benefited and not harmed? It is certainly not because humans are essentially good to themselves and to the world. In fact, humans are too frequently violent against each other and against the world. And, more often than not, the world opposes us more than it helps us. That is why we have to work so hard in order to survive in an often hostile, impersonal world. Accordingly, we cannot look to either ourselves or to the world to ground the sanctity of human life. Therefore, it is more plausible to say that humans are the objects of God's concern, a concern whose source cannot be located in either ourselves or in the world. The ubiquitous human concern to find God would be futile if humans did not hope that God is concerned with us. That seems to be the best explanation of the human intuition that we are created in *the image of God*.[22] So, how can we justify to ourselves harming or not benefiting the human objects of this unique divine concern? In other words, how can we justify transgressing the precepts of natural law that teach us how to do good and not evil to each other? 'The Lord is creator of the heavens; he is the God who formed the earth, making and setting it up. He did not create it to be chaotic (*tohu*), but to be a dwelling (*la-shevet*) did he form it' (Isaiah 45:18). Discovering natural law is discovering how to make the world a just and peaceful habitation for all humankind because that is what God seems to want for God's unique, purposeful human creatures.[23] Natural law, then, is the way humans make God's creative purposes for all humankind our own active purposes.[24]

---

[21] When Jewish law seems to provide permission for unjust acts committed by Jews against gentiles, the law is rectified so that God's reputation as a just universal lawgiver is not tarnished (*hillul ha-shem*, literally 'the profanation of God's name'). See B. Baba Kama 113b. And when Jewish law seems only to mandate concern for the personal needs of Jews (called *gemilut hasadim*, 'acts of kindness'), thus implying its moral myopia, the law is emended to include concern for the personal needs of non-Jews with whom Jews interact (see *Tosefta*: Gittin 3.13–14; B. Gittin 61a). These two rectifications are based on natural law principles, viz., injustice is to be corrected anywhere; peace with everybody is to be pursued.

[22] See *Mishnah* [hereafter 'M.']: Avot 3.14 re Gen. 5:1.

[23] See M. Gittin 4.5.   [24] See M. Avot 2.4.

The communal created nature of humans involves the integrity of humans as religious (that is, God-related) beings, the integrity of the human body, the integrity of human sexuality, and the integrity of human property. The protection of these forms of human integrity is enacted in the Noahide laws, which (as we have seen) as natural law apply to all humankind in their active humanity. Noahide-natural law is learned when we fully reflect on the practical meaning of our communal created nature.

3.2. Natural Law is the Precondition of the Covenant

In some recent discussions of natural law in Judaism, especially among more traditionally oriented Jewish thinkers, the debate has been between those who deny there is any Jewish doctrine of natural law and those who see at least some evidence for it. However, even those who do see some evidence of natural law in Judaism seem to see it as only supplemental, a very secondary supplement to the revealed law of Scripture and the rabbinic writings.[25] It would seem that they are somewhat fearful of ascribing any more fundamental role to natural law in Jewish law and theology because, in principle anyway, that seems to constitute a surrender of revelation and its authority to human reason. Looking upon natural law as akin to human invention, instead of looking at it as a form of human discovery of what is not of human making, makes some Jewish thinkers fear that an a priori role for natural law will block rather than open up the revelation of God's higher law of the Torah to Israel.

For natural law thinking to be developed again (let alone thrive) among Jewish thinkers committed to the authority of the Jewish tradition (that is, for whom the Jewish tradition is essentially *Torah*), the defects of hyper-traditionalism (what some have called 'fideism') will have to be avoided. That can be done best when natural law is affirmed only as the subjective precondition *for* human acceptance of revealed law, but not as the objective ground *of* that law itself. A 'precondition' is what enables or prepares human subjects to accept revealed law intelligently and not just because that law was forced upon them by a greater power. The prior acceptance of natural law by

---

[25] See, e.g., J. David Bleich, 'Judaism and Natural Law' *Jewish Law Annual* 7 (1988) 5–42.

a society enables its members to accept revealed law as coming to build a community in the social space that acceptance of natural law has opened up for it. As such, natural law is not the foundation of revealed law, but only its receptacle. Natural law does that by limiting the pretensions of human creatures to invent their own fulfilment. And that is what Noahide-natural law does: all its norms limit human pretension, whether that pretension be in relation to God (idolatry and blasphemy), or in relation to their vital bodies (murder), or in relation to their sexuality (family destructive sexual activity), or in relation to their use of the goods of the world as if they were one's own creation (robbery). Nevertheless, natural law does not eclipse or overcome the revealed law of the Torah, because none of its norms provide any positive content for human fulfilment. The Noahide commandments are all negative (with the exception of the positive precept to establish courts of law, but whose function is to adjudicate violations of the negative precepts). The empty social space resulting from the acceptance of natural law cannot by itself constitute a true community, since it supplies no interhuman content. That content comes from revelation. Thus revealed law always has ontological priority. Natural law only has logical priority insofar as it makes revealed law truly intelligible *for us*.[26] And natural law only has epistemological priority insofar as it was known *before* the Torah was revealed to Israel.[27]

The careful analysis of natural law's function in the economy of God's higher law gives it heuristic value far richer than the more circumspect exponents of Noahide law can admit. It is not just an add-on (a posteriori); it is what makes the intelligent acceptance and development of revealed law possible. Yet it is not as foundational as some of its modern enthusiasts have wanted it to be, which is to make it the foundation of Jewish morality. To them, we can quote the Talmud: 'when one grasps too much, one grasps nothing; when one grasps something less, something is indeed held onto.'[28] A true precondition always accompanies what it has enabled to come to appear in the world. That accompanying precondition should never be overcome

[26] As such, it functions very much like a Kantian a priori. See *Critique of Pure Reason*, A34–5.

[27] See Novak, *Natural Law in Judaism*, 55–60.

[28] B. Rosh Hashanah 4b and parallels.

either by making it a foundation of revealed law (the liberal error) or by making it merely tangential to revealed law (the fideist error).

3.3. Natural Law is the Criterion for Human Legislation of Interhuman Relationships

One of the things most of the opponents of natural law in Judaism forget is that Jewish law pertaining to interhuman relationships, especially Jewish civil and criminal law, is an area where, as the Mishnah put it, 'there is little from Scripture and much more from tradition'.[29] Now one can see much of the 'traditional law' that was developed by the rabbis and recorded in the Talmud being based on ancient, inherited traditions, believed to go back to the time Moses was also receiving the Written Torah. These ancient traditions are taken to be concomitant specifications and elaborations of the norms revealed in the Written Torah or Scripture. However, most of the literary evidence suggests otherwise. It represents most of this civil and criminal law to be the development of human legislation by the rabbis themselves.[30] But, surely, the rabbis did not exercise their legislative authority arbitrarily as some sort of expression of their political power? Was not their political power, instead, to be justified by some objective criterion taken to be true? In other words, did not the justification of their legislative enactments have to be by persuasion? And can persuasion be anything but rational? And reason discovers what is true before it devises ways to instantiate that truth.

Most Jewish civil and criminal law is that it is based on what the rabbis discerned to be universally valid standards of justice. There being so little in this area from Scripture itself, the reasoning of the rabbis had to be far more conceptual than exegetical. Here is where the idea of natural law is needed for the coherent development of that type of conceptual reasoning in matters of human experience and practice that can hardly be taken as unique to Jewish thought. The rabbinic concept of this type of ethical criterion is called *tiqqun ha`olam* (literally, 'the moral rectification of the world').[31] This concept seems to more or less correspond to the natural law concept of

---

[29] M. Hagigah 1.7.
[30] See Maimonides, *Mishneh Torah*: Mamrim, Chapter 1.
[31] See M. Gittin 4.2–7.

the 'common good' (*bonum commune*), which is what makes the community more of a community by enabling the persons who are parts of the community to interact with one another with less fear of injustice and more expectation of communal peace. When this line of thought is followed, it shows how natural law criteria of justice limit the pretensions of humanly made positive law, and how natural law criteria of peace enable humanly made positive law to further true communion among the permanent members of the community and all those transients who can rightfully claim the community's shelter and hospitality.[32]

3.4. Natural Law is a Cultural Construct

Perhaps the greatest vulnerability of natural law theory, in both antiquity and modernity, is its seeming oblivion to and disrespect of cultural diversity, especially regarding normative issues. Natural law is taken to be what is universally true and right. But where does one actually experience this moral universe? Where is the 'nature' in natural law to be found? Furthermore, those who take their natural law inspiration from Aristotle must also be aware of the fact that he was speaking Greek to Greeks. It would seem that he largely followed the presumption of his culture that non-Greeks, or at least non-Greek speakers, are really subhuman 'barbarians'.[33] Consequently, they were, in effect, attempting to conceptualize what was regarded in their own culture to be optimal human standards, that is, when being 'Greek' and being 'human' were taken to be synonymous. Accordingly, Aristotle provided the rationale for the hellenization of the larger world conquered by the army of his most famous student, Alexander the Great. That process of hellenization included the proposal of Greek ethical standards to be universally authoritative. Also, the Roman concept of the 'law of nations' (*ius gentium*), without which their concept of *ius naturale* cannot be understood, was originally the name of an institution of Imperial Rome, conceived for the rule over certain non-Romans living under Rome. And natural law as conceived by Roman Catholic theologians is part of the authoritative teaching (*magesterium*) that explicitly attempts to

---

[32] See, eg, Lev. 19:33–34 and 24:22. cf. Gen. 19:9.
[33] See Plato, *Republic*, 469B–C.

include all humankind within herself. Jews too must admit that much of what could be termed 'Jewish universalism' is the hope of a kind of 'judaizing' of the world, as it were.[34] All of this leads to a considerable problem for the inherent 'universality' of natural law. In fact, has not natural law advocacy usually been part of a programme of reducing many cultural particularities to one particularity, which only becomes universal by the most dominant culture eliminating all its rivals?

The problem here is not only ethical-political. There is also an epistemological problem. Universal thinking by very particularly formed persons seems to be an imaginative attempt to constitute a world that exists apart from the culture of any particular people in the world. But does this abstraction correspond to anything actually experienced. Is it not a *utopia* ('no place'), what one contemporary philosopher has called 'the view from nowhere'?[35] Any attempt to locate some universal phenomenon is so vaguely general as to be normatively useless. Of course, our imagination can tentatively abstract us from our own cultures from time to time, but we cannot transcend our own cultures by means of some culturally neutral Archimedean fulcrum in order to escape them, destroy them, or re-create them. And we cannot cogently propose that our own culture be the universal standard to which every other culture should aspire to become or be forced to become by our conquest or seduction of it.

Perhaps it is more truthful and more useful to see natural law as the constitution of a normative universal horizon by thinkers *in* a particular culture *for* their own culture? Only thereafter can they negotiate transcultural space with thinkers from other cultures based upon an analogous constitution of a universal horizon in and for those other cultures. In that sense, then, it is truly multi-cultural speculation rather than 'mono-cultural' dictation. The coherence of that imaginative construction makes it plausible, even though it corresponds to nothing we actually experience in the world. Nevertheless, that imaginative-cultural construct is not the projection of an 'ideal'. It does not propose the realization of an idea we ourselves have thought up. Too often that kind of ideal projection is the philosophical justification of a process of the totalizing imperialism of one

---

[34] See David Novak, *Jewish-Christian Dialogue* (New York: Oxford University Press, 1989) 57–67.

[35] Thomas Nagel, *The View from Nowhere* (New York: Oxford University Press, 1986).

particular culture progressively swallowing up all other particular cultures in its march forward into a future it is constantly casting ahead of itself.[36] In modern times, that has been the rationalization of the cultural imperialism of a national culture that presents itself to be 'in the vanguard of progress'. Instead, the imaginative-cultural construction I am suggesting here as the way the idea of natural law operates in Jewish thought is the imagination of a real order Jewish thinkers can assume actually exists. Therefore, that imagination is not only an epistemological exercise; it is also an ontological exercise in its assumption of the extra-mental reality of its object. The reality of that order is not the product of human creativity, and the imagination of that order does not claim for itself universal authority. It is like imagining or inferring the blueprint of a building by examining the structure of the building. We can assume there is indeed such a blueprint, and we can discover that it has significant points in common with the blueprints of other buildings similarly constructed, even though we can never actually find a copy of it. Furthermore, we do not claim to have made the imagined blueprint ourselves, and we do not impose it on, or even propose it for, anyone else. We only share our thinking about it with others who are thinking about something similar. As such, imagining the blueprint is an heuristic enterprise rather than a political programme.

3.5. Natural Law is What Makes Jewish Moral Discourse Significant in an Intercultural World

The interest in natural law throughout Jewish history has been in proportion to the worldly involvement of Jews at any particular time and place. Thus in those times and places when Jews have either not been included as participants in an intercultural world, or have not wanted to be included in that world, the interest in natural law has been negligible or dormant. The best and most persistent example of this Jewish worldview has been that of almost all the kabbalists. For them, any world outside the inner unity of God-Torah-Israel is unreal or demonic.[37] The converse of this worldview has been that type of

---

[36] See G.W.F. Hegel, *Lectures on the Philosophy of Religion*, R.F. Brown, P.C. Hodgson, and J.M. Stewart, trans. (Berkeley, CA: University of California Press, 1988) 202, 371–4.

[37] See Novak, *The Image of the Non-Jew in Judaism*, 267–8.

Jewish theology that has seen affinities between some of the doctrines from the classical Jewish sources and some ideas of western philosophers, like the idea of natural law. But until modern times the worldliness of the Jews was largely an academic affair, mostly conducted through the exchange of thoughts written in books than through person-to-person discourse. When it came to social contact, however, the vast majority of Jews lived in their own walled-off ghettos.

The three great events (or perhaps periods) that have determined so much of modern Jewish life have, in effect, catapulted Jews personally into an intercultural world. As such, Jews have been thrown into a world of real political interaction. Here natural law has had to play an even greater role in Jewish life than it did in antiquity and the Middle Ages. These three great events have been: (i) the emancipation of West European Jews from being noncitizens of the larger polities in which the lived (the key date here being the French Revolution of 1789); (ii) the murder of at least half of European Jewry in the Holocaust (the key date here being the beginning of the Second World War in 1939); and (iii) the establishment of the State of Israel in 1948.

(i) In terms of the political emancipation of the Jews, natural law was at the heart of arguments for the enfranchisement of Jews as individuals in modern, secular nation-states. Citizenship was to be a human right dependent on the acceptance of a universally valid moral law. Since the end of the eighteenth century, all Jewish claims to be free of any kind of discrimination or second-class citizenship (bordering on being tolerated as resident-aliens) have been made in the language of natural or human rights, even when they have been made in a conceptually obtuse way.[38]

Now, if one thinks that this modern political claim has no precedence in the Jewish tradition (which has been all too frequently presumed), then one will have to separate the demand the Jewish tradition makes upon a modern Jew for ultimate loyalty from the claim a modern Jew makes for equal recognition in a secular polity. And, since the demand and the claim inevitably clash, a Jew will often have to make a choice of one over the other. All too frequently, modern Jews have chosen secular polity over Judaism and have,

---

[38] See Jacob Katz, *Tradition and Crisis* (New York: Schocken Books, 1971).

thereby, distorted the meaning of both the traditional demand on Jews and the modern demand of Jews on the new kind of polities where they live and want to live justly and peacefully. Well-thought-out (philosophically) and well-researched (historically) natural law arguments, which are more than political strategies, can persuasively make the case for proactive Jewish citizenship in secular polities that is consistent with the prime loyalty Jews owe to God, the Torah, and the Jewish people.[39] And they can do so without succumbing to the outrageous secularist demand that one must totally privatize (and thereby trivialize) one's religious tradition in order to be a citizen of a secular democracy in good faith.

(ii) In terms of the Holocaust, natural law enables Jews to argue that the mass murder of European Jewry by the Nazis and their cohorts to be a genuine crime against humankind per se. The universality inherent in any natural law argument saves the need many Jews feel to remind the rest of humankind of the agony of the Holocaust victims from being dismissed as an example of special pleading. The subjects of natural law are all human beings. And the Nazis attempted to justify their murder of the Jews by arbitrarily eliminating Jews from the definition of humankind. As such, they denied the humanity or human nature of the Jews.

The affirmation of natural law means that certain acts are never to be committed against any other human being, and certain acts are always to be committed for any other human being. And since natural law is in accordance with human nature as we find it and not human nature as we invent it, no one born of human parents can be cogently eliminated from the rights and duties prescribed by natural law for all those naturally human. In other words, the ontological falsehood employed by Nazi racism has to be seen as the presupposition of their morally indictable crimes.[40] It must, therefore, be refuted before their crimes can be returned to moral criteria for rational judgement and condemnation. That is why the first violation of the natural human right to life is the arbitrary elimination of any human being or class of human beings from the nature that makes one the subject of that right. It is an assault on truth before it is an assault on human

[39] See David Novak, *In Defense of Religious Liberty* (Wilmington, DE: ISI Books, 2009) 3–28.

[40] The most notorious formulation of this thesis is found in the 1930 book, *Der Mythus der 20, Jahrhunderts,* by Alfred Rosenberg, the leading Nazi racist theorist.

rights. And the only way to prevent those humans so removed from natural human status from claiming it, as they surely will, is to kill them. Furthermore, the reason humans enjoy unique rights, as we have seen, is because they are uniquely created by and uniquely related to God. That is why Nazi racism also denied the Creator God by replacing Him with the idolatry of the people (*Volk*), the state (*Reich*), and the *Führer*.[41] And idolatry is a violation of Noahide-natural law. For some Jewish thinkers, its prohibition is the first Noahide commandment.[42]

(iii) When it comes to the establishment and development of a Jewish polity in the ancestral land, which is now the State of Israel, the most fundamental political question is what sort of polity it is to be. Heretofore, it has been designated by its government to be both a Jewish and a democratic state. Yet many have seen an inherent paradox in that dual designation. Some religious Jewish thinkers have argued that a Jewish state cannot possibly be the same as a western-style democracy, and many secularist Jewish thinkers have argued that a religiously founded state would necessarily be a theocracy which, for them, could only be the inherently anti-democratic dictatorship of a rabbinical oligarchy.

Perhaps, though, a natural law perspective can begin to overcome this impasse. An affirmation of natural law that is Jewishly cogent is the affirmation of a set of rights and correlative duties seen as constituting God's law for all humankind, and knowable through human reason. In fact, we Jews would have been in no position to accept the Mosaic Torah intelligently unless we had already been governed according to this more general law. Is not this, then, something that could be the basis of a certain compromise between religious and secularist Zionists? Of course, like any compromise, it would involve a each side accepting at least part of a position it had not been able to accept in the past, and not asserting or bracketing a position it did advocate in the past.

For the religious, this would mean bracketing its advocacy of a Jewish state governed according to the full law of the Mosaic Torah, especially as administered by a rabbinical establishment. That would

[41] See Emil Fackenheim, *Encounters Between Judaism and Modern Philosophy* (New York: Basic Books, 1973) 188–95.

[42] B. Sanhedrin 56b re Exod. 32:8 and Hos. 5:11; Maimonides, *Mishneh Torah*: Melakhim, 9.1.

have to be bracketed if for no other reason than that, for that kind of Torah to have moral authority, it would have to have the support of the overwhelming majority of not only Israeli Jewry, but of world Jewry. What it would require, in fact, is a total Jewish reiteration of the covenant God made with all Israel at Sinai.[43] That is, of course, at present a messianic desideratum, not a political likelihood at all. But would not the acceptance of Noahide-natural law, itself the precondition for the acceptance of the law revealed at Sinai, be better than the merely positive human law according to which the State of Israel is now governed?

For the secularists, this would mean their acceptance of a law Jews have seen as being divine law. That would involve a bracketing of the public atheism many of them avow. But would that acceptance of the idea of divinely mandated natural law, however hypothetically, not connect them to the Jewish tradition in a way they have blocked in the past? Is that not better than the charge made against them that they have no real connection to the Jewish tradition, and that in their whole worldview they are only Hebrew-speaking pagans, who have not even affirmed what is best learned from human reason and experience? Would acceptance of a natural law philosophy, which could be shown is definitely within the Jewish tradition, not give them something authentically Jewish in common with religious Jews, that is, if religious Jews could be persuaded of its theological authenticity?

Perhaps a rethinking of natural law by Jews can contribute to the greatest intellectual challenge to the Jewish people today, which might be to find a cogent definition of a Jewish state that can find favour in the eyes of God and all humankind, that is, a definition of the Jewish state that can find both theological and philosophical justification.

---

[43] See B. Shabbat 88a.

Part IV

Medieval and Modern Politics: Maimonides and Spinoza on Reason and Revelation

7

The Politics of Fear: Idolatry and Superstition in Maimonides and Spinoza

Daniel H. Frank

This essay, which is a comparative study of Maimonides and Spinoza on the origins and ends of political society, is illustrative of Jerusalem's enduring presence. Spinoza will be seen to respond in his own way to Maimonides and the latter's view of the human good, a view that itself adapts Greek philosophical insights to monotheistic culture. As a result of this rich and deep dialogue, spanning two millennia, the enduring presence of Jerusalem may perhaps best be seen not so much as foundational, in the way Greek philosophy surely is, but rather as an intermediary, a brilliantly creative force carrying on and transforming Greek wisdom for its own purposes *and* setting the stage for what is to come. Jerusalem's enduring presence is Janus-faced, looking both back and to the future. Better to understand Athens and Jerusalem not as parallel streams, never intersecting, but rather as interconnected tributaries contributing to and feeding off each other. While Plato and Aristotle demonstrably influenced Maimonides, the latter fructified the ancients, and in so doing presents a set of philosophical views that, amongst other things, provided some starting points for Spinoza.

For present purposes, the starting point for political theorizing for both Maimonides and Spinoza is a manifest human weakness, a propensity for miscalculation and misevaluation grounded in hope and fear, that which Maimonides deems idolatry and Spinoza superstition. Such 'errors' have deleterious political effects, and to compensate for this Maimonides and Spinoza offer differing political solutions. I present these, but not before I outline in some detail what occasions them. So, this is an essay that has something to say about human nature and fear.

1. MAIMONIDES ON IDOLATRY AND THE LAW

For Maimonides, the first intention of the divine law is the extirpation of idolatry,[1] worship of false gods. Such idolatrous worship always looms as a possibility, and Maimonides presents in both *Mishneh Torah* and the *Guide of the Perplexed* a proto-history of humankind indicative of the propensity for lapsing into idolatry (*avodah zarah*).[2] From contemplative repose in Gan Eden to idolatrous worship already in the time of Enosh (two generations after Adam), Maimonides is intent on showing us the historical swing between right and wrong belief, grounded in the apparent human propensity to appease powerful forces in times of distress. So, humankind flailed about until Abraham (the 'pillar of the world'), the first monotheist. Maimonides presents Abraham as a philosopher amongst idolaters, who extracts monotheism from cosmological arguments. A veritable Socrates suffering at the hands of the unenlightened masses, Abraham, unlike Socrates, goes into exile, a journey both spiritual and geographic, the former indicative of the incommensurability of monotheism and idolatrous practice, and the latter grounded in a kind of Platonic pessimism founded on the fate of Socrates and the unlikelihood of the reform of idolatrous practice from within.

The biblical narrative of course does not end here. We are still at the front end of human history. But a pattern emerges. Abrahamic monotheism gives way to idolatrous worship once again in Egypt. The pain of servitude causes a forgetting of true worship. Consider also that Abrahamic monotheism is, as noted, grounded in philosophical speculation, not revelation. For Maimonides, there is a strong suggestion about the relative weakness of philosophy, philosophical speculation unaided, in sustaining true worship. Theory without materialization in ritual practice is far too weak to sustain itself. Again, the fate of Socrates, who attempted to instruct all and sundry solely by means of philosophical argumentation, and whose failure

---

[1] *Guide* 3.29.
[2] *Mishneh Torah*, H. Avodah Zarah 1.1–2; *Guide* 3.29.

motivated Plato into institutionalizing a 'sentimental education' prior to dialectic, can be seen in its own way to stand behind Maimonides' psycho-historical narrative. Abrahamic monotheism gives way to idolatry which (finally) gives way to Mosaic prophecy.

For Maimonides, Mosaic prophecy is unique.[3] Not only did Moses have a divine experience (encounter) like no other before him— Maimonides is clear that the imaginative faculty played no role in Mosaic prophecy—but his prophecy took a peculiar form. Moses did not attempt to instruct the masses by means of philosophical argumentation, as apparently did Abraham, unsuccessfully. Rather Moses presented a legal code, in fact a constitutional (constituting) structure for a nation. I think we must read this grand historical narrative from Gan Eden to Mosaic prophecy, from theoretical repose to idolatry to discursive argument to idolatry (again) to finally law-giving as suggestive of a philosophical anthropology. I shall flesh this out momentarily, and with it the political corollaries, but first let us note that a keen empiricism is at work in Maimonides' account. In one of the great chapters in the *Guide* (3.32) Maimonides is at work on the genesis of the law in general and of the *qorbanot* (sacrifices) in particular. He writes:

> When one considers the works of God as seen in nature, one will become conscious of God's subtlety and wisdom in creating the animal body with the interlocking functions of its organs and their complicated layout. One will also realize how wisely and subtly God arranged for the successive stages of the development of the whole individual. Many items in our Law exhibit the same careful planning . . . It is impossible to pass all at once from one extreme to another; it is therefore not in keeping with human nature for man to abandon suddenly all he has been used to. (Rabin, trans.)

These remarks are preliminary to his discussion of the continued need for sacrifices, and laws governing their appropriate functioning, and the comments are crucial for an understanding of why the (divine) law takes on the particular form it does. Maimonides is clear that the divine plan is grounded in the current state of human kind, the status quo. For Maimonides, past history (and human nature as it is) cannot be effaced, and, as he notes, '[i]t is impossible

---

[3] *Guide* 2.39–40; also *Commentary on the Mishnah*, Sanhedrin 10 (*Pereq Heleq*), principle 7.

to pass all at once from one extreme to another; it is therefore not in keeping with human nature for man to abandon suddenly all he has been used to.' At the time of the Mosaic legislation, the people were not far from slavery and idolatrous worship. Forty years' wandering reduced the number of those who once dwelled in Egypt. For Maimonides, this time span is part of the divine plan to properly prepare the people for the law, and provides the reason why the law was not given to the first generation of ex-slaves. But the aura of false worship still hovered. Backsliding was possible (inevitable?). As a result, sacrifices were not eliminated, but their referent was transferred, from 'created beings and figments of the imagination' to God Itself. Sacrificial practice is maintained, even as it becomes a part of divine worship.

Maimonides is invariably sensitive to time, place, and context. In response to one who wonders what prevents God from 'causing an inclination to accomplish the acts of obedience willed by Him and to avoid acts of disobedience abhorred by Him, *to be a natural disposition in us?*' (Pines, trans.; my emphasis), Maimonides responds tartly, 'God does not change at all the nature of human individuals by means of miracles' (*Guide* 3.32). God works with human nature as It finds it at a given moment in time, and it would be nothing less than miraculous to change the nature of humanity at an instant. As a result, Mosaic prophecy is the modality for legislation for the newly free, and a legal code presented in imperatival form, and consequentialist in its trajectory, is appropriate at this early stage of nation building. Ultimately the hope is that fear of punishment will give way to a more mature, deontological outlook, but the significant point now is that it is quite impossible to hasten such a change.

A bit more of this robust contextualism can be seen in Maimonides' discussion of prophecy in general. Following immediately upon his celebrated discussion of creation in part two of the *Guide*, Maimonides presents three views of prophecy,[4] and the one he labels 'our' view, and is presumably the one he supports, is a view of prophecy grounded in the prior state of the would-be prophet. Prophecy is given (when it is given) only to those 'wholly perfect and virtuous. As for an ignorant vulgar person, it is in our opinion utterly impossible that God should make him a prophet, any more than it would be

---

[4] *Guide* 2.32.

possible that he would make a prophet out of an ass or a frog' (*Guide* 2.32; Rabin, trans.).

In both his discussions of the law in general and of prophecy Maimonides is intent on grounding his comments on the status quo. Whatever we take the modality of 'impossibility' to entail about divine power, God works with humankind as It finds it. Humanity is not amenable to swift and radical change, even as Maimonides shifts the paradigm in his biblical narrative from one in which monotheism is grounded in pure theory to one in which true divine worship is grounded in law and commandment. The historical narrative from Gan Eden to Moses seems to indicate a rather deep pessimism about the durability and sustaining influence of philosophical argument in effecting deep change. The establishment of a proper character is key, and the law both sustains and develops this.

Maimonides, however does not give up on theory, and its power to motivate. Instead, he embeds it in the law. More than once he makes clear that the law, the Mosaic constitution, has two purposes, the welfare of the soul and the welfare of the body (politic). The latter precedes 'in the order of nature and of time' (*Guide* 3.27), and concerns itself with the administration of the state. Crowd control, and correlatively physical well-being, are necessary conditions for anything more exalted, and the purpose of the law is at first to ensure a just order and a citizenry committed to this. We might describe the welfare of the body (politic) as the 'secular' part of the divine law. The divine blueprint in very large part is thus concerned with inculcating a law-abiding attitude and the social virtues inclined to bring this about. But the divine law is not exhausted by its 'secular' part, for it is also concerned with the welfare of the soul, the communal inculcation of correct beliefs and opinions. The welfare of the soul, which is 'indubitably greater in nobility', is sensitive to the differing intellectual capacities of the members of the community. Maimonides is clear that the rational excellences are not equitably shared, and that philosophical speculation is available to just a few.

Nevertheless, and importantly, this does not lead Maimonides to alienate the intellectual from the community. On the contrary, the whole point of the *Guide* is to draw the intellectual back into the community from which he is temporarily estranged by imagining that the tradition does not support, and is not supported by, scientific speculation. For Maimonides, to speculate as you are able and to rectify belief is a divine imperative, embedded in the law. Philosophy is a religious obligation, for those so able.[5] At the far, upper end of speculation one unsurprisingly finds cosmological speculation and metaphysics (no less than Aristotle, Maimonides understands the *summum bonum* as theoretical engagement),[6] but also included in the perfection of the soul is the foundational study of the law, *ta'amei ha-mitzvot*. To ascertain the reasons for the commandments, to go beyond mere behaviour, is a desideratum, and obligatory for some.

As noted, the twofold purpose of the Mosaic legislation, the welfare of the body and the welfare of the soul, answers to perceived differences amongst human beings. Minimally, 'good citizenship' is what can reasonably be hoped for; for a few, more is possible, a reflection on foundations and on supra-political ends. All play their allotted part, and minimally live sociable lives through communal worship and fear of the consequences. The divine law is meant to bind the community in a kind of worship and way of life that is the antithesis of idolatrous worship. In this sense, love of God replaces irrational fear and communal worship replaces idolatrous practice.

For his part, Maimonides believes that the Mosaic legislation, a legal code supporting both civil order and supra-political ends, provides the means whereby *all* overcome idolatry, each in his own way, and achieve a portion of happiness. Although Maimonides is clear that the *summum bonum* is theoretical activity, and the ultimate perfection is to become rational *in actu*, the divine law was given to a collective. Given this reality, philosophy and politics mix, inasmuch as idolatrous practice may be overcome through both ritual (communal) worship and, at its highest level, philosophical speculation. Such speculation is, or leads to (what Maimonides, following the sages of old, calls) 'worship of the heart'.[7] Worship of the heart is given to but a few, but is not beyond the law. We are *commanded* 'to love God, and to serve Him with all your heart and with all your soul' (Deut. 11:13). Again, the law binds the collective, as it allows, better demands, that each achieve a portion of happiness commensurate with individual abilities.

---

[5] H. Davidson, 'Philosophy as a Religious Obligation' in S.D. Goitein (ed.), *Religion in a Religious Age* (Cambridge MA: Association for Jewish Studies, 1974) 53–68; D.H. Frank, 'The Duty to Philosophize: Socrates and Maimonides', *Judaism* 42 (1993) 289–97.

[6] *Guide* 3.54.

[7] *Guide* 3.51 (*Taanit* 2a).

To return to our starting point: the first intention of the divine law is to extirpate idolatry, misguided and irrational belief leading to wayward practice. The audience for the law is just those who stand in need of it, a motley crew. Crucial is that the law is for all, and no one is beyond it, even as the law addresses the differing needs of the collective. At its fundamental level the law supports, indeed commands, the study of physics and metaphysics. That these latter are part of the law, and not in opposition to it, sets Maimonides' view of the *summum bonum* at odds with his detractors, like Spinoza, who offers physics *in place of* Torah. The political implications of this bifurcation are considerable, and we now turn to Spinoza.

2. SPINOZA ON SUPERSTITION AND THE DIVINE LAW

Superstition (*superstitio*) plays much the same role for Spinoza in his political theorizing and philosophical anthropology that idolatry plays for Maimonides. They are the driving forces for instability. Both mental states are universal, grounded in fear and a human desire to curry divine favour and to counter presumed divine inconstancy. Imagination (*phantasia*) has run amok, and both idolatry and superstition are species of irrational belief.[8] The antidote for such irrationality is reason and the (rational) structure of law. As we have seen, for Maimonides the goal of law is social order and justice, and the first intention of the divine law is the extirpation of idolatry and the rectification of belief. The political implications of the rectification of belief are significant, for a just social order, grounded in supra-political ends, follows. Maimonides clearly distinguishes between secular politics, with mundane goals of social justice and healthy interpersonal relations, and a politics that is 'more' than this, with extra-mundane goals in view. As different as the trajectory of the political order, so is its instigator, according to Maimonides.[9]

---

[8] For Spinoza on *superstitio*, see especially the Preface to the *Theological-Political Treatise* (hereafter, *TTP*).

[9] *Guide* 2.40.

In this way Maimonides demarcates a sharp distinction between politician and prophet. The former is a true 'cave-dweller' in Plato's celebrated sense, whose only perfected mental faculty is the imagination.[10] Unsurprisingly the happiness aimed at is 'imaginary,' a semblance of true happiness. Contrarily, the prophet, the direct cause of the political regime established for both political and supra-political ends, is one whose rational faculties are perfect, and hence has a clear view of the true ends of human existence. The prophet is also able to apportion to each the requisite life plan, and the law that the prophet promulgates institutionalizes the distribution of happiness. It has long been noted that there is a marked similarity between the prophet as described by Maimonides (and Farabi) and Plato's philosopher-king. Both advance the cause of human well-being precisely because they are able to apply a transcendent insight to the material realm.[11]

Published anonymously in 1670, Spinoza's *Tractatus Theologico-Politicus* (hereafter, *TTP*) counters Maimonides and the latter's view of the foundations of political well-being. We shall see that for Spinoza a social order grounded in supra-political ends is disastrous, the cause of interminable warfare and social disruption. The potentially happy marriage between theology and politics, indeed the (Maimonidean) necessity of there being a prophet—a philosopher-king—to establish a political order that could finally defeat idolatry, is for Spinoza doomed to failure. Indeed, a theocracy, a political order grounded in divine law, will tend to institutionalize irrationality, and immaturate its citizenry by divinizing its leader and decreasing general autonomy, much as traditional religion 'has snuffed out the light of the intellect entirely'.[12] By contrast, it is freedom of thought, not its alienation to those with a presumed higher wisdom, that must be the goal of political life, if ever the individual and the state are to prosper.

Spinoza counters Maimonides quite directly. He construes prophecy as a species of imagination and the prophets as (no more than)

---

[10] *Guide* 2.37, 40.

[11] For the influence of Farabi's theory of prophecy on Maimonides, see L.V. Berman, 'Maimonides, the Disciple of Alfarabi', in J.A. Buijs (ed.), *Maimonides: A Collection of Critical Essays* (Notre Dame IN: University of Notre Dame Press, 1988); J. Macy, 'Prophecy in Alfarabi and Maimonides: The Imaginative and Rational Faculties', in Y. Yovel and S. Pines (eds), *Maimonides and Philosophy* (Dordrecht: Nijhoff, 1986).

[12] *TTP*, Preface (8, Gebhardt).

political leaders, charismatic to be sure.[13] What the prophets lack for Spinoza—philosophical wisdom—is precisely what Maimonides invested them with, and with this subtraction the traditional divine law (Torah) loses all claim to timelessness and geographical ubiquity. The Mosaic constitution comes to be understood as a particular law for a particular people at a particular time and in a particular place.[14] For Spinoza, the Mosaic law can lay no greater claim than any other constitutional structure to bring about the human good. Indeed, its theocratic nature with increasingly hierarchical and monarchical tendencies, perhaps understandable given the historical context of its promulgation, is viewed with suspicion.

One may be tempted to see in Spinoza (an uncharacteristic) agreement with Aristotle's remark at the very beginning of the *Ethics* that politics is the architectonic master science that studies the human good and the goals of human and civic life.[15] Spinoza's critique of Maimonides entails a subverting of the foundational role of prophecy in statecraft. With Hobbes and later Rousseau, Spinoza holds that there must be secular control over sacred matters and a manifest unconcern with any supra-political ends.[16] For Aristotle himself, the foundational role of politics is grounded in a view of humanity as, by nature, social. Since human beings are social, and the (human) good is in accord with (our) nature, the end of human life is to be construed in social and political terms. And what subject other than political science, a practical science that takes as its subject human beings in their natural environment, could be primary?

With the dethroning of prophecy and theology and the empowering of the secular over the sacred, it appears that for Spinoza politics and the secular trajectory of political and civic life reign supreme and define the horizon for the human good. And in a way this is the case. Political stability requires a principled non-interference between

---

[13] *TTP*, Chapters 1–2 ('On Prophecy' and 'On Prophets'). For commentary, see W. Z. Harvey, 'A Portrait of Spinoza as a Maimonidean', *Journal of the History of Philosophy* 19 (1981) 151–72; H.M. Ravven, 'Some Thoughts on What Spinoza Learned from Maimonides on the Prophetic Imagination, Part Two: Spinoza's Maimonideanism', *Journal of the History of Philosophy* 39 (2001) 385–406; H. Kreisel, *Prophecy: The History of an Idea in Medieval Jewish Philosophy* (Dordrecht: Kluwer, 2001) 544ff.

[14] *TTP*, Chapter 5 ('On Ceremonies and Narratives'), 72, Gebhardt.

[15] *Nicomachean Ethics*, I.2 (1094a–b).

[16] For a general treatment of Spinoza's political philosophy, see D.H. Frank and J. Waller, *Spinoza on Politics* (London: Routledge, forthcoming).

church and state, and between religion and politics. The decoupling of politics and traditional religion, and an understanding of 'true' religiosity and piety as a commitment to the practice of justice, charity, and biblical neighbourliness, are requisite, if ever religious strife is to be overcome, and, as importantly, intellectual maturity is to be advanced.[17] Political stability is advanced by commitment to acts of loving-kindness, indeed by the adaptation of true religiosity to political reality. The state has much to gain by supporting, morally if not financially, the Salvation Army and Habitat for Humanity (and the Peace Corps, one might add), and side-lining less tolerant religious initiatives. In Chapter 14 of the *TTP* Spinoza presents a *religio catholica*—a universal religion—which is taken to represent a distillation of the dogmas consistent with a religious way of life, and the vital importance of this *religio* is precisely that the commitment and self-fulfilment such a life engenders is also *politically* efficacious. In the end, for Spinoza, 'true' religion is morality, and surely the state has good reason to support the moral development of its citizenry.

However, at just this point, the Aristotelian 'perfectionism' that we might have imagined Spinoza was committed to, namely an understanding of human beings as perfected through social integration and deeds of loving-kindness, and a political order established for that very end, begins to come apart. For Spinoza, no less than Hobbes, both writing in times of terrible religious strife, the state is a protector against religious warfare and persecution, and in this role as guarantor of the peace it enables the citizenry to live without fear. But living without fear of persecution is less than what one gets from Aristotle, who grounds human well-being in a *natural* sociability. At the very end of the *TTP* Spinoza writes:

> [The state's] ultimate purpose is not to exercise dominion nor to restrain men by fear and deprive them of independence, but on the contrary to free every man from fear so that he may live in security as far as is possible . . . It is not the purpose of the state to transform men from rational beings into beasts or puppets, but rather to enable them to develop their mental and physical faculties in safety, to use their reason without restraint and to refrain from the strife and the vicious mental

---

[17] *TTP*, Chapter 14 ('On Faith and Philosophy'). Spinoza's decoupling of piety from its traditional religious moorings, and the intentional linking of it with (secular) notions of political and economic justice is Spinoza's way of adapting core virtues within traditional religion for purposes of political stability.

abuse that are prompted by hatred, anger or deceit. Thus the purpose of the state is, in reality, freedom.[18] (Shirley, trans.)

The foregoing comment about the role of the state sounds more like Mill (even Locke) than Aristotle. There is an (unAristotelian) pluralism, and a strong sense that the state as guarantor of security is decidedly neutral when it comes to the *summum bonum*. As we have noted, the state is concerned, for its own self-preservation, with the moral improvement of its citizenry, but beyond this it would appear to be studiously neutral, lest it recapitulate the divisive role of religion.[19]

We should note that for Spinoza, the freedom '*to* develop their mental and physical faculties in safety...' emerges from a quite different kind of freedom, freedom *from* fear of persecution. This latter (negative) freedom has a Hellenistic pedigree. Fear grounded in irrational superstition (ignorance of true causes) enslaves us, and the goal of life is to overcome such ignorance and the psychic disturbance consequent upon it. The antidote to fear is development of a rational and scientific outlook on the world. Analogously, the salvational role the Epicureans and the Stoics give to reason, Spinoza gives to the state, as the guarantor and enabler of freedom (from fear). In fact, his extreme (Epicurean-influenced) hostility toward traditional religion, as the product of imagination and vainglory, makes the state appear almost as the embodiment of Reason, promising fulfilment and happiness to all.

But just here a tension lurks. The dethroning of theology and the privatizing of traditional religion does no more than offer the *possibility* of happiness (by removing its impediments), and for Spinoza, no less than his Hellenistic forebears, this possibility of happiness is realized only if one adopts a rational outlook. No less than his ancient forebears, Spinoza indexes (true) happiness to a study of natural science. Only a deep, scientific study of the natural world order will

---

[18] *TTP*, Chapter 20 ('A Free State'), 240–1, Gebhardt.
[19] I reiterate the positively unAristotelian aspect of Spinoza's political theorizing. The state is not in the business of inculcating a 'thick' morality (M. Walzer, *Thick and Thin: Moral Argument at Home and Abroad* (Notre Dame IN: University of Notre Dame Press, 1994)). But perhaps, for Spinoza, it is concerned with inculcating those 'thin' (liberal) virtues, such as toleration, which are necessary conditions for a healthy cultural pluralism. If so, then Spinoza may perhaps be deemed a liberal republican, and less Hobbesian than often suggested.

free one from the kind of mental disease (superstition) that holds one in thrall. Short of this, one can at best be a good *citizen*.

For Spinoza, to study nature is to study the divine, for the divine law is the laws of nature.[20] This is an identity claim, and as such, it undercuts Maimonides' (traditional) view of the divine law in two distinct ways. First, for Maimonides, the divine law is a law for human beings, and has no direct application outside the human sphere. Second, the divine (Mosaic) law entered history at a certain time. Although it is eternal, being binding evermore *from* the time of its promulgation, it is not eternal in the sense of being uncreated. In both these regards, the laws of nature, as conceived by Spinoza, are at odds with the traditional conception of the divine law. They are applicable to the entire natural world, now inclusive of the supra-lunar and sub-human realms, and everything in between, and they are eternal and ungenerated. Indeed, Spinoza is perfectly entitled to denominate his laws of nature 'divine', as they possess a (kind of) changelessness and universal applicability.

However, his revisionism here should not hide his tacit agreement with Maimonides on the possibility of human happiness.[21] For Spinoza, living in accordance with nature, that is, living with a deep and abiding understanding of one's place in the cosmos and an understanding that all is as it must be and cannot be otherwise, is 'rare'.[22] Rare, because difficult, and difficult, because of the power of our passions. The state cannot change this, although it can remove an obstacle. For Spinoza, true happiness, freedom from (existential) fear, is the prize of but a few. A life committed to justice, charity, neighbourly love, and freedom from persecution is the goal of the state for all its citizenry, but this laudable goal provides no more in its own way than what Maimonides dubbed 'the welfare of the body'.[23] But there is more to human well-being than this for *both* Maimonides and Spinoza.

In their own (elitist) ways, both thinkers set the bar for human happiness very high. Prophecy for Maimonides is the *summum*

---

[20] And, correlatively, 'knowledge and love of God' is for Spinoza the *summum bonum* (*TTP*, Chapter 4 ('On the Divine Law'), 60–1, Gebhardt). Maimonides does not disagree, and both understand the *summum bonum* in 'theoretical' terms. I elaborate a bit more on this commonality in 'Divine Law and Human Practices' in S. Nadler and T.M. Rudavsky (eds), *The Cambridge History of Jewish Philosophy: From Antiquity through the Seventeenth Century* (Cambridge: Cambridge University Press, 2009) 804–6.

[21] See n. 20 above.   [22] See the very end of the *Ethics*.   [23] *Guide* 3.27.

bonum, while for Spinoza it is the study of physics, and the understanding of the cosmos attendant upon such study. Both are clear that this highest activity is quite solitary, and tends to remove the agent from the social sphere.[24] But a difference is to be noted in the final analysis. The Mosaic prophet, the analogue to the philosopher-king, uses his knowledge for humankind.[25] Alas, there is no political role I see for the Spinozist sage, except perhaps to write the *TTP* itself for the benefit of all![26] Spinoza's decoupling of theology from philosophy, and faith from reason, assures this.

In the end, I think it must be said that the picture of human society that Maimonides offers has a certain unity lacking in Spinoza's. For Maimonides, the divine law, like the biblical text itself, has something in it for everyone. For the mass of the community it offers stability and a form of life devoted to the extirpation of idolatry. For the more serious intellectual it refreshes with all manner of scientific knowledge and cosmological speculation, whose quest it explicitly commands. For Maimonides, science and philosophy are part of the law, and the particular means that binds the intellectual to the general community of believers, through knowledge and (consequent) love of God. On the other side, for Spinoza, the deep division between science and religion leaves the community itself deeply divided. While it may be held together by the moral principles that enrich Judaism and Christianity, it leaves the would-be sage to his own devices.

---

[24] For Maimonides, note in particular his gloss on *Song of Songs*, 5.2 in *Guide* 3.51.
[25] *Guide* 3.54; see D.H. Frank, 'The End of the *Guide*: Maimonides on the Best Life for Man', *Judaism* 34 (1985) 485–95.
[26] Or maybe 'for the benefit of just *some*', namely the 'philosophical reader' of the text (*TTP*, Preface, 12, (Gebhardt)).

8

Torah as Political Philosophy: Maimonides and Spinoza on Religious Law

Edward C. Halper

Both Maimonides and Spinoza are rationalists. Both stress the importance of reason as a tool to arrive at knowledge and as a faculty whose cultivation is the principal human end. Since religious law is not generally thought to be rational, it must seem counterintuitive to argue, as I will here, that both philosophers justify it rationally. By 'religious law' I mean a part of what Maimonides calls 'divine law'.[1] This latter includes both (a) the moral laws 'whose utility is clear to the multitude' (*misphatim* or judgments) and (b) the commandments 'whose utility is not clear to the multitude' (*ḥuqqim* or statutes) (III.26.507). Among the former are the prohibitions against theft and murder; among the latter the prohibition of eating meat with milk. (The way Maimonides distinguishes these two classes implies that together they comprise *all* the commandments, though the *ḥuqqim* have traditionally been taken to be a narrower class.)[2]

---

[1] M. Maimonides, *The Guide of the Perplexed*, Part II, chapter 40, 384, S. Pines, trans. (Chicago: University of Chicago Press, 1963). Hereafter cited as: II.40.384. On this chapter, see J.L. Kraemer, 'Naturalism and Universalism in Maimonides' Political and Religious Thought' in *Me'ah She'arim: Studies in Medieval Jewish Spiritual Life in Memory of Isadore Twersky*, G.B.E. Fleischer et al (eds) (Jerusalem: Magnes, 2001) 47–81.

[2] *Babylonian Talmud*, *Yoma* 67b distinguishes *ḥuqqim* and *mishpatim* with examples but does not say that this distinction is exhaustive. J. Stern, *Problems and Parables of Law: Maimonides and Nahmanides on Reasons for the Commandments (Ta'amei Ha-Mitzvot)* (Albany: SUNY Press, 1998) 33–4, notes that Maimonides extends *ḥuqqim* beyond their traditional bounds by including sacrifices. However, Stern, following tradition, takes *ḥuqqim* to be commandments whose *reasons*

Spinoza reserves 'divine law' for 'the universal law that consists in the true way of life', a class whose content is identical with Maimonides' (a), and he contrasts it with what he calls 'ceremonial observances', clearly class (b).[3] Clearly echoing Maimonides (as we will see), Spinoza claims that the Torah sets out *both* classes as of utility to the Hebrew state, though he objects that the commandments in class (a) are better understood as *universal* moral injunctions. Nonetheless, both agree that the Torah's commandments consist of: (1) moral laws that are valuable in all societies and (2) laws the Torah gives to Jews alone. The latter I term 'religious law'. Again, it is odd to propose that two rationalists endorse 'religious law'. Still odder is the thought that Spinoza, despite emphasizing love of God over the Mosaic commandments, recognizes an important role for *particular* religious practices in the state. Oddest of all, perhaps, is the notion that the Torah espouses a political philosophy.

The Torah is not explicitly philosophical, but both Maimonides and Spinoza see it as philosophical in a subtly qualified sense. My aim here is to explain this sense, to argue that it is virtually the same for both thinkers, and to explain its enduring importance. In particular, I think that both appreciate the Torah as, among other things, a kind of political programme, based upon philosophical truths, that aims both to inculcate the moral laws by regular practice and to use religious laws as what I call 'devices' to attain political ends. Since they think that everyone recognizes the content of moral law, they find the Torah's religious law more philosophically interesting. As Maimonides notes, it is because of Israel's religious laws (*ḥuqqim*) that other nations declare it a 'wise and understanding people' (Deut., 4.6; *Guide*, III.31.524). The benefit of religious law is not apparent because it is collective rather than individual, and religious laws aim to motivate individuals to acts that cultivate socially beneficial virtues. Whereas Maimonides aims to explain religious laws and to show their enduring benefit for diverse segments of the Jewish community,

---

are unknown (39), whereas Maimonides thinks it is their *benefits* (פאידה) that are unknown. The former definition would exclude from *ḥuqqim* Sabbath and festivals because their reasons are well known, whereas Maimonides' definition includes them because their benefits are not (cf. III.32.531). Since Maimonides' usage is nonstandard, it seems to me best to avoid the term *ḥuqqim* and use 'religious law' to designate all commandments besides the *mishpatim*.

[3] B. Spinoza, *Theological-Political Treatise*, S. Shirley, trans. (2nd edn., Indianapolis: Hackett, 2001) chapter 5, 59–60. Hereafter: *TTP* 5.59-60.

Spinoza maintains that the Torah's religious laws are fatally flawed and he advances what amount to secular alternatives, different sets for different types of states, that are not subject to this defect.

Their treatments of religious law are of enduring importance in the normative sense that motivation is a significant, albeit neglected portion of political philosophy. Both think that the Torah aims to motivate individuals to perform actions necessary to sustain the sort of community in which individuals can fulfil their human nature. In this context, to motivate is not to induce a particular choice but to mould the *desire* to sustain the community. This sort of motivation receives little or no attention in contemporary political theory. Instead, the latter focuses on determining political principles and the acts or choices that put them into practice. Maimonides and Spinoza see that between principle and action lies motivation and that without motivation, principle never becomes action. Since they also think that true principles and actions appropriate to them are clear to all, their political philosophies focus on creating motivation, specifically, through laws and institutions that serve as 'political devices'. In my view, modern liberal democracies ignore motivation to their detriment and suffer a host of problems in consequence. I will not justify this contention here. Instead, I aim to show how both Maimonides and Spinoza regard the Torah as a model set of political devices and, thereby, to make an indirect case for the importance for political philosophy of both motivation and the Torah. I note that this essential dimension of their thought has received little or, in Spinoza's case, virtually no attention.

1. POLITICAL DEVICES

What are 'political devices' and how do religious laws serve as political devices? Aristotle mentions some examples of political devices ($\sigma o \phi i \sigma \mu a \tau a$—see 1297a34–6) in his *Politics* (4.13): wealthy property owners can be induced to sit on juries if they will be heavily fined for their absence, whereas the poor can be induced to sit on juries if jury members are paid. The former device might be used by an oligarchy, the latter by a democracy. It is important that the appropriate type of device depends on the type of state it sustains and that these devices target particular classes, rather than the whole state. Important, too, is that neither device is perfect: the wealthy can choose to pay the fine, and the poor can forgo the reward. A device can *motivate*, not guarantee action. A final characteristic of devices is that they can be tweaked for more specific results. For example, to make it more likely that offices will be held by people in the middle class, the fine for property owners' not serving should be relatively small. Then, owners of large estates would be likely to decide to pay the fine rather than serve, whereas small farmers would find the fine onerous and serve. It is hard to imagine a single device that would induce all citizens to hold office: a state that would *both* fine the rich and reward the poor would risk excluding the middle class.

Aristotle's treatment of devices is seldom discussed because it appears in his account of the best possible state (1288b21–39) in *Politics* 4–6, whereas most contemporary readers have focused on his account of the best state and its principles in books 1–3. Aristotle sees the state as a self-sustaining configuration of offices. In the *best* state a wise and virtuous ruler (cf. *N.E.* 6.8.1141b23–25) ensures that each office is filled by a person ideally suited to it. Lacking such a ruler, the *best possible* state, as well as lesser states, need devices to motivate people to serve in the offices that sustain the state. Devices are, as it were, institutionalized substitutes for the knowledge possessed by those capable of ruling the best state.

My contention is that religious laws serve as political devices. Maimonides sometimes speaks of a 'divine ruse', as, for example in III.32, where he argues that the Torah's institution of sacrifice is a ruse because it uses a mode of worship associated with idolatry to wean people away from idolatry and towards the apprehension of God. Often, though, he describes ruses without using this term.[4] Thus, in III.46 Maimonides accounts for details of specific sacrifices by referring to specific idolatrous practices.[5] At the end of the chapter, speaking specifically of pilgrimages on certain festivals, he mentions the 'renewal of the Law' and the 'fraternity' that comes from the festivals. He is referring to the assembly that takes place on Succot at the end of the Sabbatical year and also to the second tithe. The

---

[4] Maimonides' Arabic verb for device is תלטף. It means literally acting graciously, and it suggests that religious laws are acts of Divine grace. The Hebrew translation, עשה תחבולה, means literally making a ruse. Pines translates variously as, e.g., 'gracious ruse', 'wily graciousness'; see, e.g., III.32.525, 527, 528, III.33.532, III.45.580.

[5] In his introduction to the *Guide*, Pines calls sacrifices 'contrivances' that Moses uses 'to hammer into shape the religious and national community'.

latter was generally sold and its proceeds used to buy food that had to be eaten in Jerusalem. Since there was usually too much food to be consumed by the farmer and his family, food was given to the poor, fostering fraternity. (Every third year, the second tithe was simply given to the poor.) Likewise, on the three festivals the Torah commands pilgrimages to Jerusalem with offerings for the Temple, some of which were to be eaten in festive meals by those bringing them. At III.43.570, Maimonides notes that these festivals along with Rosh Hashannah and Shemeni Atzeret were instituted not only for 'rejoicings and pleasurable gatherings, which in most cases are indispensable for man' but also for 'the establishment of friendship, which must exist among people living in political societies'. Additionally, he claims that Passover and Succot foster humility and submission by commanding people to live in tabernacles and eat unleavened bread (III.43.572).

Maimonides notices that the Torah prohibits eating meat with milk in conjunction with a discussion of pilgrimage to the Temple, from which he infers that such a meal belonged to an idolatrous practice and that the Torah prohibits it to undermine idolatry (III.48.599). If the pilgrimage and the festive meals promote friendship among the Hebrews, then we can infer that idolatrous practices are inimical to this friendship and that prohibiting them is a way to foster friendship. Why, though, does the prohibition against milk and meat endure—Maimonides says that *ḥuqqim* are 'absolute and eternal' (III.34.353)—when the idolatrous practice has long ceased?[6] The answer, I think, is that all the religious laws continue to separate Jews from other groups and, thereby, to draw them together into a community.

The benefits Maimonides describes are not apparent to the person who observes these religious commandments. He supposes himself to be acting for God's sake, but the result is fraternity and friendship that are necessary for a state as well as a disposition to submit to authority

---

[6] The issue is generally considered in terms of the *reasons* for the commandments, rather than the *benefits* from them (see n. 1). Thus, A. Hyman, 'A Note on Maimonides' Classification of Law', in *Proceedings of the American Academy for Jewish Research* (1978–9) 46, 334, suggests that some laws are 'conditioned by historical circumstances'. Referring to III.41.563, J. Stern, *Problems and Parables of Law* (1998) 40–1, suggests two reasons why the *ḥuqqim* cannot be changed: (a) the *ḥuqqim* would be liable to corruption and (b) changes would lead people to think that the *ḥuqqim* did not come from God.

that makes citizens willing to obey laws. Thus, he who observes these commandments unwittingly acts to preserve and enhance the state or, now, after the destruction of the Hebrew state, when charity is substituted for sacrifice, the community. Since a person is more likely to observe the festivals if he does not recognize their political ends, these ends should be considered candidates for what Maimonides would suggest but conceal from his readers (Introduction.6–7).

Whereas Aristotle's devices are rewards or punishments intended to motivate actions, Maimonides' devices consist of legislated *actions* (commandments) that mould dispositions for other sorts of actions. Thus, observance of the festivals disposes a person to friendship from which, in turn, he tends to avoid acts of wrongdoing (III.27.510) and to perform acts of love, pity, and mutual benefit that Maimonides calls 'the greatest purpose of the Law' (III.49.601–2). In short, the Torah's devices foster character traits that are essential for a community.

Whereas the benefits of religious laws are indirect and thus not apparent, Maimonides denies that anyone 'was ever so perplexed for a day as to ask why we were commanded by the Law that God is one, or why we were forbidden to kill or steal, . . . or why we were ordered to love each other' (III.28.513). He is talking about moral laws that are recognized by all states and about a belief in God that he thinks is essential. No one puzzles about them because their utility is clear: they 'communicate correct opinion', 'abolish reciprocal wrong-doing', and 'inculcate a noble quality'. The last refers to moral virtue, for by repeatedly practicing these commandments, a person comes to possess those dispositions that Maimonides, following Aristotle, regards as moral virtues.[7] It is different with religious laws. Someone who follows the commandment not to steal comes to be disposed not to steal, whereas someone who observes the festivals becomes disposed to something quite different, namely, to become friends with others in the community and to perform acts of kindness for them.[8]

Spinoza has the same understanding of the religious commandments. As I noted, he calls them 'ceremonial observances' and

---

[7] This is a major theme of Maimonides' *Eight Chapters* (see chapter 4 in R.L. Weiss and C.E. Butterworth (eds), *Ethical Writings of Maimonides* (New York: Dover, 1975) 71–2)), that I think Maimonides tacitly assumes in the *Guide*. Puzzlingly, moral laws in chapter 4 include all forbidden foods, whereas the prohibition of eating meat with milk is mentioned in chapter 6 as a *ḥoq*.

[8] See *Eight Chapters*, chapter 6.

distinguishes them from what *he* terms 'divine law'. This latter 'consists of the true way of life' that is 'inscribed in the heart, or mind'. It is 'by nature', whereas ceremonial observances are 'by convention' (5.59–60). Divine law leads to 'blessedness'; ceremonial observances promise nothing more than material advantage and pleasure. These latter are attained through the state, and Spinoza stresses the role in preserving and strengthening the Hebrew state played by ceremonial observances 'so adapted to the nature of their government that they could not be practiced by the individual but involved the community as a whole' (5.59). Apart from the laws commanding these observances and, thus, the nature of their state and 'social organization', the Israelites' beliefs and virtues were indistinguishable from those of other nations (3.46–8).

What does Spinoza understand by 'ceremonial observances' and how do they lead to material advantages? Referring to Isaiah and the Psalms, he mentions under this head sacrifices and festivals (5.59). These and other observances were designed 'to give them the constant reminder of obedience. This, then, was the object of ceremonial observance' (5.65). He means that in performing the ceremonial observances, a person comes to develop obedience as a character trait. Thus, whereas Maimonides explains the commandments individually or in groups, Spinoza lumps them all together and declares that all serve the same end, obedience. Now obedience to the law is necessary for every state, for all states require their citizens to set aside their own perceived individual good to obey the sovereign's laws and to work for the common good. Obedience can always be and usually is motivated by fear of the sovereign. However, Spinoza thinks that Moses was able to institute a state religion that made people 'do their duty from devotion rather than fear', for he encouraged the people with prospects of *reward* rather than threats of punishment (5.62–5, 17.198–200). In particular, the festivals ('the requirement to give themselves up to rest and rejoicing at certain seasons of the year') encourage people to desire what the laws command; indeed, Spinoza claims that 'no more effective means can be devised to influence men's minds' (17.199). In short, Moses used 'ceremonial observances' to make men obey the law out of love of God rather than fear of punishment (cf. 3.46–7).

This account is close to that of Maimonides. Whereas Maimonides thinks the pilgrimages and festivals promote friendship and fraternity that motivate people to follow the commandments and mentions 'submission' only in conjunction with eating unleavened bread and dwelling in tabernacles, Spinoza evidently thinks that joyous celebrations of festivals are *rewards* that motivate citizens *to obey* the laws. In other words, Spinoza substitutes obedience (=submission) for Maimonides' friendship. Spinoza is also following Maimonides when he emphasizes the material value of religious commandments for the state and individuals (cf. 5.60 with III.27.510–11). However, Maimonides thinks the *moral* commandments are also materially beneficial and, apparently, that both kinds have a hand in inculcating correct opinion in the soul. I will return to opinion in section 4.

The one important point on which they differ is the continuing value of the Torah's religious laws. Because he focuses on the value of tithes and sacrifices to the *donor*, Maimonides can easily substitute charity for sacrifice and ensure the same utility.[9] Spinoza, however, focuses on the value of these donations for their *recipients*, the priests and Levites. Inasmuch as there is no longer a Hebrew state, a Temple, or people serving in the Temple, and since Mosaic laws were instituted to maintain the state, Jews are no longer bound by them (5.61–2, 65). He knows, of course, that these laws enable Jews to maintain a separate identity within the larger communities in which they live, but he thinks such a separate community is an unwarranted rejection of the sovereignty of the state (4.44–7).

Spinoza argues that the elevation of the tribe of Levi to religious service was the fatal flaw in a state that might otherwise have lasted indefinitely (17.203). The Torah's original plan was that the first born in each family would be responsible for Temple service, but this was changed—from anger and vengeance, Spinoza thinks—when all but the Levites worshipped the golden calf (17.200–3). The Levites were rewarded with Temple service but also, in consequence, deprived of any portion in land and, thus, they were unable to support themselves. They were forced to rely on tithes and gifts from other tribes.[10] People would have been willing to maintain their relatives as religious functionaries, and all the tribes would have been equal; but they deeply resented supporting a separate tribe in 'idleness', especially

---

[9] He may also have in mind Aristotle's argument in *Nicomachean Ethics* 9.7 that the donor is more likely to love the recipient than the reverse.

[10] T. Verbeek, *Spinoza's Theological-Political Treatise: Exploring the 'Will of God'* (Hampshire, England: Ashgate, 2003) 132–3, does not see that Spinoza's issue is the Levites' material sustenance.

since the Levites were constantly rebuking their religious observance. Moreover, since even kings were barred from performing Temple rites, there was an ongoing struggle between temporal and religious authority.

Strikingly, the festivals, sacrifices, and donations that Maimonides claims promote friendship and harmony are, according to Spinoza, the root of the strife that tore apart the Hebrew state. But, again, the issue is confined to the Levites. Spinoza has the highest praise for the festivals, as we saw, and he has no issue with sacrifices and donations in themselves. His criticism needs to be understood in the context of his overall claim that the Torah's religious laws did an extraordinary job of motivating people to obey the sovereign out of love. Like Maimonides, he regards religious laws as political devices, and he sees their end to lie in the stability and material prosperity of the Hebrew state, a state that, absent its flaw, would have endured indefinitely.[11]

This praise of the Hebrew state is not undermined by Spinoza's famous claim that Jesus' teaching is morally superior to Moses' Law (5.60). Jesus expounded his teachings 'because he was intent on improving men's minds rather than their external actions', whereas Moses was 'concerned to found a good commonwealth' (7.91–2).[12] The 'substance' of Christianity 'consists essentially in moral teachings' that can be 'grasped by everyone by the natural light of reason' (11.142). Christianity has nearly nothing to say about how to organize a state, yet we know from the *Ethics* that man lives more freely in a state (IVP73).[13] Given the importance Spinoza attaches to the state, we must wonder whether his praise of Christianity belongs to a rhetorical strategy designed to mask his implicit criticism of its missing political dimension and his own effort to make it more like

[11] A.V. Garrett, *Meaning in Spinoza's Method* (Cambridge: Cambridge University Press, 2003) 134, claims that Spinoza thinks 'Scripture should be . . . viewed . . . as the primitive and superstitious ramblings of a tribe of on again, off again desert nomads.' Rather, Spinoza insists that as long as it is properly interpreted, 'we shall find practically nothing in Scripture that can be shown to contradict the light of nature' (6.83).

[12] A. Donagan, 'Spinoza's Theology' in *The Cambridge Companion to Spinoza*, D. Garrett, ed. (Cambridge: Cambridge University Press, 1996) 370, notes that even though Spinoza claims Jesus is superior to Moses in having adequate perception of eternal truths, he regards Jesus as a man, not God.

[13] Spinoza acknowledges that some Christian ceremonies had political ends (5.65), but he denies that they are essential to Christianity.

Judaism. There is, in any case, no doubt that the *TTP* aims to supplement Christianity with a suitable state.[14] Spinoza does not introduce ceremonial observances—only a prophet could do that. Instead, as we will see, he suggests a way that freedom of religion and collective political decisions enable citizens to put into practice the morality Jesus preached, but only when accompanied by political devices modelled on those of the Torah.

2. MAIMONIDES' JUSTIFICATION OF RELIGIOUS LAW

We have seen that both Maimonides and Spinoza see the Torah as expounding not only universal moral laws, but also religious laws that serve as political devices. Let us now consider why they think such devices are necessary. Neither makes a direct case. Surprisingly, their arguments emerge from their treatments of the Garden of Eden parable and from their organization of the parts of philosophy.

Maimonides examines this parable in his much-discussed second chapter of the *Guide*.[15] This chapter begins by mentioning a challenge from a 'learned man': how could Adam and Eve's expulsion from the garden be a punishment if the result of Adam's disobedience is his becoming more perfect by gaining knowledge of good and evil? Before answering, Maimonides barrages the absent questioner with abuse. Indeed, his remarks are so strong and the question so seemingly innocent that the reader can hardly help being distracted and confused. Eventually, Maimonides answers that since Adam is made

---

[14] H.M. Ravven, 'Some Thoughts on What Spinoza Learned from Maimonides on Prophetic Imagination. Part Two: Spinoza's Maimonideanism', *Journal of the History of Philosophy* (2001) 39, 212, writes: 'Spinoza envisioned . . . all modern polities . . . along the general lines of the democratic political constitution of the original Jewish commonwealth.'

[15] Recent studies include: L.V. Berman, 'Maimonides on the Fall of Man' *AJS Review* (1980) 5, 1–16; M. Fox, 'Interpreting Maimonides', in *Interpreting Maimonides: Studies in Methodology, Metaphysics, and Moral Philosophy* (Chicago: University of Chicago Press, 1990) 173–98; S. Pines, 'Truth and Falsehood vs. Good and Evil: A Study in Jewish and General Philosophy in Connection with the *Guide of the Perplexed*', in *Studies in Maimonides*, I. Twersky, ed. (Cambridge, Mass.: Harvard University Press, 1990) 95–157; H.T. Kreisel, *Maimonides' Political Thought: Studies in Ethics, Law, and the Human Ideal* (Albany: SUNY Press, 1999) 71–5, 100–6; J. Stern, 'The Maimonidean Parable, the Arabic *Poetics*, and the Garden of Eden', *Midwest Studies in Philosophy* (2009) 33, 224–44.

in God's image, he is endowed with intellect (see I.1.22); and in respect of his intellect, Adam grasped the truth of God's command-ment not to eat from the tree. However, Adam also had faculties of sensation and imagination that led him to desire the fruit of the tree, despite what he knew.[16] Hence, he was punished 'measure for mea-sure' (*midah keneged midah*) by being deprived of (some part of) his intellect and by coming to know what is commonly accepted as 'good and evil'. This latter is what judges (*elohim*) have. In other words, Adam loses his thoroughly 'intellectual apprehension' of the truth and comes to grasp in its stead what is generally accepted as good.

Maimonides is claiming that the apprehension of truth and falsity belongs to the intellect, whereas the apprehension of good and bad belongs to some other faculty, a faculty of opinion. It is sometimes objected that Adam could not have known that he should obey God's commandment unless he already grasped good and evil. However, with a perfect intellect, Adam must have fully understood the com-mandment, and this knowledge should have sufficed to make him obey it. It did not. Even perfect knowledge can be overcome by desire and imagination. Adam's punishment is a kind of permanent loss of the intellect that they had overcome and the substitution of common opinions as an additional motive force in his soul.

Maimonides agrees with Aristotle that knowledge can be overcome by desire; this is, incontinence (*akrasia*). Further, his distinction between the intellect and opinion is rooted in Aristotle's distinction between theoretical and practical sciences. Whereas the-oretical sciences demonstrate necessary truths about subjects that cannot be otherwise, practical sciences, dealing with subject matters that admit irregularity, arrive at conclusions that are only as precise as their subjects (*N.E.* 1.3.1094b11–28). Physics and mathematics know truths. Ethics and politics, both of which aim at the human good,

---

[16] At II.30.356–7 Maimonides, drawing on a Midrash, stresses the intermediation of Eve between Adam and the serpent, and claims it was Satan, riding on the serpent, who misled Eve. Satan plausibly represents imagination and the serpent the soul's non-intellectual side. The lesson is that when the former persuades the latter, the latter can undermine the intellect, H.A. Davidson, *Moses Maimonides: The Man and His Works* (New York: Oxford University Press, 2004) 346–7. Alternatively, Satan is lust and the serpent is imagination, and the former uses the latter to turn away reason, Sforno, *Commentary on the Torah*, R. Pelcovitz, trans. and ed. (Brooklyn, NY: Mesorah, 1997) 22.

explore 'common opinions' (*endoxa*) about what is likely to contribute to this good.[17]

It is striking, then, that Maimonides thinks that the truth of a commandment about how to live, which clearly falls under ethics, was grasped by Adam's intellect, rather than opinion. He is proposing that, contrary to Aristotle, there is a *theoretical* science of ethics and that Adam had this science before he was expelled from the Garden of Eden. Given that Maimonides identifies knowledge of good and evil with generally accepted opinions, the commandment not to partake of knowledge of good and evil is tantamount to an injunction not to rely on opinion. That is to say, Adam grasps with his intellect that he ought not to rely on opinion: he understands that he cannot understand anything except through the understanding, that is, the intellect. There is, thus, a reflexive, self-certifying character to God's commandment to Adam. Possessed of this knowledge, Adam hardly needs a divine commandment not to rely on opinion.

All the more surprising, then, that even such a self-certifying knowledge could be unseated by desire and imagination. This possibility is evidently the lesson of this Torah parable. Adam had the truth, but he was unable to hold on to it. Incontinence is possible because the intellect cannot protect itself from the blandishments of the sensation of beauty and the imagination of pleasure. Although Adam is deprived of a portion of his intellect in punishment, God grants him a kind of substitute: knowledge of good and evil consists of *generally accepted* opinions about right and wrong that constitute a legitimate basis for a judge's decisions. So Maimonides in I.2.

What is really striking here, but easy to miss, is that accepted opinions about good and evil are both normative and universal. Since we are *all* descendants of Adam, we are all like judges knowing good and evil. The recognition of morality is a common possession of mankind. We do not need the Torah to instruct us in moral values.

Why, then, is religion valuable? What role can Judaism and the commandments possibly play in moral life? I.2 does not answer these questions directly or even ask them. However, I think Maimonides

---

[17] D.H. Frank, 'Reason in Action: The "Practicality" of Maimonides' *Guide*', in *Commandment and Community: New Essays in Jewish Legal and Political Philosophy*, D.H. Frank, ed. (Albany: SUNY Press, 2002) 76, 78–9, argues that the *Guide* resembles Aristotle's *Nicomachean Ethics* in being a practical science that aims to bring readers to a theoretical grounding of what is known by common opinion.

suggests answers when he abuses the imagined person who asks about
the parable, and I think he includes the abuse just to make this point.
Before mentioning the question, Maimonides says, 'every Hebrew
knew that the word *Elohim* is equivocal' (I.2.23). Since the interlocutor is assumed not to know this equivocation, we can safely
assume that he is not a Hebrew. The same can be surmised from
Maimonides' suggestion, on the next page, that the questioner regards
the Torah as a work of history or poetry (24), a perspective Maimonides thinks no Hebrew would take. Maimonides goes on to accuse
the questioner of trying to engage in theoretical speculation with the
first notions that come to him 'when, in some of your hours of leisure,
you leave off copulating and drinking'. Much later in the *Guide*
Maimonides divides all the Torah's commandments into fourteen
groups, the last two of which are devoted to moderating eating and
drinking (III.48.600) and desire for sexual intercourse (III.49.602). He
thinks moderation preserves and protects the body, thereby allowing
the intellect to thrive. Thus, his rebuke of the questioner in I.2 is a
pointed declaration that the questioner has not benefited from the
Torah's commandments. Maimonides seems to be saying that only
someone mired in lower order passions could suppose that being
guided by sensation and opinion would be better than following the
intellect and that the Torah's commandments aim to lift a person out
of sensation and desire so that he could act on correct opinions and
pursue knowledge (I.5.29). If this is right, Maimonides' abuse of the
questioner is a powerful clue to what is otherwise missing in this
chapter, namely, the role that the Torah's commandments play in
moral life; and it makes clear that the Torah, or something like it, is
essential for moral life.

Again, inasmuch as all the descendants of Adam are like judges or
rulers in being able to tell right from wrong, there is no need for the
Torah to teach men right and wrong. What the Torah needs to do is
remove the obstacles to the *exercise* of these opinions. As proposed
earlier, the Torah's course of training has two dimensions. The first is
the repeated observance of the moral laws, the *mishpatim*, for the
sustained practice of virtuous acts cultivates moral virtue, Aristotle
claims (*N.E.* II.1.1103a31–b2). Second, the training includes the performance of the religious laws, for Maimonides thinks that the
religious commandments are designed to promote the friendship
that disposes a person to perform the moral commandments and,

thereby, to promote the moral virtues and create a community in which these virtues as well as intellectual pursuits can thrive.

Both types of commandments aim to moderate desire and control the imagination. Hence, in performing them all, a person is removing just those obstacles to the intellect that overcame Adam.[18] Practising the divine law, he places himself in a position to recover the intellectual apprehension of truth that Adam is said to have had.[19] Just this, 'intellect in actu', is the highest end of man, Maimonides thinks (III.27.511). To obey the religious commandments is, then, to reshape and, as it were, tame the faculties that undermined Adam's intellectual apprehension: it is to replace the sensation of the fruit's attractiveness and the imagination of pleasure in eating it with the love and pity for others that result in acts of mutual benefit (cf. III.49.601–602). Properly oriented, desire and imagination cease to be inimical to the intellect. In sum, the Torah's religious commandments refine desire and imagination so that those who obey the Law can recover the knowledge originally possessed by Adam, knowledge that is not, of itself, sufficient to ward off the threat that desire and imagination pose to it.[20] Indeed, part of this Adamic knowledge would have to be the understanding of the human faculties that I.2 and I.1 present.

We see implicit in I.2 a threefold distinction of knowledge or opinion. There is (1) the theoretical knowledge of truth possessed by Adam before his expulsion. This includes not only metaphysics and physics, but also ethics and politics. Then, there is (2) knowledge of good and evil that he and all his descendants come to possess. This division consists of opinions whose truth is not proven but confidently asserted by all people. Finally, there are (3) the religious commandments in the Torah that are distinctive of the Hebrew

---

[18] W.Z. Harvey, 'A Portrait of Spinoza as a Maimonidean', *Journal of the History of Philosophy* (1981) 19(2), 171, notes this point without elaborating on the mechanism.

[19] Daniel H. Frank, 'The Politics of Fear: Idolatry and Superstition in Maimonides and Spinoza', in this volume, 178, makes this point as a general observation: 'Theory without materialization in ritual practice is far too weak to sustain itself.'

[20] Stern, 'The Maimonidean Parable', 225–7, notices that in I.1 Maimonides presents his own position in the first person singular, whereas in I.2 he uses the first person plural. This shift supports my interpretation. In I.1 Maimonides is himself ('I') speaking universally about the nature of man and responding to popular views. In I.2 his target is a non-Jewish questioner, and he responds with 'We' so as to suggest the Jewish understanding of the relation of the faculties.

state. These last commandments are not universally accepted and their benefits are not apparent.

The problem Maimonides is implicitly raising is how to protect the intellect from being corrupted by imagination and the pleasures of the senses. Enhancing the power of the intellect is not the solution; for Adam is supposed to have a perfect intellect, and the inability of the intellect to preserve itself generates the problem in the first place. Nor will shared opinion about the good protect the intellect; for it allows us all to condemn, like judges, the abuses of one person against another and, thus, to live and work together, but not to overcome the private indulgence of the senses of which Maimonides accuses his interlocutor. Indeed, few people can acknowledge the threat either because they imagine their own intellect as more powerful than it is or because they suppose their own nature to lie in other faculties. If, then, the intellect is to be protected, a person must be tricked into protecting himself. The Torah's religious laws are just such a ruse. By directing desire and imagination towards festival meals and sacrifices, the Torah allows for their moderate satisfaction, but also, as we have seen, refines them into, respectively, love for others (friendship) and pity for their (imagined) condition, both character traits essential for a community. So refined, these faculties no longer threaten the intellect and, moreover, play a positive role in the community's providing for the bodily welfare (III.27.510) that makes intellectual development possible.

In sum, Maimonides' implicit argument is that the intellect cannot, by itself, resist the power of desire and imagination. But man's essential nature lies in his use of the intellect. Hence, in order to realize his nature, man requires something from *outside of himself* to neutralize the power of desire and imagination. The Torah contains devices that reorient these latter faculties so that they promote the state and, thereby, make possible the conditions in which the intellect can thrive. Hence, the Torah, or something like it, is necessary for the realization of human nature. Desire and imagination are responsible for human motivation. Hence, in directing these faculties towards friendship, the Torah is reorienting human motivation towards the conditions essential for a state and for human fulfilment. Obeying the commandments, an individual supposes himself to act for the God's sake, but the benefit is his own.

3. SPINOZA'S JUSTIFICATION
OF POLITICAL DEVICES

Spinoza makes the same threefold division of knowledge or opinion that we find in Maimonides. His *Ethics* sets out the knowledge that Adam might be supposed to have had before his expulsion. His *Theological-Political Tractate* sets out mechanisms for a kind of moral action that is based upon opinion rather than knowledge; and his unfinished *Political Treatise* expounds what amount to secular 'religious laws' that are modelled on the Torah. Apart from helping to explain Spinoza's philosophy, drawing out the structural parallel with Maimonides' parts of philosophy will allow us to see his argument for political devices. Let me begin by explaining my characterization of each of the three works.

In a passage in the *Ethics* that strikingly recalls Maimonides' interpretation of Adam's sin, Spinoza argues that men who are born free would not form a concept of good or evil (IVP68). He means that they would live in accordance with the true and the false. His argument here depends on his earlier account of an adequate idea, an idea that is intrinsically true (IID4) because it is known entirely through its cause. No idea of a partial cause could be adequate, and our experience would seem to be inevitably partial. However, there are things (such as the law of inertia) that exist equally in a part and its whole and that can, therefore, be conceived adequately by grasping the part (IIP38). To be acted upon by something else is not to be free. Someone with an inadequate idea knows only partially and, thus, Spinoza argues, is acted upon by other ideas (IIIP1) and so comes to have an 'affection' or, as we would say, an 'emotion' (IIIP1C). Knowledge of good and evil is an affection (IVP8), for knowledge of evil is an inadequate idea (IVP64). It is, thus, clear that only a person who has exclusively adequate ideas is free and that such a person has no knowledge of evil nor, because good is its correlate, knowledge of good (IVP68; IV64C).

The Scholium to IVP68 announces that no man could actually be born free, but it explains that insofar as we can conceive of God as the sole cause of man's existence, man would be conceived to be free.[21]

---

[21] In the *TTP*, Spinoza interprets the commandment not to eat of the tree of knowledge of good and evil as an injunction to do good from 'knowledge and love of good' rather than from 'fear of evil' (4.55–6). He adds that he who does so acts freely.

This, Spinoza claims, is how Moses conceives of God and the first man. Thus, the first man was prohibited from eating of the tree of knowledge of good and evil. If he ate from it, he would fear death rather than desiring to live, and thus not be free. Spinoza proposes that Adam lost his freedom when he came to believe that he was like the other animals and came, through his *imagination* (IIIP27), to imitate their affections. The passage adds that the patriarchs enabled men to recover freedom by introducing the idea of God.[22]

This passage needs to be understood in the context of IVP68. Insofar as man is conceived entirely through his cause, namely, God, he is known adequately, that is, truthfully. When Adam conceived of himself as created by God, he knew himself adequately and was, to this extent, free. The free man acts from his intellect's adequate ideas, not from affection. Whereas desire to live belongs to man essentially (IVP6–7), fear is an affection. Hence, the Scholium is claiming that Adam's intellect was undermined by this affection. Spinoza thinks that a man cannot actually be born free because everyone belongs to nature and is, consequently, affected by what surrounds him (IVP4). Embedded in nature from birth, every man is subject to the fear of the external things that could destroy him. However, a man can come to be free by overcoming this and other affections.

Thus, the Scholium is proposing three stages: If we conceive of man as somehow being created directly by God and aware of his own creation, we would have to suppose that (i) man's intellect grasps its cause and is, thereby, adequate. This is an idealization, but it is, Spinoza claims, the basis of the Torah's account of Adam—or rather, as we have seen, the basis of Maimonides' interpretation of it. In any case, (ii) the initial purity of intellect cannot be sustained because Adam recognizes himself as like other animals, that is, subject to outside influences that he cannot understand or control. In this

---

In this work someone who acts from love of the good is free, whereas the person who fears is controlled by something else. Hence, the injunction not to eat from the tree is an injunction to be free. Spinoza does not commit himself to this interpretation.

[22] In a pioneering paper arguing that Spinoza shares many of Maimonides' views, W.Z. Harvey, 'A Portrait of Spinoza as a Maimonidean', *Journal of the History of Philosophy* (1981) 19(2), 155–61, shows that Spinoza interprets this passage as Maimonides does, that is, as a conflict between reason's grasping truth and, on the other side, imagination and opinion about the good. Harvey notes that these latter faculties are the source of Spinoza's first type of knowledge (IIP40S2).

context, (iii) the patriarchs' introduction of the idea of God was liberating because it is a way to grasp the causes of the whole of nature, and it is by grasping the whole and the forces necessarily at work in it that we come to be free.

The stages are familiar from Maimonides. But the *Ethics* differs on the way Judaism effects a recovery of Adamic knowledge. Whereas Maimonides implicitly points to the *Torah*'s *commandments*, Spinoza ascribes the recovery to the *patriarch's idea* of God. But Spinoza is being coy. If any source provides an adequate idea of God and a way to overcome affections, it is Spinoza's own *Ethics*. It begins with God and ends, famously, with the intellectual love of God (VP42), a love through which a person restrains lusts and achieves 'blessedness', the state of mental autonomy that is the model of what the *TTP* claims Jesus' teaching brings (*TTP* 5.65). In other words, unlike Maimonides, Spinoza thinks that there is a rational, deductive path towards the recovery of the perfect knowledge ascribed to Adam. The intellect alone can subdue the affections that would corrupt it. The *Ethics* is intellect's manual.

A potential objection to this conclusion is that the *Ethics* does not confine itself to truth but also speaks of good and evil. My response is that the *Ethics* gives these terms functional meanings that are *opposite* to accepted opinions: 'good' is useful, and 'evil' distances us from some good (IVD1–2). It follows that any sort of power is good and any lack of power is bad. This equation troubles readers.[23] However, the philosopher knows that his own good lies with that of others. Thus, Spinoza argues—substituting 'free' for 'good'—that free men are 'joined to one another by the closest bond of friendship' (IVP71, drawing on IVP35 and IVP35C) and that a man guided by reason

---

[23] E. Curley, 'Kissinger, Spinoza, and Genghis Khan', in *The Cambridge Companion to Spinoza*, D. Garrett, ed. (Cambridge: Cambridge University Press, 1996) esp. 318–22, denies that Spinoza has the conceptual resources to criticize a tyrant. W.Z. Harvey, 'Maimonides and Spinoza on the Knowledge of Good and Evil', *Binah: Studies in Jewish Thought* (1989) 2, 136, Article orig. in *Iyyun* (1978) 28, 167–85, acknowledges a 'pedagogic' use of 'good' to denote intelligible entities and recognizes that this must be its use in the Preface to part IV (at 144), but he insists that goods are objects of imagination that are merely compared by reason. A.L. Motzkin, 'Maimonides and Spinoza on Good and Evil', *Daat* (1978) 24, fn. 50, usefully distinguishes Spinoza's identification of the 'good' as power (efficient cause) from Maimonides' claim that 'good' refers to what conforms to our final cause (III.13.453); but he, too, denies that Spinoza gives an adequate account of morality and compares him to Nietzsche.

lives more freely in a state where he follows law than he does living in solitude and following his own reason (IVP73). Guided by self-interested *reason*, the philosopher enters into relationships of friendship, love, and citizenship that other people enter from *love* for others and *fear* of the state of nature or the sovereign.

Few people have the intellectual power to live this way. Most are, rather, governed by their affections and by accepted opinions. Whereas the *Ethics* expounds Adamic knowledge, the *TTP* belongs to Maimonides' second class of knowledge, accepted opinions about good and evil. Here Spinoza relies on religions, specifically, Christianity, to teach people what they need to know to be citizens, namely, love of other people and love of God. The essence of all legitimate religions comes down to these two well-recognized *moral* principles. They are popular versions of two philosophical notions we saw in the *Ethics*: friendship among free people and intellectual love of God. Religions convey these precepts through imagination, rather than reason, and in the process they invert them.[24] Whereas a free man has rational grounds for attaching himself to other free men, ordinary citizens form attachments by giving up their individual *desires* (what Maimonides calls sensation) and acting for the other's good or the collective interest. Philosophers are free because they are motivated by reason; citizens imitate freedom by stilling the desires that are inimical to reason, namely, the self-regarding desires.[25]

The *TTP* proposes two mechanisms for fostering this citizen morality. The first is freedom of religion. Spinoza thinks that someone who freely chooses his own religion will be most likely to subject himself to it and, so, to mould his own character in accordance with

---

[24] Spinoza rejects imagination in the *Ethics* (VP39S), but endorses it in the *TTP*. See H.M. Ravven, 'Some Thoughts ... Part Two: Spinoza's Maimonideanism' *Journal of the History of Philosophy* (2001) 39, 187–8, 209–11. Y. Yovel, *Spinoza and Other Heretics: The Marrano of Reason* (Princeton: Princeton University Press, 1989) 130, notes Spinoza's development of 'mental and institutional mechanisms that will transform the imagination into an external imitation of reason'. Similarly, H.M. Ravven, 'Some Thoughts...', claims that Spinoza as well as Maimonides contrast rational morality with 'morals instituted imaginatively by political authority'.

[25] See E. Halper, 'Spinoza on the Political Value of Freedom of Religion' *History of Philosophy Quarterly* (2004) 21, 167–82, for a fuller discussion of this point and what is said in the next paragraph.

the two precepts which are the same for all religions, precepts that require him to limit his own desires and interests. One who does so becomes obedient and, thereby, fit to be a citizen.[26] Second, Spinoza recommends, as a kind of substitute for reason, a joint sovereignty and collective process of decision making. His thought here is that whereas an individual who makes decisions by himself will be strongly influenced by desire for his own interest, one who decides by reaching consensus with others will need to act in the common interest. Since by appetites 'all men are drawn in different directions' (16.175),[27] joint decisions cannot be made by appetite and are, thereby, more rational. In a democracy, an ordinary citizen is able to act with a degree of rational autonomy that approaches, even if it falls short of, that of the free man (16.178).[28] In sum, the *TTP* expounds a citizen morality and a popular politics that are based upon common opinion and manifest the Torah's moral laws (*mishpatim*).

Just as Maimonides' third division of knowledge is religious law, Spinoza has a third work that sets out laws for particular states, the unfinished and little discussed *Political Treatise* (*TP*). Spinoza does not claim to be a prophet, and these laws are secular. However, they are clearly modelled on the Torah.

The *TP*'s introductory chapter reminds readers that, though a person could control his affections (desires) with reason, most people find this path too difficult (1.5.35–36). On the other hand, religion and love of others 'have no weight in law-court or palace'. Yet, insofar

---

[26] S.B. Smith, *Spinoza, Liberalism, and the Question of Jewish Identity* (New Haven: Yale University Press, 1997) 152–4, thinks that the main lesson Spinoza derives from history is 'the necessity of political control over religious authority'. He infers that the task of the state is to liberate 'the individual from the power of the clerics'. Smith does not appreciate the very important, positive role that Spinoza accords religious observance in the liberal state. He does rightly note that Spinoza sees the Torah as 'an exclusively political legislation' (74).

[27] Also, B. Spinoza, *Political Treatise*, S. Shirely, trans. (Indianapolis: Hackett, 2000) chapter 8, para 6, 98. Hereinafter: *TP* 8.6.98.

[28] Spinoza's idea that a collective decision by citizens would approach rational autonomy is a close cousin to, if not the direct basis of Kant's notion that a universal law is a rational law; see E. Halper, 'Spinoza on the Political Value of Freedom of Religion', *History of Philosophy Quarterly* (2004) 21, 177. In contrast, Frank, 'Politics of Fear', 187, claims that because, in the *TTP*, the state's end is freedom, rather than virtue, 'there is an (unAristotelian) pluralism, and a strong sense that the state as guarantor of security is decidedly neutral when it comes to the summum bonum'. In my view, freedom for Spinoza is no more morally neutral than it is for Kant. That democracy is the best form of government because it is most guided by reason and most likely to achieve the material ends of the state, namely, peace and security, is argued by W. Sacksteder.

as a state's preservation depends on some such control, the state must be so organized 'that its ministers cannot be induced to betray their trust or to act basely' (1.6.36). It is clear that Spinoza has shifted his attention from the morality of ordinary citizens, where religion has a role to play, to the affections of those who administer a state. Ordinary citizens acquire a semblance of morality by stilling their self-regarding affections, but scarcely anyone would undertake the tasks of government without some measure of ambition (7.6.80; cf. *Ethics* IIIP31S). Unchecked, their ambition would undermine the common-wealth. Hence, the state must be so constituted that it provides an attractive sphere to which talented individuals can come and remain in power only by working for the welfare of the whole state. Spinoza's general technique is to divide the offices and assign them to progressively more powerful assemblies. An individual is motivated to obey the law by the prospect of holding office, and motivated to execute his office well by the prospect of more important offices. Other ambitious officeholders prevent him from abusing his power. Since citizens obey laws from fear of punishment or the expectation of reward (*TP*, 2.10.42; 3.3.49; 4.4.59), which latter motive Spinoza calls 'love,' a civil order that offers citizens prospects for advance is apt to inspire obedience.

Spinoza distinguishes three kinds of state, monarchy, aristocracy and democracy. The *TP* begins with monarchies, probably because that is the form of government of the Hebrew state. It proposes a large advisory council whose members are appointed in equal numbers from each clan and proportionally from cities (6.15.68). Importantly, he counts on citizens' hopes that they themselves will eventually be on this council as a key incentive inducing them to uphold the state's laws (7.6.80). At the same time, he thinks that the king is likely to be sufficiently afraid of opposing a large group of citizens that he will either ratify the council's decisions or work to reconcile opposing views (7.11.81–2). The king's power will be further restricted by an unpaid citizen army (7.16.84). In this state people will not be able to own land, for Spinoza thinks this will make them less anxious to go to war. To promote trade, citizens are allowed to lend money at interest, but only to fellow citizens (7.8.80).

The 'clans' here are clearly modelled on the tribes of Israel; the council of the elders recalls the council of 70 elders—Spinoza greatly increases their number—that Moses drew from all the tribes (Num. 11:16) and that later became the Great Sanhedrin. The land distribution may be inspired by the Torah's allotment of portions of land to tribes as permanent possessions. (The tribes allotted the land to individual families who could, in turn, rent it out for up to 50 years, but not sell it.) The citizen army is also modelled on the Torah, as is the prohibition of interest, though Spinoza shrewdly reverses the latter to promote trade *within* the state rather than between states.

Aristocracy is, in turn, based on monarchy. Since sovereignty is divided between a large number of patricians, there is no need for clans because there is no monarch to oppose (8.8.99). Rather, there should be equality among patricians, and there is some concern about factions among them. Hence, Spinoza looks for ways to promote *unity* rather than the *opposition* he promoted in monarchies. Those on the council will be divided by their affections, but unified when they rely on reason to pursue honourable ends (8.6.98). Unlike monarchies, aristocracies can have professional armies, but all patricians should be capable of leading them (8.9.99–100). Land ownership gives subjects an incentive not to desert in war (8.10.100–1), and the prospect of a role in political institutions induces citizens to defend their country. A national religion, required of all patricians, further serves to unify the population (8.46.118). Clearly modelling himself on the Torah, Spinoza even suggests that a census be conducted by having people contribute a small coin (8.25.105–6; cf. Exodus 30:13–14).

Spinoza completed only a few pages on democracy. Like aristocracy, it is governed by a supreme council, but membership is open to all citizens and appointments to offices are made 'not as being the best men, but by law' from among the wealthy or the eldest sons (11.2.135). Recall that the eldest sons were to be appointed priests according to the Torah's original plan, a plan that Spinoza thinks would have given all families a larger stake in religious life. So this measure is likely to be a means of unifying citizens, an important end when everyone is equal.

We need not go deeper into the details of the *TP*, for it is clear that Spinoza begins with the Torah's religious laws and modifies them so as to achieve stability in different forms of government. He arranges benefits from the political order so as to *motivate* citizens to obey its laws and to undertake governing positions from love, as he thinks people obeyed the Torah. Few individuals living in, say, the monarchy he sketches would understand why they could not lend money to foreigners at interest or why their council takes the form it does. For most, these laws would resemble the Torah's religious laws. But these laws can achieve their ends without citizens' understanding them. Ironically, led by their own hopes for *individual* gain, citizens obey laws that preserve order and balance and, thereby, check individual ambition so as to benefit all citizens collectively.

Taken together, all three works constitute an implicit argument for political devices: Whereas philosophers do not need devices because they can rationally deduce the benefit of the state, those who cannot grasp this benefit rationally will obey the laws and work for the state only if they are motivated in some other way. Since their contribution is essential for the collective benefit, it is legitimate to motivate them. To obey a law a person must set aside his immediate desire and act in the common interest. Since religion aims to limit immediate desires, it promotes obedience to law. On the other hand, only self-interest could motivate citizens to undertake the jobs that sustain a state, even though those so motivated tend to work against the common interest. If a state is to sustain itself, it must provide its citizens opportunities to realize their ambitions in ways that promote the order and welfare of the state. Spinoza's institutions and laws are devices designed to motivate citizens in this way. Hence, they, or something like them, are necessary to secure the state and, thereby, to allow the (quasi-)moral and intellectual activities it makes possible.

4. THE COGNITIVE VALUE OF RELIGIOUS LAW

In short, Spinoza's secular statutes serve the same political ends Maimonides ascribes to religious laws. Both philosophers also think that these devices preserve the intellect. For Maimonides, though, they shield it from corrupting faculties, whereas for Spinoza they allow a citizen to exercise in political deliberations a measure of judgement that is not dictated by his affections. They differ more fundamentally in that Maimonides thinks that the Torah's religious laws instil true opinions about God. Maimonides proposes that the Torah's being able to do this is evidence that it is divine law, in contrast with nomoi, whose benefit is limited to preventing injustice (II.40.383–4). This cognitive benefit of the Torah's religious commandments has no counterpart from Spinoza's secular alternatives. Because Maimonides thinks the ultimate purpose of the bodily welfare attained by the state is the perfection of the soul, it is important to say something about this function of religious law.

Maimonides explains many of the most mysterious commandments as forbidding idolatrous practices. Thus, he claims that some peoples supposed blood to be the food of the jinn and drank it to fraternize with them (III.46.585-7). In prohibiting the consumption of blood, the Torah is instilling the opinions that God is not like these jinn and that he does not require physical sustenance. Other such prohibitions teach more about what God is not. Now Maimonides insists that someone comes to know God, to the extent He can be known, by learning what He is not (I.58.135). Hence, commandments that reject idolatrous practices can bring someone who reflects on them true beliefs about God (I.60.143-4). True belief is not knowledge, but it is still valuable for its own sake (cf. I.36.85) and a step towards deeper insight. Thus, there is a path from the observance of the religious commandments to the highest human knowledge, 'intellect in actu'. The religious commandments do not merely provide conditions for the recovery of Adamic knowledge; puzzling over them belongs among the reflections that perfect the soul.[29] Again, that religious commandments serve political as well as cognitive ends is a sign they are divine.

In short, both Maimonides and Spinoza see religious law or their secular counterparts as designed for those who stand between the highest and lowest human attainments, that is, between demonstrative knowledge and slavery to the body; and all of us are in this position, at least at some time in our lives. Maimonides' intermediate good life is constituted by true beliefs and the avoidance of injustice. Spinoza accepts the latter action but substitutes the exercise of judgement in governance for true beliefs. This move allows the citizen to imitate through practice the philosopher's reason, but it also deprives him of the intellectual path Maimonides thinks the Torah provides to come closer still.

---

[29] That Maimonides sees a path towards knowledge is clear from III.51.622. J. Stern, *Problems and Parables of Law (1998)* 47-8, suggests, *alternatively, that because the historically conditioned religious commandments do a person no good, they provide him with an 'other-worldly training'.*

5. CONCLUSION

We might have expected discussions of the Torah to emphasize eternal truths, rather than devices, ruses, and motivation. Neither Spinoza nor Maimonides thinks that the Torah is primarily or exclusively a source of eternal truths. For that we are better off looking to philosophy or science. Yet, it is just because the Torah has a role to play in that murky area between truth and feeling that it has been and continues to be so important. For, inhabiting this murky area, we human beings need something to motivate us besides rigorous argument and uncontrolled feeling. We need springs of action that motivate beneficial and self-sustaining practices. Maimonides and Spinoza both see the Torah as a model source of such springs of action. Whether or not they interpret the Torah's devices rightly seems to me not as important as the now evident fact that the Torah addresses an issue in political philosophy that, despite its current neglect, remains central. Besides treating principles and actions, political philosophy ought to design laws and institutions that induce citizens to realize their abilities and to contribute to the community, particularly in an era when institutions of government strain to accommodate a population that far exceeds that for which they were designed and people grow increasingly alienated from the societies in which they live. Because laws and institutions inevitably shape people, philosophers should undertake to shape laws and institutions. It is in this normative sense that I think the Torah advances a political philosophy that is of enduring significance.[30]

---

[30] A version of this essay was delivered at the Association for Jewish Studies. I want to thank my commentator on that occasion, Hillel Fradkin, as well those who gave me comments individually: Eugene Garver, Yehuda Halper, Jonathan Jacobs, Howard Kreisel, Josef Stern, Roslyn Weiss, and Martin Yaffee. My interpretation of *Guide* I.2 was initially provoked by a very interesting paper on that chapter by Ronna Burger.

Part V

Moral Personality: Enduring Influences and Continued Borrowings

9

Dancing in Chains

The Baffling Coexistence of Legalism and Exuberance in Judaic and Islamic Tradition

Ze'ev Maghen

Judaism and Islam share many characteristics, due, inter alia, to the influence of the former on the latter and the latter (though to a far lesser degree) on the former. This paper will focus on one of the heretofore unexamined commonalities between the two religious systems: the fascinating tension in the classical texts of each faith between extensive legislation, on the one hand, and the persistence—seemingly in the very face of that legislation—of a spirit of unfettered spontaneity and irrepressible vitality that pervades the narrative sections of the same literature. This eclectic, even oxymoronic quality is shared uniquely, I would aver, by early Jewish and Muslim sources, serving to underscore the strong familial relationship between these two spiritual civilizations while simultaneously setting them apart from the vast majority of their religious, cultural and ideological counterparts.

Judaism and Islam are arguably the two most legalistic traditions in human history, and their tendency to regulate nearly every aspect of quotidian existence is already on display in well-developed form in their founding documents: Bible and Talmud, Qur'an and Hadith. A large share of the proscriptions, and not a few of the prescriptions, laid down in these documents are geared toward curbing the destructive capacity of people's instinctual impulses and animal appetites: human nature must not be allowed to undermine human society.

Now, it seems a plausible enough assumption that communities hemmed in on all sides by hundreds and thousands of ordinances specifically designed to prevent the id from having its way, will produce individual members, and especially literary exemplars, who are scrupulous and dutiful, subdued and submissive, even ascetic and puritanical—who are, in a word, saintly. The diametric opposite is true, however, in the case of Jewish and Muslim sacred lore. There are no saints therein, nor any room or desire for them.

The exponential proliferation of 'thou shalt's' and 'thou shalt not's' that informs the early Judaic and Islamic canons stands in stark contrast to the boisterous and rambunctious personalities of the heroes and leading ladies that people those same canons from end to end. Tamar and 'Aisha, Samson and 'Ali, David and Muhammad, Jacob and 'Amr, Bathsheba and Zaynab, Judah and Hashim, Yael and Ju'da, Joab and 'Umar—all of them dance their tempestuous existences around and under and through the colonnade-like array of their stalwart nemeses: the entrenched, immutable laws, as stable as the heroes are reckless, as restrictive as they are obstreperous, as cerebral as they are visceral, as conservative as they are revolutionary.[1]

This pregnant juxtaposition within the bounds of the same sacred literary tradition of, as it were, both classicism and romanticism, of Nietzsche's Apollo and his Dionysus, of Kierkegaard's Either and his

---

[1] One way to try to mitigate the power of this paradox might involve wielding the old Wellhausian notion—connected to the JEPD thesis—that Israel evolved over biblical time from *ein volk* to *ein kirk,* and claiming that the antithetical approaches to life that we attempt to draw out in this essay, rather than evincing a counterintuitive coexistence of opposites within a single literary-theological system, merely reflect the contributions of diverse elements and traditions as isolated from one another chronologically as they were socially or politically. Without opening up such a vast subject, it suffices to respond that (1) the phenomenon we will strive to elucidate is one in which a particular trend or worldview within the Judaic (and Islamic) canon *interacts with and emphatically rejects* another trend or worldview within the same canon: at least one side of the 'debate' cannot have been blissfully unaware of the other. Indeed, as far as the subject under examination here is concerned, the trend would seem to move in the opposite direction of Wellhausen's '*ein volk* to *ein kirk*' process: it is the 'vital' or 'exuberant' elements which appear to be administering a corrective to the pietistic or priestly elements. (2) Moreover, and perhaps most basically, the redactors of these canons, as well as the popular reception and perception of them over time, both doggedly maintained these discordant dimensions of the classical texts side by side, welding them in the national–religious consciousness into a beaten whole. If it is easier to accept, then, I am willing to replace the schizophrenia of the Jewish and Muslim *canon* with the schizophrenia of Jewish and Muslim *traditional consciousness* as the object of this essay's scrutiny.

Or, of rigid precepts and refractory protagonists all wrapped up together in a single package with neither side willing to give an inch—this apparent paradox invites examination. How shall we understand this Judeo-Islamic 'bi-polar disorder', this strange *entente cordiale* in the context of both creeds between two radically antagonistic and uncompromising worldviews inhabiting a single set of seminal sources, the one fanatically legalistic, the other no less fanatically dedicated to the proposition that laws were made to be broken?

1. THE ORDER OF THINGS

Few who have immersed themselves in the pages of the Bible for any considerable length of time can have failed to note the following salient instance of the phenomenon described above. Pentateuchal law, in common with the legal systems of nearly every society and religion co-extant with it in the ancient *oikumene*, firmly upheld the practice of primogeniture, that is, the policy of granting preference and privilege to first-born children over their younger siblings. Somewhat indirect (but nevertheless incontrovertible) confirmation of this fact may be found in Deuteronomy 29, verses 25–6:

> When a man has two wives, one whom he loves and one whom he hates, and both the loved and unloved wives have sons, but the first-born is that of the unloved one; on the day that this man wills his property to his sons, he must not give the son of the beloved wife preference over the first born, who is the son of the unloved wife. Even if the first born is the son of the hated wife, the father must recognize him as to give him a double portion of all his property. Since this son is the first fruit of his father's loins, the birthright is legally his.

It is an argument a fortiori—did we need one—that since the father is enjoined in this passage to favour his first-born son even when he is emotionally prejudiced against him, he is all the more obligated to do so when such extenuating circumstances are absent. This was the law of the land, and the law of the Hebrews. It was the law of God. When Jacob on his death bed places the more auspicious right hand on the head of his *younger* grandchild in preparation for pronouncing the blessing, Joseph hurries to correct him: 'Not so, my father, not so: for *this* is the first born. Put thy right hand upon *his* head.' (Genesis 48:18). But Jacob is not moved by this traditionalist appeal to the divine norm—and neither is anyone else in the Bible.

Let us begin from the beginning and race through for lack of space. Adam and Eve's first-born child was Cain, while their youngest was Seth. But Cain was 'disinherited' and all of his descendants died in the deluge,[2] whereas Seth—whose name means something like 'foundation'—became the father of humanity. Noah's first-born was Japheth (read Gen. 10:21 as a clarification of Gen. 9:18), yet the begetter of the truly important genealogical line from the biblical perspective—that is, the Semites—is of course Shem. Abraham's first-born was Ishma'el, but the Pentateuchal text shunts him aside in favour of his younger brother, for (as the Almighty informs Abraham) 'through *Isaac* shall thy seed be called' (Gen. 21:12).

What of Isaac's offspring? Here the scriptures ensure that there is no room for confusion and place an almost explicit rejection of primogeniture—or at least of its applicability in this particular case—into the mouth of the Deity:

> And God said to Rebecca: 'Two nations are in thy womb, and two peoples shall be separated from thy bowels; and the one people shall be stronger than the other, *and the elder shall serve the younger*'. (Gen. 25:23)

The first fruit of Jacob's loins, Reuben, fared no better than any of his predecessors: he and his progeny dwindled to insignificance. Meanwhile, of Jacob's fourth son we read that 'The scepter shall not depart from Judah, nor the ruler's staff from between his feet, until the coming of Shiloh; and unto [Judah] shall the obedience of the peoples be' (Gen. 49:10). That remnant which is left today of the Hebrew tribes—the 'Jews'—is named after this fourth son.[3]

Judah had three boys. The first was killed by God for an unspecified iniquity, the second was killed by God for a specified iniquity.[4] When

---

[2] Or beforehand. See, e.g., Genesis Rabbah 23:12. The Midrashic notion that Noah's wife was Na'ama, a descendent of Cain, is debunked in a variety of ways by the same stratum of Talmudic sources that advances the claim.

[3] 'Judah is king, therefore let him sit at the head of the table, and let Reuben the first-born take the second seat' (Louis Ginzburg, *The Legends of the Jews* (Philadelphia: The Jewish Publication Society, 1968) vol. 2, 96).

[4] According to the Talmud they were both executed by heaven for the same offence, viz. anal intercourse (see Yebamot, 34a).

Judah was reticent to send his third son on the mission that had led to the demise of his second, that is, levirate marriage with Tamar, the latter tricked her father-in-law into doing the job himself.

> And it came to pass in the time of her travail, that, behold, twins were in her womb. And it came to pass, when she travailed, that one put out a hand; and the midwife took and bound upon his hand a scarlet thread, saying: 'This came out first.' And it came to pass, as he drew back his hand, that, behold his brother came out; and she said: 'What a break-through thou hast made!' Therefore his name was called Peretz. And afterward came out his brother, that had the scarlet thread upon his hand; and his name was called Zerah (Gen. 38:27–30).

Once again, the first-born has been circumvented in dramatic fashion—albeit in this case while still inside the womb—and the younger sibling has 'cut in line' and usurped his elder's legitimate rights. From this 'Breakthrough' (for such is his name) is descended none other than King David (1 Chron. 2:5–14), who was himself chosen over all of his brothers for the position of sovereign even though he was, as the text makes sure to emphasize, 'only the youngest' (1 Samuel 16:5–12). And before David there was Saul, who challenged Samuel's adumbration of his future ascendance to the throne with the words: 'Am I not a Benjaminite, of the youngest tribe of Israel, and is not my family the youngest of all the clans of my tribe?' (*u-mishpahti ha-tze'ira mikol mishpehot shivtei Binyamin*—1 Samuel 9:21). And before Saul there was Gideon, who asked the Lord: 'How shall *I* save Israel? My clan is the smallest in Manasseh, and *I am the youngest* in my father's house' (Judges, 6:15).

In case the message has yet to sink in, Genesis sums the whole business up with a resounding thunderbolt, in the final story it has to tell. Joseph has brought his two sons to receive their grandfather's blessing. Jacob/Israel places his right hand on the head of the youngest and his left hand on the head of the oldest, 'crossing his hands'. Joseph remonstrates with his father, whose reply represents the culmination of a life spent—from its very 'heel-grabbing' inception—in relentless struggle against the law of primogeniture: from his purloining of both birthright and blessing from Esau, to his seeking of the hand of Laban's younger daughter instead of the elder, to his favouritism towards 'the son of the beloved wife (i.e. Joseph son of Rachel) over the first-born, who is the son of the unloved wife (i.e. Reuben son of Leah),' in direct violation of the Deuteronomic precept adduced at the

outset of this section. Jacob, the indefatigable rebel, refuses to recon-
figure his hands and explains:

> I know it, my son, I know it. He (Manasseh) shall also become a people,
> and he also shall be great. *But his younger brother shall be greater than
> he*, and his seed shall become a multitude of nations (Gen. 48:19).

Jacob's 'sign of the cross'—his insistence that individuals should be
judged not by the order of their birth but by the content of their
character—should be regarded as the coat-of-arms for the entire book
of Genesis. By means of it the Bible declares to us regarding its own
emphatic strictures and unequivocal injunctions: 'Do not believe
everything you read.'

2. GLORIOUS BASTARDS

Thus, long before the 'killing of the firstborn' during the Exodus from
Egypt, Genesis left no doubt regarding its distaste for the biblically
backed precept of primogeniture. But this is not the only instance of
biblical lore undermining biblical law. Even without leaving the realm
of reproduction we can point to several more examples, including the
extremely sensitive issue of pedigree. In brief, the eighteenth chapter
of the book of Leviticus contains a lengthy delineation of the various
permutations of the crime of incest, the collective penalty for the
perpetration of which is nothing less than being 'vomited out' from
the Promised Land (Levit. 18:27). The bastard issue (*momzer*) of such
illicit coition 'may not enter into the congregation of the Lord even
unto the tenth generation' (Deut. 23:3). These proscriptions against
sexual abomination and consequent contamination of the *stemma* are
clearly among the most weighty in the Pentateuch.

Or are they? Is it a coincidence that the biblical text goes out of its
way on more than one occasion to reveal to its readership that the two
most important and revered figures in the entire Hebrew scriptures,
Moses and David, *are themselves the products of incestuous unions*?
Of David we already know from the above that he was descended on
the one side from a flagrant infringement of Lev. 18:15 ('Thou shalt
not uncover the nakedness of thy daughter-in-law'), when Judah slept
with Tamar. But the Bible is not satisfied with showing its favourite

son and most revered monarch to be the offspring of bastards from only *one* side. And so the text takes the trouble to regale us with the tawdry tale of how Lot's daughters, having fled from a burning Sodom to a cave in the surrounding mountains, plied their father with drink and bedded him down, the first girl giving birth to a son named 'Moab' (which sounds in Hebrew like 'from father' [*me-av*]— Gen. 19:30–8). Not for nothing is Ruth, David's famous progenitor from the other side, repeatedly introduced as 'the Moabitess' (beginning with Ruth 1:22).[5]

But if David is *descended* from bastards, Moses is . . . well . . . *himself* a bastard (the pen recoils, but the truth must out). In Levit. 18:12 we read: 'Thou shalt not uncover the nakedness of thy father's sister'; in Exodus 6:20, we read: 'And Amram took him Jochebed, his father's sister to wife; and she bore him Aaron and Moses.'[6] It is hard to imagine a more glaring contrariety than this, and it is no less difficult to imagine that this contrariety was coincidental (one does not publish such damning material by mistake).

But we are not finished yet: the Midrash asks what Genesis 37:35 intends by 'All of Jacob's sons *and daughters* rose up to comfort him (for the putative mauling of Joseph).' Whence had Jacob daughters beyond Dina? The answer is that each son of Jacob was born together with a twin sister to whom they were wed, in flagrant infringement of Leviticus 18:9 ('Thou shalt not uncover the nakedness of thy sister').[7] The entire Israelite people, then, can proudly trace their lineage back to . . . illegitimacy. What's more, Cain, Abel, and Seth are said by many Rabbinic sources to have married *their* sisters.[8] In short: we are *all* bastards.

---

[5] The story of Lot and his daughters is, of course, also, and perhaps primarily, a dig at a longstanding enemy of the Israelites, but the Bible is a very sophisticated book and it is not difficult to attribute a dual purpose to that anecdote.

[6] There are several half-hearted Talmudic attempts to extricate Moses from this unpleasant predicament (see Yebamot, 4:13, Kiddushin, 3:12 and Sanhedrin, 58b).

[7] Genesis Rabbah, 84:21: '[Jacob] had only one daughter, and would that she too had been buried' (Dina is tainted in Rabbinic literature with the stain of promiscuity— *hada havat vehalvai qavra*). 'R. Judah says: [the eponyms of] the tribes were married to their sisters (*le-ahayoteihem nus'u ha-shevatim*).' What is perhaps gained by this legend in the realm of ethnic purity and nationalist exclusivism, is offset by what is lost in the realm of genealogical legitimacy.

[8] For a concise review of the midrashic material ses Ginzburg, *Legends,* vol. 5, 145, fn. 42.

3. STRANGE BEDFELLOWS

The intra-biblical contradictions, or at least tensions, sketched thus far have been stark and focused. But they partake of a more general dichotomy or dialectic described in the introduction to this essay that runs like a thread through the books of the Old Testament. This is the juxtaposition, or rather contraposition, within the same sacred literary canon of an already highly developed and ramified moral-legal system, on the one hand, and a flamboyant, free-wheeling, almost Byronesque cast of characters, on the other. Here we are not interested in any *specific* paradox between the behaviour of vaunted figures in the narrative sections of scripture and a particular Pentateuchal regulation. What exercises us is rather a more basic, gut feeling that the personalities and activities of the Bible's preeminent protagonists do not seem to fit in well with the legalistic and pietistic spirit of the document as a whole, almost as if they were characters from another book who had taken a wrong turn.

Let us be honest: as a rule, we do not tend to associate romance with regimentation, swashbuckling with codification, poetry with legislation, virility with subordination, or the appreciation of beauty with the enforcement of modesty. Sanctity, strictness and fastidiousness do not dwell easily in our minds with brashness, tenderness and libido; restriction and limitation do not jibe naturally in our consciousnesses with wildness, passion, comedy and carnality. The modern (and medieval) notion of a 'religious' man is far closer to *The Simpsons'* goody-two-shoes neighbour Ned Flanders—puritan, pedantic, prudish, even sissified—than it is to, say, Don Juan or Cyrano de Bergerac. A literature infused with divinity and saturated through and through with rigid and detailed ordinances geared to restrict human activity on every side, is where we would expect to encounter paragons who are more akin to automatons: the paint-by-numbers types who have been tamed, trained, habituated and ultimately emasculated by an all-encompassing system of psycho-social conditioning. It is definitely *not* the venue in which we would anticipate running into daredevils, schemers, troubadours, and bad-boy *caballeros* who 'ooze sex'. We would certainly understand if the *villains* of such a literary tradition were portrayed in this manner, as a sort of 'control group' against which to offset the cultural ideal. But it is, rather, the *heroes* of the Hebrew scriptures who are thus depicted, by those scriptures themselves and by their Rabbinic elaborations and embellishments.[9] These unpredictable, irrepressible, indomitable individuals are *anything but* poster-boys for the Pentateuchal or Talmudic codes of conduct, are *anything but* the cowed minions and impotent cookie-cuts that are so often the products of rigidly regulated ideological/behavioural systems.

4. THE FLESH IS STRONG

There is *amour* in the Bible, and one need not venture as far as the Song of Songs to find it. One look at Rachel coming down the hill surrounded by her flocks, and Jacob was inspired to 'roll the great stone from atop the well's mouth' which it normally took many men to move. 'And Jacob loved Rachel', the text goes on, and he 'labored seven years for her hand', a period which 'seemed to him but a few days because of his love of her' (Gen. 29:1–27). For sheer romance, these lines are hard to beat.

The pedantic legal minds that authored Bible and Talmud (or at least eventually approved the redaction of the canon) somehow managed to maintain quite the predilection for aesthetics. Isaac was stunning, Joseph was a dream-boat (one look at him, and a hall full of Egyptian noblewomen sliced off their fingers instead of peeling the oranges on their plates),[10] Rachel was 'beautiful and well endowed' and Sarah and Rebecca were so fetching that they were snapped up immediately by the ruler of any land whither they travelled with their husbands. Saul was tall, and made women swoon: when he came into town looking for his father's lost donkeys and asked the local girls a simple question—'Is the seer here?'—they responded with a three-verse long barrage of interminable chatter designed (say the rabbis) to keep the Benjaminite beau standing there so they could gawk at him.[11] Abigail, wife of Nabal and then of David, was one of the 'four most gorgeous women in the world', together with Sarah, Esther

---

[9] I am the first one to admit that the Talmud frequently does the exact opposite, turning the virile and vital characters of the Bible into a bunch of bookworms, pietists and teacher's pets.

[10] See Ginzburg, *Legends*, vol. 2, 51.

[11] See RaSHI to 1 Samuel 9:12: *ma'arikhot hayu badevarim kedei lehistaqel be-yofyo shel Sha'ul.*

and Rahav the harlot.[12] Samson 'the Judge' picked fights, preferred Philistine girls, visited prostitutes, and was a sucker for the tears of the fairer sex. Said Rabbi Yohanan of Ruth without wincing: 'Whoever saw her immediately ejaculated.'[13]

One need not go beyond the biblical David to discover (I hope the female readership will pardon me) every young woman's dream. David was a handsome, winsome shepherd and dashing warrior-poet. He was a chivalrous outlaw, a lute-playing bandit, cruel to his enemies and devoted to his friends. Enraptured, he could strip down to a loincloth and dance ecstatically in front of thousands. Not for nothing did the ladies love him (1 Samuel 18:8)—and he loved the ladies.

The rabbis, far from endeavouring to whitewash or mitigate this depiction of David, portray him as insatiable. 'Late one afternoon [the king] rose from his bed and strolled on the roof of the royal palace' (2 Sam. 11:2). What was David doing in bed at that hour? the Talmud wants to know, and quickly furnishes its own answer:

> David would cohabit by day instead of by night (the celebrated commentator RaSHI explains: 'so that he would get his fill of coition in the morning and would not think about women all day'). [In doing so, however,] he forgot a well known fact of nature, to wit, that there is a small organ in man which when satisfied becomes hungry, but when left hungry becomes satisfied (*evar qaṭan yesh ba-adam, masbi'o ra'ev u-marvi'o save'a*—RaSHI explains: 'He who tries to satisfy his male member through frequent copulation finds himself craving more of the same and increases his lust').[14]

David's drive was strong, and so he made it a practice (one forbidden by Jewish law)[15] to have sex in the morning, in order to free his mind up for

---

[12] Megillah 15a: *arba'nashim yefeifiyot ba-olam . . .*

[13] Ruth Rabbah 2:4 and Megillah 15a: *kol ha-ro'eh et Rut merik keri.*

[14] Sanhedrin 107a. On David's ongoing battle with his libido (*yetzer*), see Baba Batra 17a, Yerushalmi Berakhot 9:5, Sukkah 52a, Sanhedrin 107a, Yerushalmi Sanhedrin 2:3.

[15] Niddah 16b and 17a: 'It is forbidden for a man to have conjugal relations during the day' (*asur lo le-adam leshamesh mitato bayom*—it is considered 'brazenness' ['*azut metzah*]; one rabbi even claims that this prohibition derives from the verse 'love thy neighbor as thyself' [Leviticus 19:18], the 'neighbor' in this case referring to a man's wife and the danger of daytime intercourse being that he might perceive some bodily imperfection that would cause him *not* to love her). Even 'that wicked one' (Ahasuerus) is praised by the rabbis because he 'would not have intercourse during the day' (Megillah 13a—Esther is described as 'coming [to the royal palace] in the evening and returning [thence] in the morning' [Esther 2:14]), whereas the otherwise righteous Isaac is censured for sleeping with Rebecca while the sun still shone (see the

matters of state. This method was ineffective, however, as he soon felt the need for another encounter, and then another, and before long it was late afternoon (and even at that point his growing appetite remained unsatiated, for from the roof upon which he was strolling he espied—and then summoned to his quarters and had intercourse with—Bathsheba).

The rabbis may have critiqued David's *handling* of his powerful biological urge, but that does not mean that they did not revel in it. See, for instance, the following glorification of the celebrated sovereign's prowess:

> Rabbi Judah said: Rav said: Even when David was ill he fulfilled eighteen marital duties (*afilu bi-sh'at ḥelyo shel David qiyyem shmoneh 'esreh 'onot*), as it is written (Ps. 6:7): 'I am weary with my groaning, all the night I make my bed to swim, I water my couch with my tears.'[16]

In sickness as in health, the rabbis are stressing here, David was man enough to satisfy his many wives, one after the other. Elsewhere in the Talmud the rabbinic authorities furnish an illustration of David's virility that can only be characterized as a macho boast:

> It is written: 'And the damsel (*viz.* Abishag the Shunamite) was very fair, and she became a companion to the king and ministered unto him, but the king did not have relations with her' (1 Kings 1:4). She said to him, 'Let us marry,' but he (*viz.* David) said: 'You are forbidden to me.' She mocked him: 'When courage fails the thief, he becomes virtuous' (i.e. you reject me only because you are old and impotent). So he commanded his servants, 'Call Bathsheba!' And we read: 'Bathsheba went to the king into the chamber' (1 Kings 1:15). Rabbi Judah said in the name of Rav: On that occasion Bathsheba wiped herself with thirteen napkins (i.e. cleaned off the residue of thirteen male ejaculations—*be-otah sha'ah qinḥa Batsheva' be-shlosh 'esreh mapot*).[17]

There are a great many other examples that could be adduced of such unabashed 'robustness', and a great many areas and fields in which the biblical characters, whether in their purely scriptural or more ornate Rabbinic guise, can be shown to be shockingly human. We

---

commentaries to Genesis 26:8). The rabbis similarly look the other way when David violates regulations such as that of *yiḥud* (being alone with a member of the opposite sex) with Abishag (see Sanhedrin 21a).

[16] Sanhedrin 107a. The reference may be to any illness or to his final one. The tears of the verse are made into a metaphor for sperm. As for the groans . . .

[17] Sanhedrin 22a. Whether it is 18 wives one time each, as above, or one wife 13 times, the point is the same.

could also go on to demonstrate that the rabbis describe *themselves* in terms no less straightforward and surprising. But space does not permit, and it is time to offer some brief remarks on several corresponding phenomena in the Islamic tradition.

5. NO STANDER ABOVE MEN

The Qur'an and Hadith—which may be (very loosely) compared to the Bible and Talmud—play host to a curious contrariety that is quite reminiscent of the multi-pronged paradox discussed in the previous pages. Islam is easily the most 'legislated' or legalistic religion after Judaism, and the *shari'ah* (Muslim law) has a great deal in common with the *halacha* (Jewish law). The seminal documents of the faith that Muhammad brought are filled to overflowing with celestial decrees and terrestrial enactments that are swiftly dissected, delineated, developed and especially *expanded and elaborated*—by jurists and 'proto-jurists'—into a vast system of tens of thousands of positive and negative precepts and sub-precepts. Easily over a third of the Qur'an consists of exhortations and admonitions to observe these duties, and the Hadith literature (an immense genre that consists of an almost incalculable number of 'reports' concerning the actions and statements of the Prophet Muhammad and his Companions) similarly lays heavy emphasis on the reward or punishment awaiting those who are obedient or disobedient to the religion's prescriptions.

But in Islamic tradition, as in Jewish, we find heroic figures whose devil-may-care exuberance strikes us as more than a little out of place in such severe surroundings. The Qur'an tells us, for instance, that God instructed Muhammad to issue the following warning to his flock:

> Command the believing men, that they lower their gaze and restrain their sexual passions. That is purer for them. Surely, Allah is aware of what they do. And command the believing women that they lower their gaze and restrain their sexual passions, and do not display their beauty except for those parts which may be exposed, and let them wear their head coverings such that they cover up their bosom . . . and let them not strike their feet so that the adornment they hide may be known . . . (Q. 24:30–31).[18]

---

[18] The final clause quoted here is reminiscent of Isaiah 3:16.

Modesty and chastity are enjoined upon both sexes in these verses, and the Hadith, scriptural commentary (*tafsir*), and jurisprudential literature (*fiqh*) proceeded to derive from this passage alone an entire sprawling universe of complex and confining legislation, the exposition of which covered many thousands of pages in medieval exegetical and legal works. As in the previous section, we go now not in search of any *specific* violation of these injunctions or their derivatives on the part of a particular Muslim paladin. Rather, we are interested to know whether the leading men and ladies of the Islamic canon are portrayed as embodiments of the same chaste and modest spirit that informs these verses, whether they exemplify the 'pious personality' that we assume such laws are designed to construct and preserve.

The black-eyed *houri*s or virgins of paradise—constant butt of ignorant Western ridicule—represent the first clue that Islamic ideals in the legendary sphere depart quite some distance from Islamic ideals in the legal sphere: the distance of poetry and art from physics and arithmetic. These 'females with large and lustrous eyes'[19] will, explain the traditional Qur'an commentators, 'burn passionately for their husbands, desire them and crave them'.[20] Their skin will be 'as delicate and diaphanous as the inner membrane of an egg', and their faces so beautiful that 'when one of them removes her veil the sun will pale in comparison to her radiance'.[21] They will be endowed with 'round swelling breasts' (*ku'b*), upon one of which will be inscribed the name of Allah and upon the other the name of the *houri*'s husband,[22] and they will excite the carnal urge through a lascivious motion of the hips (*ghunj*).[23]

On earth as it is in heaven: neither condemnation nor inhibition but rather comfort and approbation informs the treatment of matters carnal by the early Islamic canon, and nowhere is this more true than in the case of the faith's most venerated hero and Model for all Muslims, the Prophet Muhammad. His beloved wife 'A'isha reported that her husband's 'three favourite things in this world were food,

---

[19] Qur'an 56:22.

[20] Muḥammad b. Jarīr al-Ṭabarī, *Jāmi'al-Bayān 'an Ta'wīl Āy al-Qur'ān* (Beirut: Dār al-Fikr, 1995) vol. 27, 244–5: *'ushaqqan li-azwajihinna ... yashtahina ... yashtaqna*.

[21] Imad al-Din Isma'il b.'Umar b. Kathir, *al-Bidaya wa'l-Nihaya* (Riyad: Maktabat al-Nasr al-Haditha, 1968) vol. 2, 284.

[22] *Encyclopedia of Islam*, 2nd edn., *s. v.* 'Hur' (A.J. Wensinck and C. Pellat).

[23] Tabari, ibid 246.

women and perfume'.[24] Muhammad's personal servant, Anas b.
Malik, testified that 'the Messenger of God, may God's peace and
blessings be upon him, surpassed all others in four things: generosity,
courage, fierceness and frequency of intercourse'—qualities more
suitable to a cross between Sir Lancelot and Casanova than to our
'nerdy' notions of what a holy man should be.[25] Hisham transmitted
the following from the Companion Qatada (strong echoes of David):

> The Prophet used to make the rounds of his wives in the space of a
> single day or night—and they (i.e. his wives) were eleven in number.
> I (i.e. Qatada) asked Anas: 'Did he really have the stamina for that?'
> (*a wa-kana yutiquhu?*). He replied: 'We used to say that he had been
> given the strength of thirty men.'[26]

'I am flesh and blood!' Muhammad used to emphasize, and he would
go on to excoriate any followers who thought to deprive themselves of
the good things of this world. With Walt Whitman, the Prophet of
Islam could confess himself 'turbulent, fleshy and sensual, eating,
drinking and breeding . . . no stander above men or women, or apart
from them, no more modest than immodest.'[27] His Companions, for
the most part, took his advice:

> 'Abd Allāh b. 'Umar (son of the second successor to Muhammad and one
> of the ten believers promised paradise while still alive) had a voracious
> sexual appetite. He would break his [Ramaḍān] fast on sexual intercourse
> (*kāna yafṭūru bi'l-jimāʻ*), and sometimes he would even have intercourse
> *before* the Sundown Prayer, perform the greater ablution, and then pray.
> Once he cohabited with three of his concubines in one night during the
> month of Ramaḍān—in other words, between sunset and the last meal
> (*saḥūr*) before beginning the fast of the following day.[28]

---

[24] Walī al-Dīn Tibrīzī, *Mishkāt al-Maṣābīḥ* (Lahore, Mālik Sirāj al-Dīn, n.d) vol. 1,
52: *kāna rasūl Allāh yuʻjibuhu min al-dunya thalāthun: al-ṭaʻām wa'l-nisā' wa'l-ṭīb.*

[25] Shams al-Dīn Abū Bakr Muḥammad b. Qayyim al-Jawziyya, *Zād al-Maʻād fī
Hadī Khayr al-ʻIbād* (Beirut: Iḥyā al-Turāth al-ʻArabī, n.d.) vol. 3, 147: *fuḍḍila rasul
Allah ʻalā'l-nāsi bi-arbaʻa: bi'l-sakhā' wa'l-shajāʻa wa'l-baṭsh wa-kathrat al-jimāʻ.*

[26] Zayn al-Dīn Abū'l-Faraj b. Rajab al-Ḥanbalī, *Fatḥ al-Bārī: Sharḥ Ṣaḥīḥ al-
Bukhārī* (Madīna: Maktabat al-Ghurabā' al-Athariyya/Maktabat Taḥqīq Dār al-
Haramayn, 1996) vol. 1, 298: *kana al-nabi yudiru* (other versions: *yatufu*) *'ala nisa'ihi
fi layl wahid . . . kunna natahaddathu annahu u'tiya quwwata thalathin.*

[27] Walt Whitman, *Leaves of Grass* (Philadelphia: David McKay, 1900) 'Song of
Myself,' 24.

[28] Abū Ḥāmid Muḥammad b. Muḥammad al-Ghazālī, *Iḥyā ʻUlūm al-Dīn* (Cairo:
Mu'assasa al-Ḥalabī li'l-Nashr wa'l-Tawzīʻ, 1967) vol. 1, 184. The *'ashara al-mubash-
shara* or ten believers granted paradise during their lives is also a Talmudic notion.

Examples of such hearty irreverence are as abundant in Islamo-classical as they are in Judeo-classical literature, and here again, these traits are ascribed not to malefactors or even to second-string paragons, but specifically to the faith's most sacred personages. Here, to close, is what can only be described as a 'men's locker room' story:

'Abd Allah b. Rawaha (signatory to the Second Treaty of 'Aqaba, amanuensis of the Prophet, martyr at the battle of Mu'ta) was lying in bed one night with his spouse. At a certain point he rose, betook himself to the adjoining cubicle of his maidservant, and mounted her. Sensing his absence, Ibn Rawaha's wife awoke with a start, donned her robe and went out in search of him. Espying her husband in *flagrante delicto* with the girl, she returned to the house in a jealous rage, grabbed a kitchen knife and stormed back to the scene. In the meantime, Ibn Rawaha had satisfied his urge (*faragha fa-qāma*), and on his way out of the maidservant's quarters encountered his knife-bearing wife. 'What's this?!,' he inquired. 'I'll tell you what this is,' she responded. 'If I had caught you now where I saw you before, I would have plunged this knife right between your shoulder-blades!' 'And where did you see me before?' asked Ibn Rawaha (playing dumb). 'Why, I saw you on top of the maidservant!,' cried his wife. 'Nay!,' he replied, 'You did *not* see me thus, [and I can prove it]: for the Messenger of God has forbidden us to recite the Qur'ān when we are impure as the result of a sexual encounter (*junub*).' 'Very well,' his wife demanded. 'Recite!' (Now—adds the narrator—Ibn Rawaha's wife was not well acquainted with scripture [*wa-kanat la taqra'a al-Qur'an*]). So Ibn al-Rawaha recited:

> The Messenger of God came to us
> declaiming his Book,
> Like the brilliant flash of the rising dawn,
> He came bearing guidance in wake of the darkness,
> And our hearts are sure
> that what he said is the truth,
> All night long he jumps up out of bed,
> While the polytheists sleep soundly![29]

---

[29] Ibn Rawaha's extemporaneous poetry stretches the simile of Muḥammad's light banishing *jāhilī* darkness, and may even—in the final couplet—contain a mischievous allusion to the poet's own actions immediately prior (these lines are difficult to decipher). Being one of the Prophet's amanuenses (*kuttāb al-waḥy*), Ibn Rawaha was no doubt particularly familiar with the literary style of revelation. This may, however, have been intended as a deliberately poor parody of the same.

Convinced that her husband had declaimed genuine Qur'anic verses—and that therefore he could not possibly have come from a sexual encounter—Ibn Rawaha's wife hung her head in shame. 'I believe in God,' she apologized. 'Mine eyes are belied!' On the morrow (the anecdote concludes) Ibn Rawaha went to see the Prophet Muhammad and told him all that had transpired. The Messenger of God laughed so hard you could see his back molars.[30]

There is obviously nothing exacting or scientific about the paradox I have tried to explicate in these pages so far: it is more of a feeling that gradually creeps up on the reader of these literatures, a sense of tension between two fundamental forces pulling in opposite directions, as if the narrative sections of the Bible/Talmud and Qur'an/Hadith were in defiant rebellion against the legal sections, and neither tradition—the Judaic or the Islamic—felt the need to cover up this internal conflict in favour of a smooth and unified heritage. As attractive as I find this apparent preservation of contradiction, in the final pages of this essay I would like to propose a solution to this conundrum—or at least: a direction one might follow in search of a solution—that views these seemingly antipodal tendencies not as antagonists to, but in fact as allies of, one another.

6. NO SINNERS, NO SAINTS

There are two ways to foster a moral society: one is to build strong men; the other is to build strong walls. The first method is educational, and is predicated, if not upon the perfectibility of human beings, then upon their improvability. It attempts to reach down into the hearts and minds of society's individual members and 'rewire' their psyches in such a manner as to render them, to one degree or another, resistant to transgression. This end is sought through a combination of exhortation—geared to instil a conscience that admonishes its owner against wrongdoing—and conditioning—geared to ensure that he or she possesses the fortitude to comply with the dictates of that conscience. The procedure involved is one of inurement, or immunization. A toddler's environment offers him or

---

[30] Muhammad b. Ahmad al-Ansari al-Qurtubi, *Tafsir al-Qurtubi* (Cairo: al-Maktaba al-Tawfiqiyya, 1994) vol. 5, 182–3.

her a wide range of alluring but illicit activities in which to engage: throwing food, snatching a sibling's toy, stomping in the dog's dish, etc. In most such cases, rather than removing all opportunities for the child to perpetrate the undesirable deed (for example, in the above examples: returning to bottle-feeding, separating the siblings, covering the dog's dish), parents opt for repeated instruction before the fact and regular punishment afterward, in the hope that this will facilitate the emergence of the all-important 'superego' and the development of behavioural 'antibodies' that will allow the child to withstand such enticements *independently* in the future. The key ingredients here are *full exposure* and *unimpeded access* to problematic desiderata: only under such circumstances can an evolving personality undergo the perpetual trials that will steel it; only in this fashion can it be trained to look temptation heroically in the eye and 'just say no'. Thus, by gradually taming natural instincts and subduing animalistic proclivities, do we ultimately arrive at the noblest human ideal: the saintly man of conscience, who can be trusted to do the right thing even when surrounded by a sea of opportunities to do the wrong thing. 'Sin crouches at the door,' the Lord explains to Cain (Gen. 4:7), 'and its urge is toward you; *but you can be its master.*'

But Cain did not master sin. It mastered him, and a man was murdered as a result. The second method of forging a moral society, then, while ready to concede the possibility that the human id can be moderately reformed or reined in through training, refuses to *rely* on that possibility. Because the purveyors of this approach harbour both a deeper respect for the power of the innate drives and a greater horror of the evil to which those drives can lead us, they are unwilling to take chances. Putting people to the test by leaving the door open for them to trespass may produce its fair share of moral heroes among those who do not succumb, but it will also be responsible for the corruption of many souls and the creation of many criminals among those who are unable to resist temptation and therefore *do* succumb—to say nothing of the agony of their victims. This camp therefore holds that the very opportunity to transgress must be severely curtailed, a goal best accomplished through the *erection of barriers* that both minimize exposure and impede access. To return to the example of mischievous children: there are times when we focus less on the moral development of the child and more on his or her safety or that of a valuable item or individual: parents of toddlers generally plug up sockets, lock up medicines, place precious but fragile objects out of sight or reach, and make certain that their three-year-old does not have the opportunity to pick up the newborn. In such cases the admonition-castigation system is considered insufficient to the task: it is always possible that the child will neither heed our warnings nor be deterred by our punishments, and then the consequences might be catastrophic. We do not gamble with our children's lives for the sake of personality-shaping experiments.

The analogy to the adult world may be formulated (simplistically) in terms of the following stark choice: we can either have an immoral society made up of moral individuals, or a moral society made up of immoral individuals. In other words: (a) since the creation of moral individuals requires, as we have argued, their regular exposure to the temptation to sin and their easy access to the means of satisfying that temptation; and (b) since few of the people in a given society will pass this test all of the time and at least some of them will fail it much of the time; then (c) while a significant number of moral individuals may be created by this method, a not inconsiderable number of heinous crimes will also be committed along the way, and we have thus achieved an immoral society populated by (at least a significant number of) moral individuals.

On the other hand, (a) since the creation of a moral society requires the elimination of vice; and (b) since this end is only ensured with any degree of certainty through the erection of barriers to block both exposure to temptation and the means to its satisfaction; then (c) while crimes will be reduced to a minimum by this method, moral individuals will rarely be created, and we have achieved a moral society populated (for the most part) by immoral individuals.

There is, however, another factor that distinguishes these two opposing approaches. The attempt by those who uphold the first method to breed a nobility of moral *übermenschen* is rejected by the supporters of the second method not just because it will so often end in failure, but also because *it will frequently result in success*. The procedure whereby individuals are repeatedly exposed to enticements and encouraged to resist them, when it actually works, of a necessity involves a dampening of the natural appetites and an enfeeblement of the passions. After all, the ability to control one's cravings is the end result of a bilateral process, or, perhaps better, of what are ultimately two different ways to describe the *same* process: 'will-power' becomes strong; desire becomes weak. This creeping anorexia of the id is the high road—indeed, the only road—to sainthood.

The problem is that, despite eons of official rhetoric and exhortation to the contrary, *most of us have little use for saints.* Tampering with the internal machinery of the human personality effects permanent, non-discerning change: reducing passion in the face of *illicit* temptation entails the reduction of passion across the board, including in the face of *licit* temptation, not to mention in those many other areas in life where passion is a desideratum. Indeed, passionless people are more often than not also *com*passionless people, and we certainly have no need for more of *them.*

How, then, can we achieve the best of both worlds? How can we simultaneously preserve passion while keeping transgression in check? The answer provided by the upholders of the second method is: build walls instead of rebuilding men. Locate the moral policeman not in *intra*-human but in *inter*-human space. Leave the drives and appetites intact and *dormant,* and do not awaken them until they are needed for legitimate purposes. Instead of teasing and tantalizing the human inclinations and then demanding of their owner that he or she suppress them—the 'look but don't touch' philosophy that is busy debilitating desires (and creating pathologies) throughout the Western world today—the second method seeks to leave the libido at peace, and therefore in a good state of health. Walls achieve this goal in two related ways: (1) they avoid arousing the appetite in the first place, by preventing exposure to illicit objects of desire (thus leaving the libido at peace); and (2) if, for whatever reason, the appetite nevertheless becomes aroused (through, say, the use of imagination), the wall puts a stop to any and all attempts to satisfy that appetite, but it does so *without demanding that its owner take responsibility for suppressing or reducing it.* The psychological consequences of holding *oneself* back are vastly different from the psychological consequences of *being* held back: the former eventually emasculates the subject; the latter leaves him a man (or her a woman). In the world of walls sin is rare, but sinners (or, rather, *would-be* sinners) are legion. Saints are nowhere to be seen.

Of course, the dichotomy between these two outlooks was never so clear cut as we have presented it here: most societies throughout history have employed elements of both methods in a wide variety of proportions and combinations. Nevertheless, there are noticeable differences in emphasis, with some systems leaning more toward the first and others more toward the second method. The preeminent examples of a system that seeks to build walls instead of breaking men are the Jewish and Islamic religions. Both faiths are devoted to creating a *virtuous* society, in which heinous offences hardly ever happen; at the same time they are concerned with maintaining a *virile* society, in which human beings can revel in the fleshly facts of their humanity. There are, I would venture, no other religions extant the laws of which erect higher barriers between men and women than Judaism and Islam; and there are, at the same time, no other religions extant the revered personages of which—in many cases the very figures who promulgated the laws that established those barriers— are more explicitly described engaging in more uninhibited, varie- gated and passionate carnal activity, than Judaism and Islam.

Perhaps, then, there is no paradox after all between Jewish-Islamic legalism and the exuberance that inhabits the pages of these two religions' seminal sources; perhaps these seemingly antithetical di- mensions are not only compatible, but actually reinforce one another. The *halakha* and *shari'a* are set up in such a way as to police people's actions *externally*, not attempt to reform or rewire people *internally*. The Judaic and Islamic method is to build walls, not to rebuild men. This 'non-interference policy' allows the human being's internal drives to remain fierce; it reins them in for the sake of society, but leaves them intact for the sake of the individual. This is in major contrast to the 'invasive' methods of so many other Eastern and Western religions and ideologies throughout history that have sought to perfect the personality, that have cultivated and adulated saints or supermen: from Hinduism, Buddhism and Taoism to Christianity, Communism and—perhaps most surprisingly but also most signifi- cantly—modern, post-industrial secularism, where the exponential proliferation of temptation—an entire hemisphere inhabited by strip- tease artists—is matched only by the expectation that 'decent people' will resist it: look, but don't touch.

The Jewish and Muslim traditions do not allow one to look at that which one must not touch, not just for fear that one may end up touching it, but also for fear that *one may not end up touching it*, and in so repressing one's internal urges, ultimately enfeeble and dampen them. Do not tame or 'break' the raging bull; keep him crazed but pent up until rodeo time, and then he'll deliver one hell of a show (he might also occasionally bust out of his pen and wreak havoc, but that is a risk we are willing to take: laws breed outlaws, as St. Paul was so keenly aware). We can therefore understand why Judaic and Islamic classical texts are so crowded with charismatic he-men and *femmes fatales* at the same time that they are crammed with incomparably restrictive rules and regulations (whereas the Christian canon, for instance, is stocked with neither of these): wild men and women need high walls, and, simultaneously, *high walls keep the men and women wild*. This approach, common to Judaism and Islam, represents, I would aver, the most genuine and profound level upon which 'the law can set us free'.

10

Individuality

Lenn E. Goodman

We are often told that Hebraic values are moral, where Hellenic ideals are aesthetic. That kind of sweeping stereotype, like most such caricatures, is not highly informative. The very first biblical value judgement, after all, is God's, seeing that the light He's called into being is good. That happens long before light has a use or even a name. Light, in these opening lines of Genesis, is good intrinsically—that is, it is judged aesthetically. It is beautiful and worthwhile *in itself.*

One value, not unrelated, to be pondered in the Hebrew sources and the culture and tradition that follow in their wake is individuality—not least because the individual cultivated by Hebraic norms is a moral person from the outset, a locus of dignity and deserts, to be sure, but also an agent called on to recognize the due of others. Such thinking and valuing contrasts strikingly with some familiar, modern notions of individuality, which may set individuals at odds with one another. Here each person is the moral counterpart of others, responsible not just to requite what he receives (to 'give back' as the cliché would have it) but to act in loving kindness toward others—not just for what they have done or might do but for what and who they are.[1]

Suppose, as an expository strategy, instead of moving from biblical to rabbinic to medieval texts in the present chapter, we begin with something modern and overtly philosophical, asking how and why Spinoza, notorious for his monism and determinism, focused philosophically on the individual and the scope of human freedom.

---

[1] See the ontic account of justice in Goodman, *On Justice* (Oxford: Littman Library, 2008).

Every tyro in philosophy knows that only God or nature met the criteria for substantiality that Spinoza drew from the work of Aristotle and Descartes: self-sufficiency in being and concept, dependence on no other thing. Spinoza's well known phrase *Deus sive Natura* was not meant reductively. God was not trimmed to physical dimensions. Rather, being absolute, Spinoza's God manifests Himself infinitely and in infinite ways. Only two are known to us: thought and extension. Having nothing in common with the rest, we cannot interact with them and thus know nothing about them. Thought and extension themselves are not substances but attributes, Spinoza reasons, playing on Maimonides' classic thoughts. They are two ways in which God expresses Himself. The attributes constitute God's reality. All finite things are 'modes', modifications of the attributes. Each particular pursues the logic of its nature, of necessity. For all things must be what they are. But necessity here does not extrude a 'block universe', a static fatality. The same logic that demands a thing be what it is also demands it pursue its own course.

Dissatisfied with the Aristotelian account of being, which locates the reality of things in unchanging, universal essences, Spinoza reshapes the idea: Essences are dynamic, and unique to the individual. Sidestepping confusions with the older idea, Spinoza renames essence *conatus*, striving: The essence of each individual is its tendency to affirm its reality.[2] In an early work Spinoza defines Providence as 'nothing other than that striving found in Nature at large and in each particular thing to preserve and promote its own being.'[3] Predestination, similarly, is causality, the necessity by which things enact their own character. For all things do as they do and become what they become through the action of causes, 'internal or external'.[4] God's infinite power finds 'definite and determinate' expression in particulars.

Spinoza's radical account of substance responds creatively to the endgame played out when the ancient version of the idea failed. The activity that Aristotle saw as a sure mark of reality entails passivity as well, since all things in nature are interdependent. The idea that particulars are self-sufficient, then, collapses.

---

[2] Spinoza, *Ethics* 3p6–7.
[3] Spinoza, *Short Treatise* 5.1, Gebhardt, ed. 1.40; see Goodman, *Jewish and Islamic Philosophy: Crosspollinations* (Edinburgh and New Brunswick: Edinburgh University Press and Rutgers University Press, 1999) 156–78.
[4] Spinoza, *Short Treatise* 6, esp. 6.4, Gebhardt, ed. 1.42.

Matter failed similarly as the principle of individuation: If the cosmos was a plenum, as Aristotle, Spinoza, and Descartes agreed, embodiment could no more individuate particulars than substantial forms could unify them. Species were already losing the constancy Aristotle had seen, and Cartesian extension could hardly disaggregate individuals from their mutual enjambment. But if essences are individual and dynamic, the conatus of each individual gives it an identity. And any body is differentiated from others by its internal patterns and rhythms of motion and rest.

Intension rather than extension, as Leibniz was to put it, becomes the principle of individuation. So entranced was Leibniz with Spinoza's approach that he grounded his monadology in the idea that each particular enacts its unique essence alone. Indeed, Leibniz leaned so hard on Spinoza's approach to individuation, seeing in it an escape route from the coarse materialism that others had mounted on the Cartesian idea of extension, that he scuttled interaction altogether, proclaiming proudly that 'monads have no windows', and resting change in general and mind–body relations specifically on a postulate of pre-established harmony, punting downfield towards God's will as the guarantor of contingency and freedom.

Contingency was not a notion welcome to Spinoza. It smacked too much of the arbitrary. As for freedom, the idea that we humans act arbitrariously, exercising a faculty of will imparted for just that purpose, that was anathema on several counts: Hypostatizing the will cloaked a mere renaming of effects under the cover of an occult entity, an impostor explanation. And the notion of an undetermined will violates the axiom that things must be what they are, offering in exchange only a sorry excuse for any robust idea of freedom. For arbitrary acts are irrational, and chance doings say nothing of ourselves. How are they our own?

If freedom means autonomy, Spinoza reasoned, freedom and determinism do not exclude each other (as conventional thinkers may imagine). All that happens is determined. But some outcomes cannot be explained without reference to what *we* do. Freedom is not uncaused choice (as the Epicureans once pictured it), nor is it the recognition of necessity (as the Stoics had suggested). Rather, it is self-determination: The measure of my freedom is the extent of my agency in an act.

The real question for ethics, then, is the extent to which we can make an action our own rather than the ricochet effect of external causes. We are free insofar as our doings affirm our own reality. We are passive insofar as we succumb to externals. The issue is not determinism versus indeterminism but self-determination vis-à-vis determination by other agencies. For each of us is one of those individuals in which God's will and power are expressed in finite, determinate ways. Causality, we must not forget, can be internal or external. Of all the sources of passivity, closest to hand are the ones we allow into our minds. The passions, properly speaking, are emotions that render one more a victim than an agent. At the borderland between effects undergone and acts undertaken, thought proves the gatekeeper: Our passions are inadequate ideas, products of misunderstanding, blindly linking hopes and fears to things that do not actually affect our capacities as we might imagine. We humans are adequate causes insofar as we rely on adequate ideas, understanding the real natures and causes of things.

We win our way to adequate ideas by seeing things contextually. Many of the traits traditionally branded as vices—envy, spite, egotism, complacency, arrogance, censoriousness, cruelty—and many a tendency cast in a more favourable light—the regret that dwells on what cannot be, the pity that struggles blindly or selfishly to dissociate ego from sufferers, the vainglory that hangs on others' approval, the ambition that hopes to make others like oneself—are not, as a Cartesian or Augustinian might have charged, mere products of wilfulness. They are inadequate ideas, reflecting an inadequate understanding of oneself and one's situation. They can be swept away by stronger, perhaps more wholesome emotions. But they are dissolved by the ancient purgative of understanding, its workings now explained (as no rationalist from Plato to Freud has ever done as well) by recognizing their roots in shoddy thinking. Adequate ideas displace inadequate ideas by seeing through them.

Political freedom enhances the individual's powers. Spinoza's liberalism here is anchored in his metaphysics. Far from the smothering organic state that might have been the fruit of monism, Spinoza finds civil society precious for its capacity to foster the flourishing of the individual. Universals, after all, are mere notions for Spinoza. All value is local, alive in the conatus and the projects of particulars. But self-affirmation does not mean domination. Natural kinship makes all humans potential allies:

[W]e can never attain a state where our self-preservation needs nothing outside ourselves . . . many externals are helpful to us and rightly sought. Of these none conceivable stands higher than those well matched to our nature. So if two individuals, say, of like nature join forces they form a single individual twice as capable as each alone. To a human being, then, nothing is more useful than another human being; and men can wish for nothing more helpful in preserving their being than that all should unite, their bodies and minds forming, as it were, a single body and mind, striving in concert to preserve itself and seeking the common benefit of all.

Whence it follows that those who are ruled by reason, pursuing their own advantage under reason's guidance, seek nothing for themselves that they do not desire for their fellow humans but are just, faithful, and honorable.[5]

Societies are formed not just for protection, as if fear and aggression were the prime human motives, but on a broader, more positive basis: Thinking people join hands for mutual benefit. Trust, loyalty, good faith, honour, and decency, are anchored in the recognition of shared interests. Collaboration springs from the recognition that cooperation betters human lives.

Self-interest, Spinoza writes, is as necessary as the axiom that the whole is greater than its part. So virtue, that is, strength of character, invites each of us to pursue his own advantage. But, for the rational individual, this means 'what is truly advantageous, and genuinely conducive to enhancing his perfection as a human being'.[6]

The wise individual and the well-regulated society, then, are not locked in some zero sum game. Individual rights and common interests are not adversaries. What everyone who pursues virtue desires for himself is to live by its guidance. That is easy to desire for others, since virtue promotes the complementarities that foster human unity. Virtue still pursues individual interest. But the seeds of regard for others are planted in the conatus. We seek their good and augment their power, to promote the general good, of course, but also to further *their* projects, enhancing the power of others by fostering the growth of adequate ideas in their minds. Thought here, as in

[5] Spinoza, *Ethics* 4p18s, Gebhardt, ed. 2.222 *l.* 34–223 *l.* 18; cf. 4p29–35.
[6] Spinoza, *Ethics* 4p18s, Gebhardt, ed. 2.222 *ll.* 19–20; cf. 4p24.

Socrates, is not divorced from action: Adequate ideas are not held at arm's length but grasped and lived by.[7]

Spinoza's moral psychology reflects and nourishes his liberalism. Thus, the thesis of the one complete book he published in his lifetime that was wholly his own: 'unabridged freedom of each individual to worship God as his own insight permits' is 'not only compatible with piety and civil peace, but is in fact something without which there will be neither peace nor piety.'[8] His title page unfurls the same flag more broadly: His arguments will show 'not only that philosophical freedom can be granted without harm to piety or civil peace but that it cannot be extinguished without their extinction too.'[9]

Standing on the rise created by Spinoza's rigour we can see ahead to the case for individual immortality that Mendelssohn crafted in his *Phaedon* and that Kant emulated, the idea of each human life as a project precious in God's sight, leading to the inference that God's grace must allow each individual to realize his full potential for moral growth and spiritual reunion with the Author of his being. We can see as well the imago of the moral energies that drive the philosophies of Hermann Cohen, Martin Buber, and Emmanuel Levinas, each voiced in its own idiom and in the philosophical usages of its day. We can look back from here to the biblical and rabbinic texts which rarely use the trademark devices of philosophy as we know it; and, from there, to the essays, dialogues, treatises, and summas of medieval Jewish philosophy, couched in the language of neoplatonic Aristotelianism, and see explicit affirmations and imperatives expressive of the moral regard for the individual that all these sources have in common.

Nothing, Philo will write, commending the dictum of Genesis that man was created in God's image (1:26), nothing earthborn is more God-like than man: The individual human mind reflects the universal mind of all the world, sovereign and supreme, reverenced and enshrined, in each person who succeeds God's first human individuals (*De Opificio Mundi* xxiii). Man, Saadiah will write, citing Isaiah

---

[7] See Goodman, 'An Idea is Not Something Mute like a Picture on a Pad', *Review of Metaphysics*, vol. 62 (2009) 591–631.

[8] Spinoza, *Tractatus Theologico-Politicus*, Preface, Gebhardt, ed. 3.7.

[9] Spinoza, *Tractatus Theologico-Politicus*, title page. The passage is regrettably mistranslated in Samuel Shirley's otherwise quite serviceable Spinoza, *Complete Works* (Indianapolis: Hackett, 2002) 387. The correct sense, parsing Spinoza's Latin accurately, is reflected in A.G. Wernham, Spinoza, *Political Works* (Oxford: Oxford University Press, 1958) 49.

(45:12) is the clear goal of creation, the only rational creature, rightly regnant over all the rest, as Genesis attests (1:28), endowed with free choice and urged to choose life and good (Deuteronomy 30:15, 19). Man is God's object. For man alone, personally and individually, can make the choices that will express his gratitude for God's unbounded grace.[10]

Maimonides, fighting shy of the seeming hubris of Saadiah's affirmation that man is the goal of creation, still makes the perfection of the individual the rightful object of all human endeavour ('Eight Chapters' 5). He distinguishes divine from human laws by their implicit purposes: Mortal legislators seek only the material security and welfare of those for whom they set forth laws. But a divine law seeks to institute the practices, symbols and ideas that will foster the perfection of the individual morally and intellectually, enabling each individual who makes the appropriate effort to realize the inner affinity that links the human person with God—the affinity signified by Scripture's saying that man was created in God's image (*Guide* I 1, II 40).

Leone Ebreo, the Renaissance physician and humanist philosopher, son of the famous Judah Abravanel, like Maimonides, connects the individual mind intellectually with the transcendent Active Intellect. Leone's famous circle of love anticipates Spinoza's thesis that the soul's intellectual love of God is the very love by which God loves Himself. Mendelssohn, as we have noted already and will consider in more detail, finds the key to immortality in the individual's moral quest. Cohen, the great Kantian and the teacher of Ortega y Gasset, Nicolai Hartmann, Rudolph Bultmann, Karl Barth, Boris Pasternak, and Ernst Cassirer, discovers the philosophical depth of Judaism in its normative regard for the human individual as a fellow man.

Distinctive when the Hebraic evidence is laid alongside European recensions of individualism, is the situating of the fulfilled individual of Israelite traditions in a social environment that creates a moral context. The mature or perfect person here is morally responsible.

---

[10] See Saadiah, *K. al-Mukhtār fi'l-Amānāt wa'l-Iᶜtiqadāt* IV, Exordium and 1–3 (The Book of Critically Selected Beliefs and Convictions, cited below as *ED*), J. Kafih, ed. (Jerusalem: Sura, 1970) 150–5; cf. S. Rosenblatt, trans. as *The Book of Beliefs and Opinions*, 180–7. For God's unbounded grace, see Saadiah, *K. al-Taᶜdīl* (Commentary on Job), Kafih, ed. (Jerusalem: Committee for the Publication of the Works of Rasag, 1973) 9–11; L.E. Goodman, trans. as *The Book of Theodicy* (New Haven: Yale University Press, 1988) 123–4.

Thus Buber, like Cohen, foregrounds the human person as an ethical being. The authentic encounter of individuals with one another grounds our very personhood. Levinas, for his part, repelled by the notion of 'thrownness', sets ethics ahead of metaphysics as conceived by Heidegger: The moral recognition of each human face, in its very particularity, is the philosophical cynosure. All of these Jewish philosophers, in their diverse ways, articulate core themes, and work out central axioms of biblical ethics and the philosophical anthropology and psychology that it embodies.

1. THE CANON AND BEYOND

The idioms change as readily as the languages, from biblical Hebrew to Talmudic Aramaic, Philo's Greek, the Arabic of Saadiah and Maimonides, Leone Ebreo's Italian, the German of Mendelssohn, Cohen, or Buber, the French of Levinas. The scarlet thread that runs through all the shifting tropes of myth and history, law and exhortation, song and parable, rapture and desolation: the primacy of personhood. Thus the singular origins of Adam and his counterpart; the singling out of Noah, non-conforming, upright, blameless (6:9, 18); God's covenant with Abraham, another non-conformist, humbly haggling for the mercy that would save God's justice (Genesis 18); the epiphanies, fleshed out in moral precepts and legal statutes challenging each conscience (Exodus 20:1–14, 21:1–23:19, Leviticus 19, Deuteronomy 5:6–18, 21:1–25:19). In the crowning call to commitment (Deuteronomy 6:4–9), God addresses the individual; and in exile, sincere contrition mends the breach, each heart reopened to love God (Deuteronomy 30:1–10).

Rabbinically, of course, the Torah is law. God's law is consequential communally. But the 'yoke of the kingdom of heaven', as the Rabbis call it, falls on each person (Leviticus 18:5).[11] The choice to preserve the law and the power to reclaim it are personal:

> the duty I charge thee with this day is not too wondrous or remote for
> thee. It's not up in the sky, as if to say, Who will go up to heaven and get

---

[11] cf. E.E. Urbach, *The Sages: Their Concepts and Beliefs* (Jerusalem: Magnes Press, 1975) 400–19.

it for us, so we may hear and do it. It's not across the sea, as if to say, Who will cross the sea and get it for us, so we may hear and do it. Keeping it is as near as thy mouth and thy heart. Just look: I've set before thee this day life and good, death and evil. My command to thee today: to love the Lord thy God and walk in His ways, keep His commandments, laws, and statutes. Then wilt thou live and multiply, blessed by God in the land thou art entering as thy possession. (Deuteronomy 30:11–16)

God's charge here, even when appealing to the yearning for posterity, is addressed in the second person singular. God's prescriptions are laws of life, for the individual; and, through the individual, for the nation. But the ethos of that nation, as biblically prescribed, reflects myriad personal choices. It is the tenor of those many choices that plots the futurity of all. With the same intimacy, Micah sums up God's norms: 'He hath told thee, O man, what is good, and what the Lord expecteth of thee. Just this: to act justly, love mercy, and humbly walk with thy God' (Micah 6:8).

Equally telling are the many blessings recited by an observant Jew: on rising, washing, eating, fulfilling any religious obligation, seeing any splendid or wonderful thing—a beautiful tree, a great leader, a stroke of lightning—or on hundreds of other occasions, from answering a call of nature to celebrating a milestone—and many times more within one's daily worship.

Every blessing opens *Barukh Attah*, usually translated 'Blessed art Thou'. The prayer then goes on to acknowledge God's bestowal of the occasion, or thanks Him for a commandment, say, to wash one's hands before eating, to wrap oneself in the prayer shawl, etc. Like many sacred passages in Hebrew, these blessings typically shift from the second person *Attah*, Thou, addressing God, to the third: 'who hath kept us alive, and sustained us, and brought us to this moment'—to quote the ritual expression of gratitude on attaining some landmark. But more striking is the grammatical mood of the first word of every blessing, *Barukh*. The word is in the jussive. The worshipper is *blessing* God.

Embarrassed at that thought, translators may bowdlerize—Blessed art Thou, or Blessed are You—as if the verb were in the indicative. But the blessing does not *describe* God, and the euphemistic 'Praised are You' wanders farther from the point. The force of the passive participle here is evident in the 'Call to worship', where the officiant calls on the congregation to bless God (*Barkhu et Adonai ha-mevorakh*—

Bless ye the Lord, most worthy of blessing). The congregation responds: *Barukh Adonai ha-mevorakh le-'olam va-'ed*—Blessed be the Lord, who is infinitely worthy of blessing. The *Thou* of our daily blessings (Blessed be Thou) deepens the intimacy established by that jussive: *I* am blessing God.

Many of us bless a person who sneezes. But the Hebrew blessings are not wishing God well or asking God to bless Himself. The prayers are performative, like 'I love you'. Each blessing reaches out, to connect with God. It is not a spell. It asks for nothing. The nisus is gratitude, celebration more than petition. The symmetry bespeaks mutuality, not a quid pro quo. The subtext is caring, aspiration.

Strikingly, although obscured by liturgical familiarity, the Hebrew blessings, when shifting to the third person to speak of God, assume the collective voice of the people as a whole, acknowledging His gifts and saying, for example, in the person of all Israel: 'who hath hallowed us with His commandments and charged us to kindle the Sabbath lights'. All Israel receives the blessings of the commandments, but each person who pronounces the prayer voices thanks for them individually.

The locus classicus of Rabbinic thoughts on individuality comes in the mandated warning to each witness in a capital case:

> Capital cases are not like others. In other cases a person may make monetary restitution, but in capital cases a witness is responsible for the blood of his victim, and that of all his posterity to the end of time. Notice, when Cain slew his brother, it is written, *The bloods of thy brother cry out*—not 'blood' but *bloods of thy brother*—his, and all his seed's. Why was just one human created when the world began? To teach us that if anyone is responsible for the death of a single soul,[12] it is as if he had destroyed a world; and if anyone saves a life, as if he'd saved a world. Also, for the sake of social peace, so people cannot tell each other, My ancestor was better than yours... —And to show the greatness of the Holy One, blessed be He. For a mortal stamps many coins with the same die, and all are identical. But the King of kings, the Holy One, blessed be He, stamped each man with the seal of the first, yet no two are alike. Thus each of us must say: For my sake was the world created! (Sanhedrin 4.5)

---

[12] Some oft cited texts add 'of Israel' here, but the oldest and most authoritative texts show that this was an interpolation—as the sequel confirms, since the life saved or lost is compared not with a nation but with a world. Responsibility here is by act or by omission.

Individuality, for Aristotle, in large part meant idiosyncrasy, accident, and contingency. Matter, differentiating, even isolating particulars, gave such free rein to the welter of conflicting causes that the network of interactions readily escaped analysis, letting the unwary imagine that chance rules in nature. But for the Rabbis individuality makes every person uniquely precious. Each human being is a world of possibilities, a locus of intrinsic, irreplaceable value. Glossing the striking inference at the close of the Mishnaic passage, Louis Jacobs writes:

> each individual. . . . is not simply a minute fragment of the human race. He is the human race and whatever purposes God has for creating the human race are totally realized in him. There are, of course, billions of other members of the human race but each of these, too, is an end in himself, not only a means to a more glorious, because more embracing end, that of humanity as the whole.[13]

'For me the world was created' voices the idea of irreducible worth and dignity that Kant expressed in calling each human being an end in himself. The canon reaches this ethical ideal first through its positive appraisal of being, when God in Genesis sees that what He had made was good, indeed, *very* good with humans added to the mix; second, because human uniqueness, unparadoxically, is universal: The world exists for each of us. For each of us uniquely realizes its potential. Thus, the Talmud, reflecting that one blesses God for His hidden wisdom when one sees a crowd, explains: Just as no two faces are alike, so are no two minds alike.[14] Each human being is precious through the uniqueness we share, something that our subjecthood demands we recognize in one another.

---

[13] Louis Jacobs, *Religion and the Individual: A Jewish Perspective* (Cambridge: Cambridge University Press, 1992) 3. As Jacobs goes on to note (at 5), when God promises life to the person (*adam*) who lives by and in His laws, the Rabbis stress the universal reach of that promise. See *Sifra*, I. H. Weiss, ed. 86b, B. Bava Kamma 38a. The rabbinic intent, of course, is not to extend the demands of Jewish ceremonial law to every nation but to specify that the foundational moral, civil, and spiritual laws, Rabbinically called Noahidic and identified by modern thinkers like David Novak with the norms of natural law, shed their benefits on humanity at large.

[14] B. Berakhot 58a, with Numbers Rabbah 21.15, and the note of Zvi Hirsch Chajes in the Romm edition of the Talmud (Vilna) *ad loc.*, cited in Jacobs, 126, fn. 18.

2. THE MEDIEVAL PHILOSOPHERS

Reflecting on the book of Job, Saadiah Gaon imputes to the individual knowledge of his own moral state. Our self-knowledge does not obviate but rather intensifies the obligation of self-scrutiny: We cannot judge our sufferings undeserved before examining all our doings. But self-scrutiny is not inevitable self-deception. One can know one's innocence—as Job did, pace the midrashic writers, all too eager to find some fault behind Job's anguish. Job is as sure of his innocence as he is of God's justice,[15] hence his dilemma: Job cannot, in moral honesty, accept the advice of his friends, accept guilt and blameworthiness, despite the dictates of conscience. Job knows he has committed no such crime as would warrant his sufferings; and he knows that real wrongdoers, authors of real enormities, prosper in the world. His intellectual honesty will not allow him to paper over the discrepancy between divine benevolence and his sufferings. So he calls on God, repeatedly, to name his crime or explain his torments.

Where Descartes would one day make an existential anchor point of self-knowledge, Job's self-knowledge is moral. Like Abraham, he appeals to God's justice. Descartes will reason that a perfect being is no deceiver—and thus secure the veracity of sense experience. But Job's doubts are resolved not by reassurance as to the reality of the external world but through an epiphany that reveals to him (and through the poetic report of the words he hears in the voice from the storm wind) a scale of justice far wider than the personal, in the confluence of forces that God deploys in the work and play, danger and death, that give nature its dynamic. The rough justice of the storm wind is vouched for by the grace shown in God's initial and ongoing creative act. In this cosmic perspective, every creature matters. A person cannot be God's sole object of concern. And yet, even in suffering solitude, the individual remains precious and worthy of God's love.[16]

Saadiah's ethics, like his moral epistemology, centre on the individual. Surveying the varied ends we vie for—food and drink; love, whether erotic, romantic or procreative; development, be it urban or

---

[15] See Saadiah's introduction to his translation and commentary on the book of Job, Goodman, trans. *The Book of Theodicy*, esp. 128–30.
[16] Saadiah, *The Book of Theodicy*, 382–409.

agrarian; health and longevity; political power; vengeance; rest; even knowledge, ascesis, and the joys of worship—Saadiah will find all wanting if they exclude the rest. The Torah teaches a proper mix among these goods. For we are children of this world of multiplicity. Only God is wholly one, and He did not make us of a single element. A house needs more than one sort of material. So does a good dish or a fine perfume. Fame, remembrance of the dead—whatever goods commend themselves—all have their place. But there will be time enough for otherworldliness. Our place for now is here, living the lives that can merit a place in the hereafter. It is here that we must deal with our doubts, cope with the world's vicissitudes, and find a proper balance among the many pursuits that engage us, not shunning this life but finding the way of dealing with its goods and ills that makes an individual worthy of respite, requital, and reward.[17]

Ibn Gabirol, too, declines to reject the world. Against the backdrop of the heavens, the poet philosopher traces the human soul to an origin in the divine and maps a road for its return.[18] He speaks respectfully of Saadiah in his ethical work, *On the Improvement of the Moral Traits*[19] but labours to make clear that the mingling of motives which Saadiah promotes is (as his great predecessor well knew) no random mixture but a blending balanced not by mechanical titration but by reason.

Pride, a product of biliousness, Ibn Gabirol argues, can yield to humility if we reflect on our origins, and our end. Lust, the fickle distillate of youthful sanguinity, a passion quickly turned to hatred (2 Samuel 13:15), mellows into benevolence and compassion when sublimated, as we might say, as love of God and His Law. Joy and cheer, again sanguinary traits, find due place and measure under reason's guidance. Anxiety and grief, the fruits of melancholy, are inseparable from the human condition. Yet they may be overcome by

---

[17] See Saadiah, *ED* X and the discussion in Goodman, *God of Abraham*, 142–52.

[18] Solomon Ibn Gabirol, 'The Royal Crown', Hebrew text, Israel Davidson, ed., Israel Zangwill, trans. in *Selected Religious Poems* (Philadelphia: Jewish Publication Society, 1924) 82–123. Zangwill's introduction (xlvi) quotes Heine, who called Ibn Gabirol the thinker among poets and the poet for thinkers. Bernard Lewis' sensitive translation is reprinted in B. Lewis and A.L. Gluck (eds), *The Kingly Crown* (Notre Dame: Notre Dame University Press, 2003).

[19] Written in Arabic in 1045, Ibn Gabirol's *K. Islāh al-Ahlāq* was translated into Hebrew by Judah Ibn Tibbon in 1167. Stephen S. Wise edited and translated the Arabic text, as *The Improvement of the Moral Qualities* (New York: Columbia University Press, 1902; repr. New York: AMS, 1963).

relaxing our worldly desires, inuring ourselves to loss, and pursuing ideas. For pure ideas are not so readily lost as the will-o'-the-wisps we chase and try to hold fast in the world of generation and decay. Indeed, ideas raise us towards God's world, where real peace is found.[20]

Cowardice, diffidence, and sloth are natural enough, even useful on occasion; but, unchecked by hope, good cheer, ambition, and desire, they ruin the body they were meant to protect. Ire too has its uses. But, too readily indulged, it becomes a disease akin to madness, as Galen knew. We emulate God when we control such folly (Exodus 24:6)—and its cousins, envy and niggardliness. The qualities to cultivate: awareness, generosity, courage, zeal, patience. Man, Ibn Gabirol writes, is God's noblest creature. The body is no trap if one can learn to govern it and modulate its dispositions.

Ibn Gabirol is somewhat apologetic for not perfectly coordinating and systematizing the relations of the moral with the humoral.[21] But his thesis is clear: our varying dispositions are not determinants but tendencies. As Leibniz would one day say, they incline without necessitating. Maimonides agrees. There is no innate moral goodness, and no original sin:

> It is impossible for a person to be born virtuous or vicious ab initio, just as it is impossible for one to be naturally the master of some craft. But one can be born naturally predisposed to a given virtue or weakness, readier to act so or otherwise.[22]

Like Ibn Gabirol, Maimonides links our predispositions to each individual's humoral (we might say, hormonal) makeup: One man confronts a king, another cowers before a mouse. A brain less overloaded with fluids is readier to learn. But no one learns without effort, study, and stimulation. Warmer tempers are naturally closer to courage. But even they must learn that virtue, or any other. For finding the ways, means, occasions and modalities of any virtue demands not just inclination but insight, thought and thoughtfulness, made active and habitual.

---

[20] The strategy is Kindi's, spelled out in his 'Essay on How to Banish Sorrow'.

[21] Ibn Gabirol, *The Improvement of the Moral Qualities*, ed., Arabic 45, trans. 102.

[22] Maimonides, 'Eight Chapters' 8, in *Haqdamot le-Perush ha-Mishnah*, M.D. Rabinowitz, ed. (Jerusalem: Mossad Ha-Rav Kook, 1961) 201; Joseph Gorfinkle, ed. and trans. as *The Eight Chapters of Maimonides on Ethics* (New York: Columbia Univesity Press, 1912; repr. New York: AMS, 1966), English, 85.

With practice and experience, Maimonides argues, even a cold temperament can acquire the virtues of a hero.[23] Any man can grow wicked as Jeroboam or righteous as Moses. But the onus is on the individual. For it is not the stars, the humours, or the accidents of birth that make our choices. God Himself does not determine the tenor of one's acts (Lamentations 3:38–40). We humans, for better or for worse, make the crucial moral judgements—just as if we were gods. For even now one might reach out and pluck the fruit, still near at hand, and win eternal life (Genesis 3:22).[24]

There are those, Maimonides writes, who are troubled by the thought that God's Law serves purposes. But the alternative is to make revelation otiose, idle, or vain. God needs nothing from humans. The purpose of His law is our betterment—most elementally, by seeing to our material welfare and security, as any human code of laws might do. But, beyond that, a divine law fosters moral improvement and spiritual perfection (Psalms 19:8): The practices ordained biblically intend the refinement of our character.

Paradigmatically, God's charge to help one's enemy reload his fallen ass (Exodus 23:5) aims to aid us in curbing our natural animosity—thus the specific reference to an enemy.[25] Biblical rituals, narratives, and symbols reach yet higher. To the inquiring mind they open up avenues to intellectual/spiritual perfection, pointing to God's work in nature and helping us see God's hand in all things. Prompted by the symbolisms of the ritual commandments—the Sabbath laws, for instance—aspirants rise ever higher in contemplation of God's perfection, ever more fully realizing the individual's inner affinity with God, announced when Genesis declares that each of us, male and female, is created in God's image and likeness.[26]

Human individuals differ vastly. Some are ready to confront a lion; others quail when merely berated. Some are intuitive, others less so.[27] The wisest and most insightful most fully realize the human capacity to know God; and those specially gifted with imagination can translate their pure insights into rituals and symbols, laws, proverbs, and

[23] Maimonides, 'Eight Chapters' 8, Rabinowitz, ed., 202; Gorfinkle, trans., 85–6.

[24] Maimonides, *Mishneh Torah* I, Hilkhot Teshuvah (Laws of Repentance) 5.1–2, Moses Hyamson, ed. and trans. (Jerusalem: Feldheim, 1974) 86b–87a; the proof texts are cited here as the Rambam reads them.

[25] Maimonides, 'Eight Chapters' 4, Rabinowitz, ed., 180, Gorfinkle, trans., 65.

[26] Maimonides, *Guide* II 40, III 26–28, 31, 33.

[27] Maimonides, *Guide* II 38.

parables that give their fellows access to the fruits their minds have gleaned. Such persons are prophets. The angels on Jacob's ladder set the pattern. For they move downwards as well as up: 'after rising and reaching a given rung on the ladder comes the descent with what was gained, to govern and teach humanity, on earth'.[28] Through precept and practice, prophets, blessed with the poetic gift of imagination, impart to others less capable of sheer abstraction an implicit rapport with the ideas and values portended by an awareness of the Divine. So others too may rise, each according to his capacity, fulfilling the Mishnaic promise, that all Israel and the righteous of all nations have a share in the World to Come.[29]

Small wonder, then, that Maimonides inaugurates a trend, pursued by his admirer Ibn Aqnin and by Samuel ibn Tibbon, Samuel's son Moses, their kinsman Jacob Anatoli, as well as Immanuel of Rome, Joseph ibn Kaspi, and the astronomer philosopher Levi ben Gershom (Gersonides), breaking with rabbinic tradition and reading the Song of Songs as an allegory not of Israel's love for God but as a love song celebrating God's love affair with the individual human soul.[30]

Limitations of space deny us the chance here to study at length the emergence of personality in the biblical sources. Suffice it to say that law is not the only emergent enterprise in Hebraic scripture. There is an ethos too—'Thou shalt not seethe a kid in its mother's milk' (Exodus 23:19, etc.); 'thou shalt not take the mother bird with her young' (Deuteronomy 22:6); 'rise up before a hoary head' (Leviticus 19:32); 'thou shalt not covet' (Exodus 20:14)—and many like prescriptions, from the remission of debts and the institution of sabbaths for the land in the seventh year (Deuteronomy 15:1–11), to military deferments for the betrothed and for recent planters, and exemptions for the fainthearted—lest their fears prove contagious (Deuteronomy 20:3–9).

---

[28] Maimonides, *Guide* I 15.

[29] Maimonides, *Kitab al-Sirāj*, Commentary on Mishnah, Sanhedrin X, 'Pereq Heleq' M.D. Rabinowitz, ed. in *Haqdamot le-Perush Ha-Mishnah* (Jerusalem: Mossad Ha-Rav Kook, 1961) 109–50; cf. *Mishneh Torah*, vol 1., Laws of Repentance, Ch. III:5 ad fin., Hyamson, ed. and trans., 84b: 'the benevolent among the nations have a portion of the world to come.'

[30] See Menachem Kellner, Gersonides, ed., *Commentary on Song of Songs* (New Haven: Yale University Press, 1998), and Kellner's survey of earlier essays in the same direction, Introduction, xvi–xvii.

Alongside the explicit ethos-framing norms a parallel, narrative movement sketches heroic figures, individuals who present not a rigid ideal type but a variety of unique possibilities clustered around core values: The self-effacing Moses stands firm before God to plead for Israel, once he has ground their golden calf to dust: 'Forgive their sin', he says, 'or efface me from Thy book' (Exodus 32:32). The proud humility of Moses is balanced by prideful, self-humbling of David, the warrior-poet and one time shepherd, who 'danced with all his might' before his God, in the face of his royal princess wife's disdain (2 Samuel 6:14–22). Ruth, the gentle Moabite who gleaned in the alien corn for her widowed mother-in-law but lived to found King David's line, is balanced too, by the assertive, then exultant, Deborah, a prophet who judged Israel under her palm tree and told the cautious general Barak that if he needed her to go with him to battle, victory too would belong to a woman, honoured for making the roads safe once again (Judges 4:3–9, 31). The decisive beauty Esther, who tells her kinsman Mordecai: 'if I die, I die' (Esther 4:16) is balanced by the barren, prayerful Hannah, who speaks to God in ways unknown to an old high priest in Jerusalem but bears and weans the forthright Samuel, raised in the Jerusalem Temple and ready, if reluctant, to appoint kings over his people, to rebuke and replace those monarchs, if need be, and even to behead a genocidal enemy (1 Samuel 1:5, 12–16; 2:11; 3:21; 8:22; 15:13–35).

Focusing only on the commandments and setting aside the narratives, we can see in the Sabbath laws, and those protecting sexual privacy, and in the interlocking mandates to pursue holiness and justice (Leviticus 19:2, Deuteronomy 16:20), that Hebrew scripture cares about the individual intensely, and rather differently from what we find in the most thoughtful Greek and Roman philosophers, who see justice politically, whether in the internal councils of the mind or in the state. For them justice means parity and proportion. Biblically it means doing what is right, respecting creation, loving God's creatures, honouring their deserts. Even before the giving of the Law, the Torah reports that the midwives in Egypt evaded Pharaoh's decree that every male should be cast into the Nile—for they feared God (Exodus 1:15–19). The same love of life persists when Philo writes with horror of late term abortion and infanticide.[31] What is precious

---

[31] Philo, *De Specialibus Legibus* III 19–20.

here is each individual. And that is the valuation that shines forth rabbinically when self-incrimination is rejected, or when Akiva rules that personal dignity is God's gift, existential, as we might put it—not metred by social standing, as Akiva sees it, or waived even in the throes of poverty.[32] Perhaps it would be best, in this short chapter, to end with one further modern case study.

3. MENDELSSOHN

Moses Mendelssohn (1729–86), a pioneer of liberal philosophy and champion of religious freedom, anchored his religious pluralism in the value of individual differences: 'Brothers,' he wrote, 'if you care about genuine piety, let us not pretend to think alike. Diversity, plainly, is the plan and purpose of Providence. None of us thinks and feels just the same as his fellow man.'[33] Mendelssohn's argument is rooted in the integrity of personal conscience. Kant, a more circumspect liberal, hailed the argument of Mendelssohn's *Jerusalem* as the manifesto of 'a great reform', but cautioned that the seeds planted when Mendelssohn articulated his vision of religious freedom would be slow to bear fruit.

State meddling with religious beliefs and practices, Mendelssohn argued, is clearly unjust. In the inmost citadel of the mind, the individual holds rightful sovereignty. But, as the great Jewish philosopher's talk of *true* piety makes clear, even when conscience is crushed, dogma and conformity defeat their own intent. Their yield is hypocrisy, not devotion. Applying his brief to his own people's case, Mendelssohn judged the ritual laws of Judaism indeed binding, but only undercut, not effectuated, by sanctions. God's commandments reflect no divine need, he explains, much in the spirit of Maimonides. The Torah's precepts are for the sake of its recipients: They invite Israel to a revealed life. But the intimacy they seek is only thwarted when love, as we might say, echoing the Song of Songs (2:7) is not freely found.

---

[32] Mishnah Bava Kamma 8.6, discussed in Goodman, *Judaism, Human Rights and Human Values*, 58–9.

[33] Mendelssohn, *Jerusalem, or, On Religious Power* (1783), Alan Arkush, trans. (Hanover, NH: University Press of New England, 1983) 138.

An ancient homilist reasons much in the same vein. The *hedge of lilies* mentioned in the Song of Songs (7:3) bespeaks the work of conscience, which curbs the demands of appetite and passion. 'Was there a wall of iron or a post to hold him back?,' the midrash asks, 'Was he bitten by a snake? stung by a scorpion? . . . It was only the words of the Torah, soft as lilies!' (Song of Songs Rabbah, 7:3.2). God's law, to the free spirit, is not arbitrary or coercive. Its ethical restraints and their ritual filigree[34] are the hedge that marks a garden path, cultivated for the beauty it imparts to a way of life cherished for its lovely blossoms and the sweet, wholesome fruit of its ethos.[35]

The history and character of diverse nations, Mendelssohn argues, lead them naturally to diverse political constitutions. Diverse religions, similarly, may best suit the character of diverse individuals. Responding to a plea that he embrace Christianity if he could not or would not refute a seemingly impressive Christian tract, Mendelssohn wrote: 'Were a Solon or Confucius alive among my contemporaries, I could admire the great man in keeping with the principles of my faith, without succumbing to the ludicrous idea that I must convert a Solon or a Confucius.'[36] Personal integrity and communal loyalty join hands here, and Mendelssohn rises to stand alongside Solon and Confucius. The real challenge was not to joust in some adolescent debate but the more personal test of building and living one's own identity. Mendelssohn forged his idea of such an identity in his celebrated reworking of Plato's *Phaedo*. The clarity and confidence that made the three dialogues of his *Phaedon* so widely admired rested on his assurance that metaphysics finds a steady anchor point in human individuality.

To a great extent self-taught, Mendelssohn had entranced Enlightenment thinkers in the 1750s, when his friend Lessing published work of his. He gained intellectual celebrity in 1763 with his prize essay answering a question set by the Royal Prussian Academy as to the prospects for rigour in metaphysics. Kant took an honourable mention in the competition. But when the *Phaedon* appeared in 1767, Mendelssohn was hailed as 'the German Socrates'. The first edition sold out in four months, followed by numerous reprints, new

---

[34] See Goodman, *God of Abraham*, Chapter 6.
[35] Goodman, *Love Thy Neighbor as Thyself* (New York: Oxford University Press, 2008) 65.
[36] Mendelssohn, Open Letter to J.C. Lavater, December 1769.

editions, and translations into Dutch, Italian, French, Danish, English, and Russian.

Long fascinated by the 'great truths' and 'untrustworthy arguments' of Socrates, and entranced by the 'magnificent design' and 'unconvincing' reasoning of the dialogues in which Plato framed them,[37] Mendelssohn had taken on the ambitious task of rewriting Plato. He fell far short of Plato's dramatic flair, but he found in the dialogue form a naturally engaging format for Enlightenment philosophy[38] as he aimed to replace the arguments Plato had put in Socrates' mouth with new ones that would ring truer in modern ears. Pursuing his daring plan with vigour, he was convinced that forthright analysis of the nature of the soul would discredit the facile if fashionable materialism of atheists like La Mettrie. He chose a pagan persona, he explained, to remove any hint of appeal to scriptural authority.[39]

The one argument left standing as Plato's *Phaedo* closes is the thought that immortality may be won insofar as knowledge of the Forms draws one closer to their timelessness. But Plato's Forms are universals. So individuality, here, far from being fulfilled as we advance, is an obstacle to be overcome. If immortality means loss of personhood, however, Mendelssohn wants none of it. Replacing knowledge of the Forms with knowledge of God, the aspiration of medieval monotheists, and indeed of Spinoza,[40] Mendelssohn drops Plato's appeal to *anamnesis*. Even on its surface level Plato's account was hobbled by its Pythagorean overtones and the all too familiar images of transmigration. On a deeper level, *anamnesis*, for Plato, was meant to lead to the discovery that the soul, timelessly in touch with the Forms, is divine. But individuality suffered on either reading, muddled with subsequent and prior selves or submerged in the All.

---

[37] Altmann, *Moses Mendelssohn: A Biographical Study* (Tuscaloosa: University of Alabama Press, 1974) 141, 145.

[38] See Aaron Hughes, *The Art of the Dialogue in Jewish Philosophy* (Bloomington: Indiana University Press, 2008); cf. Michael Prince, *Philosophical Dialogue in the British Enlightenment Theology, Aesthetics, and the Novel* (Cambridge: Cambridge University Press, 1996; 2005). As Hughes notes, Mendelssohn was translating Shaftesbury even as he wrote his *Phaedon*.

[39] Mendelssohn, letter to Abbt, July 22, 1766, quoted in Altmann, *Mendelssohn*, 147; cf. 156.

[40] See Spinoza, *Ethics* 4p36. For the medieval cynosure, see Goodman, 'Happiness', *Cambridge History of Medieval Philosophy*, Robert Pasnau, ed. (Cambridge University Press, 2010) 457–71.

Mendelssohn's aim was not to discover divinity in the soul but the monotheist's counterpart: Virtue would clear a pathway to ever growing knowledge of God's perfection.

Where Plato had played with thoughts of symmetry, having Socrates opine that all things stem from their opposites (life counterbalancing death), Mendelssohn sets the strong claim that nothing in nature is utterly destroyed. Death, then, cannot annihilate the soul. But incorruptibility will hardly suffice—as if all human yearnings might be met by endless, dreamless sleep. Individual souls must live on, to think, feel, and will, and so continue to desire wisdom and pursue virtue.[41]

Simmias' famous argument in Plato's dialogue, that the harmonious tuning of a lyre cannot survive its dismantling, becomes Mendelssohn's surrogate of the French materialists' claims. So Mendelssohn's Socrates counters: Matter cannot think. Following Plotinus, Mendelssohn reasons that non-thinking parts cannot be arranged to make them think.[42] A chord, he says, capping Plato's lyre image, is not just the tones that compose it. But what makes the difference must already be subjective— either a phenomenon or the product of some act of mental synthesis. In either case consciousness is presupposed! The mind, then, cannot be a mere machine.

Mendelssohn rises higher in the final frame of his triptych. Setting aside Plato's timeless psyche, he speaks of man's vocation—thus, of a dynamic soul: 'All finite spirits have innate faculties'—not just innate ideas. These 'they develop and perfect through exercise'. Like the ancient rabbis Mendelssohn finds moral norms in God's command, 'You shall be holy, for I the Lord your God am holy' (Leviticus 19:2). Like Maimonides, he fuses this imperative with Plato's challenge ('to become as like to God as we can'—*Theaetetus* 176b). For Maimonides, this goal was to be pursued intellectually, by an asymptotic approach to knowledge of God's infinite perfection. But Mendelssohn, like the Rabbis, sees the moral virtues as no mere propadeutic to the intellectual quest but its very means: 'By imitating God one may gradually come closer to his perfections, and the happiness of spirits consists in this approximation. Yet the road to it is infinite and cannot be traversed in an eternity.' Hence the need for infinite duration of individual moral and intellectual powers, a need forecast in the most primitive expressions of the appetite for life: 'In essence,

---

[41] Altmann, *Mendelssohn*, 152, 154.
[42] See Plotinus, *Enneads* IV 7; Altmann, *Mendelssohn*, 154.

every human desire projects itself into the infinite . . . this striving for perfection . . . is the vocation of rational beings and, hence, the ultimate purpose of creation.'[43]

In 1780, just months before his death in February 1781, Lessing published his own version of his friend's idea of the soul's unending quest, reframed in intellectualist guise and draped once again in the language of transmigration. Kant recasts Mendelssohn's vision more faithfully: The holy will, to which we are called by the moral law 'can be found only in an endless progress'. Since the moral law cannot be frustrate, the soul must be immortal, forever pursuing its infinite goal.[44]

As early as 1756, Mendelssohn had argued 'One who denies immortality must prefer to see all creation perish, if only he can preserve himself.' The *Phaedon* doubles down on these high stakes, arguing that if death is the end for all, everyone has an equal right against everyone else. The result: a Hobbesian war of each against all, where even God cannot find for one side over another. Christian Garve found this argument of Mendelssohn's suppositious: Moral worries cannot warrant metaphysical claims, he reasoned. So Mendelssohn must have presupposed higher ends than life itself—and thus begged the question in behalf of immortality.

Challenged to show that the argument for which he had made his strongest claims to originality did not secrete among its premises the assumption of a transcendent realm, Mendelssohn responded in the appendix to his third edition: He had not presumed immortality, he wrote. Even Epicurus, Hobbes, and Spinoza had grounded

---

[43] Altmann, *Mendelssohn*, 155, quoting *Phaedon*, 105, 113–14.

[44] Kant, *Critique of Practical Reason* (1788), Lewis White Beck, ed. (Indianapolis: Bobbs-Merrill, 1956) 126 (Prussian Academy edn., 122–3). Kant here makes immortality a postulate of pure practical reason, moving beyond his argument in the *Critique of Pure Reason* that 'human endowments,' so far transcend mere notions of advantage or even posthumous fame as to demand 'a better world' (B 425–6). Beck writes: 'I have not been able to find any anticipation, in other writers, of the moral argument proper; but the doctrinal belief based on man's moral nature, which was Platonic in inspiration, was widely accepted in the eighteenth century. It was formulated by Addison (*Spectator*, No. 111 [1711], who said he did not remember having seen this, the "strongest" of the arguments for immortality presented elsewhere; by Platner (*Philosophische Aphorismen* §§1176–9 [1782]; by Mendelssohn (*Phaedon* [1769 [sic]); by Crusius (*Anweisung vernünftig zu leben*, Part I, Thelematologie, §§ 79ff. [1780]), all of whom had been read by Kant.' *A Commentary on Kant's* Critique of Practical Reason (Chicago: University of Chicago Press, 1960) 266 n.

moral demands for a supreme sacrifice without appeal to thoughts of immortality.

It is here that the energy driving Mendelssohn's argument is clearest: He *is* deriving metaphysical propositions from moral premises. Our concern is not with his success in proving the soul's immortality, the high longing of Enlightenment theism, but with what his arguments reveal about the precious worth of human individuality to him. Rock bottom for Mendelssohn, solid enough to give him footing when he vaults to an everlasting project of soul making, is the insatiable quest for self-improvement. This is what Mendelssohn judges indestructible and worthy of immortality, a groping for immortality presaged in every breath we take, every morsel of food and sip of water, every loving smile and caress.

Each human being, as Mendelssohn reads the human condition, is embarked on an 'infinite progress toward perfection'. The yearning that orients that quest is the clearest mark of human dignity. The trajectory of our aspirations, he argues, points, arrowlike, toward immortality. But we cannot ignore the yearning itself and the course it plots: the quest not to leave behind our moral and intellectual personhood but to perfect it.

Mendelssohn was right in insisting that he had not invoked immortality, a deus ex machina from high above the proscenium arch.[45] His reasoning was anchored not in heaven but near at hand, in the recognition that principle and honour, dignity and decency can trump even survival. That thought does not depend on any hopes or fears of sanction or reward. Its object is intrinsic worth, a goal that lies at the heart of Scripture's moral teachings. Recognition of the worth of that path and the truth of the insights that lead to it is fostered by those teachings but does not depend on them. That is the deeper message of the *Phaedon*, plainly visible when we excavate the footings of its argument. Alongside the inestimable worth of the human individual and the open ended quest for perfection, thoughts of mere immortality are little more than lightshow.

***

---

[45] The parallel with Kant is instructive here. As Ernst Cassirer wrote of Kant's claims for immortality: 'This assumption is in no way necessary *for* morality, but rather is necessitated *by* it.' *Kant's Life and Thought*, James Haden, trans. (New Haven: Yale University Press, 1981; first German edn., 1918) 264.

Reading Thomas Aquinas' famous 'Five Ways', we learn more than the methods traditionally deployed to demonstrate God's existence. We learn as well five ways in which God has been conceived: as prime mover, first cause, necessary being, highest good and source of goodness, and architect of nature. Similarly, the ways in which the Hebraic sources conceive of individuality speak eloquently of their conception of the human person. The individual is precious intrinsically, as an end, never a mere means, as a moral agent and counterpart of others, persons whose projects (not excluding progeny) deserve continuance in the eyes of God and recognition in the eyes of their fellows.

The prominence of the ethical, whether in the biblical expectation of regard and support between mates, or of honour toward parents and the elderly, or in the broader expectation of communal relations that foster cooperation and collaboration rather than conflict and invidious competition, tell us that the individual in the Hebraic normative sources is not romanticized in titanic isolation from his fellow human beings. Rather, individuals are conceived as natural allies and potential friends. Each deserves, as his due, recognition of the same kind and in the same measure as one might hope for toward oneself.

The individual here—whether in Spinoza's prudential suasion that nothing is more valuable to man than man, or in Buber's thought that each of us comes alive in human terms only in encounter with another, or in Levinas' vision of the other's unique and uniquely human face—is not at odds with the interests and concerns of the community. On the contrary, the other is a fellow (*re'a*), another self, whom God commands each of us to love as one loves oneself. The Law, then, will never simply adopt the perspective of ego. The fellowship it demands extends to the stranger (Deuteronomy 10:19), and its practical demands reach further (Exodus 20:10, 22:21, 23:9; Leviticus 19:10, 34, 23:22, 24:22; Deuteronomy 1:16, 5:14, 10:18, 14:21, 29, 16:11, 24:17, 26:11–13, 27:19, 31:12), since they presume no established bonds of friendship but only common humanity. Individuality here does not breed contempt. So it does not welcome the kind of individualism that admirers used to call rugged and that Sam Beer, laughingly, called ragged individualism. Human communities matter because they are able to foster individual well-being, moral growth, spiritual and intellectual flourishing. But the individuals who grow and prosper in these ways are not costs or drags on the community. They are contributors, but valued not just for all that they contribute but for all that they are and might yet become.

Bibliography

Akenson, Donald Harman, *Surpassing Wonder: The Invention of the Bible and the Talmuds* (New York: Harcourt, Brace, 1998).

Altmann, Alexander, *Moses Mendelssohn: A Biographical Study* (Tuscaloosa: University of Alabama Press, 1974).

Annas, Julia, *An Introduction to Plato's Republic* (Oxford: Clarendon Press, 1981).

Aquinas, *Summa Theologica* (most quotations are from *Selected Writings of Aquinas*, Ralph McInerny, ed. (New York: Penguin, 1999)).

Aristotle, *Nicomachean Ethics*, Terence Irwin, trans., 2nd edn. (Indianapolis: Hackett Publishing Company, Inc. 1999).

Arnold, Matthew, *Culture and Anarchy* (New York: MacMillan and Co., 1895).

Bahya, Ibn Pakuda, *The Book of Direction to the Duties of the Heart*, Menahem Mansoor, trans. (Oxford: Littman Library of Jewish Civilization, 2000).

Baker, J., and Nicholson, E.W., *The Commentary of Rabbi David Kimchi on Psalms CXX–CL* (Cambridge: Cambridge University Press, 1973).

Berman, Lawrence V., 'Maimonides, the Disciple of Alfarabi', in J.A. Buijs (ed.), *Maimonides: A Collection of Critical Essays* (Notre Dame: University of Notre Dame Press, 1988).

Berman, Lawrence V., 'Maimonides on the Fall of Man', *AJS Review* 5, 1980, 1–16.

Bleich, J. David, 'Judaism and Natural Law', *Jewish Law Annual* 7, 1988, 5–42.

Bodin, Jean, *Colloquium of the Seven about Secrets of the Sublime* (Princeton: Princeton University Press, 1975).

Boman, Thorlief, *Hebrew Thought Compared With Greek* (New York: W.W. Norton & Co., 1970).

Buber, Martin, *Kingship of God*, Richard Scheimann, trans. (Atlantic Highlands, NJ: Humanities Press, 1967).

Burney, C.F., *The Book of Judges* (Eugene, Oregon: Wipf and Stock, 2004 (1918)).

Cassirer, Ernst, *Kant's Life and Thought*, James Haden, trans. (New Haven: Yale University Press, 1981).

Childs, Brevard S, 'The Sensus Literalis of Scripture: An Ancient and Modern Problem', in Herbert Donner, Robert Hanhart, and Rudolf Smend (eds),

Beiträge zur Alttestamentlichen Theologie (Göttingen: Vandenhoeck & Ruprecht, 1977) 80–7.

Cohen, Hermann, *Religion of Reason Out of the Sources of Judaism*, Simon Kaplan, trans. (Atlanta: Scholars Press, 1995).

—— *Ethics of Maimonides*, Almut S. Bruckstein, trans. (Madison: University of Wisconsin Press, 2004).

Cohn, Norman, *The Pursuit of the Millenium* (London: Pimlico, 2004).

Cunaeus, Petrus, *The Hebrew Republic*, Peter Wyetzner, trans. (Jerusalem: Shalem Press, 2006).

Curley, Edwin, 'Kissinger, Spinoza, and Genghis Khan', in Don Garrett (ed.), *The Cambridge Companion to Spinoza* (Cambridge: Cambridge University Press, 1996) 315–42.

Danby, Herbert, trans., *The Mishnah* (New York: Oxford University Press, 1933).

Davidson, Herbert A., 'Philosophy as a Religious Obligation', in S. D. Goitein, (ed.), *Religion in a Religious Age* (Cambridge, MA: Association for Jewish Studies, 1974) 53–68.

—— *Moses Maimonides: The Man and His Works* (New York: Oxford University Press, 2004).

Davies, W.D., *The Gospel and the Land: Early Christianity and Jewish Territorial Doctrine* (Berkeley: University of California Press, 1974).

Isma'il b. 'Umar b. Kathir, Imad al-Din, *al-Bidaya wa'l-Nihaya* (Riyad: Maktabat al-Nasr al-Haditha, 1968).

Donagan, Alan, 'Spinoza's Theology', in Don Garrett (ed.), *The Cambridge Companion to Spinoza* (Cambridge: Cambridge University Press, 1996).

Duns, Scotus, *Philosophical Writings: A Selection*, Allan Wolter, trans. (Indianapolis: Hackett Publishing Company, Inc. 1997).

Eisenstadt, S.N. (ed.), *The Origins and Diversity of Axial Age Civilizations* (Albany: State University of New York Press, 1986).

—— 'Israeli Politics and the Jewish Political Tradition: Principled Political Anarchism and the Rule of the Court', reprinted in *Explorations in Jewish Historical Experience: The Civilizational Dimension* (Leiden: Brill, 2004) 216–37.

Elazar, Daniel J., *Covenant and Polity in Biblical Israel* (New Brunswick: Transaction, 1995).

—— *Covenant Tradition in Politics* (New Brunswick: Tranacation, 1995–98).

Fackenheim, Emil, *Encounters Between Judaism and Modern Philosophy* (New York; Basic Books, 1973).

Finnis, John, *Natural Law and Natural Rights* (Oxford: Clarendon Press, 1980).

Fishbane, Michael, *Biblical Interpretation in Ancient Israel* (Oxford: Oxford University Press, 1985).

Flight, John W., 'The Nomadic Ideal in the Old Testament', *Journal of Biblical Literature* 42, 1923, 158–226.

Fox, Marvin, *Interpreting Maimonides: Studies in Methodology, Metaphysics, and Moral Principles* (Chicago: The University of Chicago Press, 1990).

Frank, Daniel H., 'The End of the Guide: Maimonides on the Best Life For Man', *Judaism* 34, 1985, 485–95.

—— 'Reason in Action: The "Practicality" of Maimonides' Guide', in Daniel H. Frank (ed.), *Commandment and Community: New Essays in Jewish Legal and Political Philosophy* (Albany: SUNY Press, 2002) 69–84.

—— 'Divine Law and Human Practices' in S. Nadler and T. M. Rudavsky (eds), *The Cambridge History of Jewish Philosophy: From Antiquity Through the Seventeenth Century* (Cambridge: Cambridge University Press, 2009), 790–807.

—— and J. Waller, *Spinoza on Politics* (London: Routledge, forthcoming).

Freyer, Hans, *Theory of Objective Mind: An Introduction to the Philosophy of Culture,* Steven Grosby, trans. and ed. (Athens: Ohio University Press, 1998 [1928]).

Friedman, Jerome, *The Most Ancient Testimony: Sixteenth-Century Christian-Hebraica in the Age of Renaissance Nostalgia* (Athens: Ohio University Press, 1983).

—— *Michael Servetus: A Case Study in Total Heresy* (Geneva: Librairie Droz, 1978).

Garrett, Aaron, *Meaning in Spinoza's Method* (Cambridge: Cambridge University Press, 2003).

Geertz, Clifford, *The Interpretation of Culture* (New York: Basic Books, 1973).

Gersonides, *Commentary on Song of Songs*, Menachem Kellner, trans. (New Haven: Yale University Press, 1998).

Al-Ghazali, Abū Ḥāmid Muḥammad b. Muḥammad, *Iḥyā 'Ulūm al-Dīn* (Cairo: Mu'assasa al-Ḥalabī li'l-Nashr wa'l-Tawzī', 1967).

Gierke, Otto von, *The Development of Political Theory*, Bernard Freyd, trans. (NewYork: W.W. Norton, 1939).

Ginzburg, Louis, *The Legends of the Jews* (Philadelphia: The Jewish Publication Society, 1968).

Gooding, D.W., 'The Composition of the Book of Judges', *Eretz-Israel* 16, 1982, 70–9.

Goodman, Lenn E., *God of Abraham* (New York: Oxford University Press, 1996).

—— *Judaism, Human Rights and Human Values* (New York: Oxford University Press, 1998).

—— *Jewish and Islamic Philosophy: Crosspollinations in the Classical Age* (Edinburgh and New Brunswick: Edinburgh University Press and Rutgers University Press, 1999).

—— 'Value and the Dynamics of Being', *Review of Metaphysics*, Vol. LXI, No. 1, September 2007.

—— *On Justice: An Essay in Jewish Philosophy* (Oxford: Littman Library, 2008).

—— *Love Thy Neighbor as Thyself* (New York: Oxford University Press, 2008).

—— 'An Idea is Not Something Mute Like a Picture on a Pad', *Review of Metaphysics*, Vol. 62, 2009, 591–631.

—— 'Happiness', in Robert Pasnau (ed.), *Cambridge History of Medieval Philosophy* (New York; Cambridge University Press, 2010) 457–71.

Gravlee, Scott, 'Aristotle on Hope', *Journal of the History of Philosophy* 38.4 2000, 461–77.

Greenstein, Edward L., 'Presenting Genesis 1, Constructively and Deconstructively', *Prooftexts* 21, 1996, 1–22.

Grosby, Steven, 'The Category of the Primordial in the Study of Early Christianity and Second-Century Judaism', *History of Religions* 36/2 (1996) 140–63.

—— 'Primordiality', in Athena S. Leoussi (ed.) *Encyclopaedia of Nationalism* (New Brunswick: Transaction, 2001) 252–5.

——, 'The Nation of the United States and the Vision of Ancient Israel', reprinted in *Biblical Ideas of Nationality: Ancient and Modern* (Winona Lake: Eisenbrauns, 2002 [1993]) 213–34.

—— *Biblical Ideas of Nationality: Ancient and Modern* (Winona Lake, IN: Eisenbrauns, 2002).

—— 'Religion, ethnicity and nationalism: the uncertain perennialism of Adrian Hastings', *Nations and Nationalism* 9/1(2003) 7–13.

Haivry, Ofir, 'The Way of the World', *Azure*, Autumn 1998, 44–53.

—— 'Selden's Theory of National Tradition', Unpublished manuscript, 2010.

Hallamish, Moshe, *An Introduction to the Kabbalah* (Albany: State University of New York Press, 1999).

Halper, Edward, 'Spinoza on the Political Value of Freedom of Religion', *History of Philosophy Quarterly* 21, (2004), 167–82.

Al-Hanbali, Zayn al-Dīn Abū'l-Faraj b. Rajab, *Fatḥ al-Bārī: Sharḥ Ṣaḥīḥ al-Bukhārī* (Madīna: Maktabat al-Ghurabā' al-Athariyya/Maktabat Taḥqīq Dār al-Ḥaramayn, 1996).

Harman Akenson, Donald, *Surpassing Wonder: The Invention of the Bible and the Talmuds* (New York: Harcourt, Brace, 1998).

Harnack, Adolph, *History of Dogma* (London: Williams and Norgate, 1894).

Harvey, Warren Zev, 'Maimonides and Spinoza on the Knowledge of Good and Evil', *Binah: Studies in Jewish Thought* 2, 1989, 131–46. Article originally published in *Iyyun* 28, 1978, 167–85.

Harvey, Warren Zev, 'A Portrait of Spinoza as a Maimonidean', *Journal of the History of Philosophy* 19, (1981), 151–72.

Hastings, Adrian, *The Construction of Nationhood: Ethnicity, Religion and Nationalism* (Cambridge: Cambridge University Press, 1997).

Hazony, Yoram, 'The Jewish Origins of the Western Disobedience Teaching', *Azure* 4, Summer 1998.

—— *The Dawn: Political Teachings of the Book of Esther* (Jerusalem: Shalem Press, 2000).

Hegel, G.W.F., *Lectures on the Philosophy of Religion*, R.F. Brown, P.C. Hodgson, and J.M. Stewart, trans. (Berkeley: University of California Press, 1988).

Hobbes, Thomas, *Leviathan* (New York: Penguin, 1985).

Hughes, Aaron, *The Art of the Dialogue in Jewish Philosophy* (Bloomington: Indiana University Press, 2008).

Hume, David, *A Treatise of Human Nature*, L.A. Selby-Bigge, ed. (Oxford: Clarendon Press, 1888).

Hyman, Arthur, 'A Note on Maimonides' Classification of Law', *Proceedings of the American Academy for Jewish Research* 46, 1978–79, 323–43.

Ibn Gabirol, Solomon, 'The Royal Crown', Hebrew text, Israel Davidson, ed., Israel Zangwill, trans., in *Selected Religious Poems* (Philadelphia: Jewish Publication Society, 1924).

—— *The Improvement of the Moral Qualities*, Stephen S. Wise, trans. (New York: Columbia University Press, 1902; repr. Mew York: AMS, 1963).

Jacobs, Jonathan, 'Reasons, Commandments, and the Common Project', *Hebraic Political Studies*, Vol. 3, No. 3, 2008, 290–307.

—— 'Judaism and Natural Law', *The Heythrop Journal*, Vol. 50, No. 6, November 2009, 930–47.

—— 'The Epistemology of Moral Tradition: A Defense of a Maimonidean Thesis', *Review of Metaphysics*, Vol. 64, No. 1, September 2010, 55–74.

—— *Law, Reason, and Morality in Medieval Jewish Philosophy* (Oxford: Oxford University Press, 2010).

Jacobs, Louis, *Religion and the Individual: A Jewish Perspective* (Cambridge, Cambridge University Press, 1992).

Justin, Martyr, *Dialogue with Trypho* (Grand Rapids, Eerdmans, 1963).

Kant, Immanuel, *Critique of Practical Reason*, Lewis White Beck, trans. (Indianapolis: Bobbs-Merrill, 1956).

—— *Groundwork of the Metaphysics of Morals*, H.J. Paton, trans. (New York: Harper and Row, 1964).

—— *Conflict of the Faculties*, Mary J. Gregor, trans. (Lincoln, NB: University of Nebraska Press, 1979).

Kantorowicz, Ernst H., *The King's Two Bodies: A Study in Medieval Political Theology* (Princeton: Princeton University Press, 1957).

Kass, Leon, *The Beginning of Wisdom* (New York: Free Press, 2003).

Katz, Jacob, *Tradition and Crisis* (New York: Schocken Books, 1971).

Kellner, Menachem, *Maimonides on 'The Decline of the Generations and the Nature of Rabbinic Authority'* (Albany: SUNY Press, 1996).

Koester, Helmut, 'NOMOS PHUSEOS: The Concept of Natural Law in Greek Thought', in J. Neusner (ed.), *Religions of Antiquity: Essays in Memory of Erwin Ramsdell Goodenough* (Leiden: Brill, 1968) 521–41.

Kraemer, Joel L., 'Naturalism and Universalism in Maimonides' Political and Religious Thought', in G. Blidstein, E. Fleischer, et al (eds), *Me'ah She'arim: Studies in Medieval Jewish Spiritual and Religious Life in Memory of Isadore Twersky* (Jerusalem: Magnes, 2001) 47–81.

Kreisel, Howard T., *Maimonides' Political Thought: Studies in Ethics, Law, and the Human Ideal* (Albany: SUNY Press, 1999).

—— *Prophecy: The History of an Idea in Medieval Jewish Philosophy* (Dordrecht: Kluwer, 2001).

Leiman, Sid Z., *The Canonization of Hebrew Scripture* (New Haven: Connecticut Academy of Arts and Sciences, 1991).

Levenson, Jon, *Creation and the Persistence of Evil* (Princeton: Princeton University Press, 1994).

Lilley, J.P.U., 'A Literary Appreciation of the Book of Judges', *Tyndale Bulletin* 1967, 94–102.

Locke, John, *Two Treatises of Government*, Laslett, ed. (New York: Cambridge University Press, 1960).

Macy, J., 'Prophecy in Alfarabi and Maimonides: The Imaginative and Rational Faculties', in Y. Yovel and S. Pines (eds), *Maimonides and Philosophy* (Dordrecht: Nijhoff, 1986).

MacIntyre, Alisdair, *Whose Justice? Which Rationality?* (Notre Dame: University of Notre Dame Press, 1988).

Maimonides, Moses, *Dalalat al-ha'rin*, Arabic original (inc. Munk's French trans.) of *The Guide of the Perplexed*, Solomon Munk, ed. (Paris: A. Franck, 1856–66).

—— 'Commentary on Mishnah, Sanhedrin X, "Pereq Heleq"', in M. D. Rabinowitz (ed.), *Haqdamot le-Perush Ha-Mishnah* (Jerusalem: Mossad ha-Rav Kook, 1961).

—— 'Eight Chapters', in *Ethical Writings of Maimonides*, eds. Raymond L. Weiss and Charles Butterworth (New York: Dover Publications Inc., 1975).

—— 'Laws Concerning Character Traits', in Raymond L. Weiss and Charles Butterworth (eds), *Ethical Writings of Maimonides* (New York: Dover Publications, Inc., 1975).

—— 'Laws of Repentance' in *Mishneh Torah Book of Knowledge*, Moses Hyamson, trans. (Jerusalem: Feldheim Publishers, 1981).

—— *Guide of the Perplexed*, Shlomo Pines, trans. (Chicago: University of Chicago Press, 1963).

—— 'Treatise on the Art of Logic', in Raymond L. Weiss and Charles Butterworth (eds), *Ethical Writings of Maimonides* (New York: Dover Publications, Inc., 1975).

Manuel, Frank, *The Broken Staff: Judaism through Christian Eyes* (Cambridge: Harvard University Press, 1992).

Mendelssohn, Moses, *Jerusalem, or, On Religious Power*, Allan Arkush, trans. (Hanover, NH: University Press of New England, 1983).

Mittleman, Alan, *The Scepter Shall Not Pass From Judah: Perspectives on the Persistence of the Political in Judaism* (Lanham, MD: Lexington, 2000).

Moore, Clifford, *The Religious Thought of the Greeks*, 2nd edn. (Cambridge: Harvard University Press, 1925).

Motzkin, Aryeh L., 'Maimonides and Spinoza on Good and Evil', *Daat* 24, 1978, 131–46.

Murdoch, Iris, *The Sovereignty of Good* (London: Routledge, 2003).

Nagel, Thomas, *The View From Nowhere* (New York: Oxford University Press, 1986).

Nelson, Eric, *The Hebrew Republic: Jewish Sources and the Transformation of European Political Thought* (Cambridge: Harvard University Press, 2010).

Nicholson, E.W., *God and His People: Covenant and Theology in the Old Testament* (Oxford: Clarendon Press, 1986).

Niditch, Susan, 'The "Sodomite" Theme in Judges 19–20: Family, Community, and Social Disintegration', *Catholic Bible Quarterly* 44, 1982, 365–78.

Noth, Martin, 'The Deuteronomistic History', *Journal For the Study of the Old Testament* 1943.

Novak, David, *The Image of the Non-Jew in Judaism* (New York and Toronto: The Edwin Mellen Press, 1983).

—— *Jewish-Christian Dialogue* (New York: Oxford University Press, 1989).

—— *Jewish Social Ethics* (New York: Oxford University Press, 1992).

—— *The Election of Israel* (Cambridge: Cambridge University Press, 1995).

—— (ed.), *Leo Strauss and Judaism* (Lanham, MD: Rowman and Littlefield, 1996).

—— *Natural Law in Judaism* (Cambridge: Cambridge University Press, 1998).

—— 'Judaism and Natural Law', *American Journal of Jurisprudence* 43, 1998, 117–34.

—— *In Defense of Religious Liberty* (Wilmington: ISI Books, 2009).

Nussbaum, Martha, *The Fragility of Goodness: Luck and Ethics in Greek Tragedy and Philosophy* (Cambridge: Cambridge University Press, 2001).

Orlinsky, H.M., 'Nationalism-Universalism and Internationalism in Ancient Israel', reprinted in *Essays in Biblical Culture and Bible Translation* (New York: KTAV, 1974).

Oz-Salzberger, Fania, 'The Jewish Roots of Western Freedom', *Azure* 13 (2002) 88–132.

—— 'The Jewish Roots of the Modern Republic', *Azure* 13 (2002) 88–132.

——, 'Social Justice and the Right of the People: The Seventeenth Century Reads the Hebrew Bible', Unpublished manuscript, 2008.

Pak, Sujin G., *The Judaizing Calvin: Sixteenth-Century Debates over the Messianic Pslams* (Oxford: Oxford University Press, 2010).

Pines, Shlomo, 'Truth and Falsehood vs. Good and Evil: A Study in Jewish and General Philosophy in Connection With the *Guide of the Perplexed'*, in Isadore Twersky (ed.), *Studies in Maimonides* (Cambridge, MA: Harvard University Press, 1990) 95–157.

Pocock, J.G.A., *The Ancient Constitution and the Feudal Law: English Historical Thought in the Seventeenth Century* (New York: W.W. Norton, 1967).

Prince, Michael, *Philosophical Dialogue in the British Enlightenment Theology, Aesthetics, and the Novel* (Cambridge: Cambridge University Press, 1996).

Pucci, Pietro, *Hesiod and the Language of Poetry* (Baltimore: Johns Hopkins Press, 1977).

Putnam, Hilary, *The Collapse of the Fact/Value Dichotomy and Other Essays* (Cambridge, MA: Harvard University Press, 2002).

Al-Qurtubi, Muhammad b. Ahmad al-Ansari, *Tafsir al-Qurtubi* (Cairo: al-Maktaba al-Tawfiqiyya, 1994).

Ravitzky, Aviezer, *Messianism, Zionism, and Jewish Religious Radicalism*, Michael Swirsky and Jonathan Chipman, trans. (Chicago: University of Chicago Press, 1993).

Ravven, H.M., 'Some Thoughts on What Spinoza Learned From Maimonides on the Prophetic Imagination, Part Two: Spinoza's Maimonideanism', *Journal of the History of Philosophy* 39 (2001) 385–406.

Ross, James, 'Justice Is Reasonableness: Aquinas on Human Law and Morality', *The Monist*, 1974, 86–103.

Rosenberg, Alfred, *Der Mythus der 20 Jahrhunderts: eine Wertung der Seelisch-geistigen Gestaliteakampfe unserer zeit* (Munchen: Hoheneichen-verlag, 1934).

Rosenblatt, Jason P., *Renaissance England's Chief Rabbi: John Selden* (Oxford: Oxford University Press, 2006).

Rousseau, Jean-Jacques, *On the Social Contract*, Judith R. Masters, trans. (New York: St. Martin's Press, 1978).

Rynhold, Daniel, *Two Models of Jewish Philosophy: Justifying One's Practices* (Oxford: Oxford University Press, 2005).

Saadiah Gaon, *The Book of Critically Selected Beliefs and Convictions*, D. Kafih, ed. (Jerusalem: Sura, 1970).

—— *Kitab al-Mukhtar fi 'l-Amanat wa 'l-I'tiqadat* (*The Book of Critically Chosen Beliefs and Convictions*), Arabic edn. with modern Hebrew translation by J. Kafih (Jerusalem: Sura, 1970).

—— *The Book of Theodicy*, (Commentary on the Book of Job), L.E. Goodman, trans. (New Haven: Yale University Press, 1975).

Saadiah Gaon, *The Book of Beliefs & Opinions*, Samuel Rosenblatt, trans. (New Haven: Yale University Press, 1976).

Sacksteder, William, 'Spinoza on Democracy' in M. Mandelbaum, E. Freeman (eds), *Spinoza: Essays in Interpretation* (LaSalle, Illinois: Open Court, 1975) 117–38.

Sanders, E.P., *Jesus and Judaism* (Philadelphia: Fortress Press, 1985).

—— *Paul and Palestinian Judaism: A Comparison of Patterns of Religion* (Philadelphia: Fortress, 1977).

Schneidmüller, Bernd, *Nomen Patriae: Die Entstehung Frankreichs in die politisch-geographischen Terminologie (10.-13. Jahrhundert)* (Sigmaringen: Jan Thorbecke, 1987).

Schniedewind, William M., *How the Bible Became a Book* (New York: Cambridge University Press, 2004).

Scholem, Gershom, *The Messianic Idea in Judaism* (New York: Schocken Books, 1971).

Schwarzschild, Steven, *The Pursuit of the Ideal*, Menachem Kellner, ed. (Albany: SUNY Press, 1990).

Seneca, *The Stoic Philosophy of Seneca: Essays and Letters*, Moses Hadas, trans. (New York: W.W. Norton & Co., 1958).

Sforno, *Commentary on the Torah*, Raphael Pelcovitz, trans. and ann. (Brooklyn: Mesorah, 1997).

Shils, Edward, *Tradition* (Chicago: University of Chicago Press, 1981).

Smith, Anthony D., 'Nation and Covenant: The Contribution of Ancient Israel to Modern Nationalism', *Proceedings of the British Academy* 151 (2007) 213–55.

Smith, Steven, *Spinoza: Liberalism and the Question of Jewish Identity* (New Haven: Yale University Press, 1997).

Soloveitchik, Joseph, *The Halakhic Mind* (New York: Free Press, 1986).

Spinoza, Baruch, *Political Works* (Oxford: Oxford University Press, 1958).

——*Opera*, ed. Carl Gebhardt (Heidelberg: Winter, 1972).

——*Political Treatise*, Samuel Shirley, trans. (Indianapolis: Hackett Publishing Company, Inc, 2000).

——*Theological-Political Treatise*, 2nd edn., Samuel Shirley, trans. (Indianapolis: Hackett Publishing Company, Inc., 2007).

Stern, Josef, 'The Maimonidean Parable, the Arabic *Poetics*, and the Garden of Eden', *Midwest Studies in Philosophy* 33, 2009, 209–47.

——*Problems and Parables of Law: Maimonides and Nahmanides on Reasons for the Commandments (Ta'amei Ha-Mitzvot)* (Albany: SUNY Press, 1998).

Stone, Suzanne Last, 'On the Interplay of Rules, "Cases", and Concepts in Rabbinic Legal Literature: Another Look at the Aggadot on Honi the Circle-Drawer', *Dine Israel* 24 (2007) 125–55.

Strauss, Leo, *Natural Right and History* (Chicago: The University of Chicago Press, 1953).

Strayer, Joseph, 'France: the Holy Land, the Chosen People, and the Most Christian King', in John F. Benton and Thomas N. Bisson (eds), *Medieval Statecraft and the Perspectives of History* (Princeton: Princeton University Press, 1971).

Sutcliffe, Adam, *Judaism and the Enlightenment* (Cambridge: Cambridge University Press, 2003).

Al-Tabari Muhammad Ibn Jarīr, *Jami' al-Bayan 'an Ta'wīl Āyāt al-Qur'an* (Beirut: Dār al-Fikr, 1995).

Al-Tibrīzī, Wali al-Din, *Mishkāt al-Maṣābīḥ* (Lahore: Mālik Sirāj al-Dīn, n.d).

Thucydides, *The Peloponnesian War*, trans. Crawley (New York: Modern Library Education, 1951).

Toomer, G. J., *John Selden: A Life in Scholarship* (Oxford: Oxford University Press, 2009).

Tuck, Richard, *Natural Right Theories: Their Origin and Development* (Cambridge: Cambridge University Press, 1979).

Twersky, Isadore, *Introduction to the Code of Maimonides* (New Haven: Yale University Press, 1980).

Ulman-Margalit, Edna, and Sidney Morgenbesser, 'Picking and Choosing', *Social Research* 44, 1977, 757–85.

Urbach, E.E., *The Sages: Their Concepts and Beliefs* (Jerusalem; Magnes Press, 1975).

Verbeek, Theo, *Spinoza's Theological-Political Treatise: Exploring the 'Will of God'* (Hampshire: Ashgate, 2003).

Vermes, Geza, *Jesus the Jew* (Philadelphia: Fortress Press, 1981).

Wach, Joachim, *Das Verstehen: Grundzüge einer Geschichte der hermeneutischen Theorie im 19. Jahrhundert* (Tübingen: J.C.B. Mohr (Paul Siebeck) 1926–33).

Walzer, Michael, *Exodus and Revolution* (New York: Basic Books, 1985).

—— *Thick and Thin: Moral Argument at Home and Abroad* (Notre Dame: University of Notre Dame Press, 1994).

Walzer, Michael, Menachem Lorberbaum, and Noam J. Zohar (eds), *The Jewish Political Tradition* (New Haven: Yale, 2000).

Weber, Max, *The Protestant Ethic and the Spirit of Capitalism* (New York: Charles Scribner, 1958).

—— *Die protestantische Ethik und der Geist des Kapitalismus* in *Gesammelte Aufsätze zurReligionssoziologie*, vol. I. (Tübingen: J.C.B. Mohr (Paul Siebeck), 1934).

Weinfeld, Moshe, 'The Transition From Tribal Republic to Monarchy in Ancient Israel', in Daniel J. Elazar (ed.), *Kinship and Consent: The Jewish Political Tradition and its Contemporary Uses* (New Brunswick: Transaction, 1997) 216–32.

Weiss, Raymond L., and Charles E. Butterworth, eds. *Ethical Writings of Maimonides* (New York: Dover, 1975).

Whitman, Walt, *Leaves of Grass* (Philadelphia: David McKay, 1900).

Wildavsky, Aaron, *Assimilation Versus Separation: Joseph the Administrator and the Politics of Religion in Biblical Israel* (New Brunswick: Transaction, 1993).

——*Moses as Political Leader* (Jerusalem: Shalem Press, 2005).

Williams, Bernard, *Morality* (Cambridge: Cambridge University Press, 1993).

Wolosky, Shira, 'Biblical Republicanism: John Cotton's "Moses His Judicials" and American Hebraism', *Hebraic Political Studies* 4/2 (2009) 104–27.

Yovel, Yirmiyahu, *Spinoza and Other Heretics: The Marrano of Reason* (Princeton: Princeton University Press, 1989).

Ziskind, Martha A., 'John Selden: Criticism and Affirmation of the Common Law Tradition', *The American Journal of Legal History* 19/1(1975) 22–39.

Index